UNIVERSITY OF CALIFORNIA
PUBLICATIONS IN HISTORY

VOLUME XXX

1943

EDITORS

R. J. KERNER
G. H. GUTTRIDGE
F. L. PAXSON

SIBERIA IN THE SEVENTEENTH CENTURY

A Study of the Colonial Administration

BY

GEORGE V. LANTZEFF

1972

OCTAGON BOOKS

New York

Originally published in 1943

Reprinted 1972
by special arrangement with the University of California Press

OCTAGON BOOKS
A Division of Farrar, Straus & Giroux, Inc.
19 Union Square West
New York, N. Y. 10003

Library of Congress Catalog Card Number: 75-159205

ISBN 0-374-94774-0

Printed in U.S.A. by
NOBLE OFFSET PRINTERS, INC.
NEW YORK 3, N. Y.

PREFACE

ONE OF THE MOST spectacular aspects of Russian history is the unique, enormous, and continuous expansion of Russia. The insignificant Muscovite principality succeeded in welding together numerous, mutually antagonistic segments of the Russian nation, creating a large state on the plain of eastern Europe. Blocked in the west by strong neighbors, this state, by the sixteenth century, had thrown tenacious offshoots and tentacles toward the East. Over the Ural Mountains went Russian merchants, wave after wave, adventurers and colonists, very much in the same way as Spanish, Portuguese, English, and French empire builders pushed across the ocean toward the Americas. The conquest of Siberia presents a picture somewhat analogous to the conquest of the American continent, and it is remarkable for the speed of the Russian advance. At the end of the sixteenth century the fall of the Siberian khanate (a small Tatar kingdom just beyond the Urals) opened the gate to Asia. By the middle of the seventeenth century the Russian Cossack conquistadors were on the shores of the Pacific. The end of the same century brought the whole of northern Asia under the hand of the Muscovite sovereign. Parallel with the conquest, presenting another human saga of heroism and viciousness, of valiant and vile deeds, went the less picturesque, but far more important process of the development and growth of colonial institutions. It is to be noted, however, that while the acquisition of colonies and their consequent administration by west European powers have aroused a great deal of interest and been studied in detail, the Russian conquest and colonial administration of Siberia have not as yet received sufficient attention.

In the twentieth century the subject of Russian expansion began to interest American historians. The ice was broken by Professor Frank A. Golder, who in 1914 published his *Russian Expansion on the Pacific*. Since then there have appeared two impressive bibliographies dealing with Russian history, compiled by Professor Robert J. Kerner, contributions toward the study of the Russian past and present. Also, in one of his numerous publications, Professor Kerner made clear the significance of the search for a food base in the Russian exploits on and across the Pacific. Under his direction several investigations were prepared treating different phases of Russian history, among them *The Russian Fur Trade*[1] by Professor Raymond H. Fisher, who analyzed the fur trade as a motive for Russian expansion. Finally, in 1942 Professor Kerner published *The Urge to the Sea*,[2] which investigates the fundamental causes and methods of Russian expansion and offers a new approach to the interpretation of Russian history. At the suggestion of Professor Kerner this study has been undertaken to show the mechanism of the early Russian colonial administration and the policies practiced in Siberia by both central and local authorities.

Perhaps an explanation should be made of Russian terms used in this study for which there are no English equivalents. Because the plural of Russian nouns is often unrecognizable to an English reader, the following system was used: For Russian nouns which form the plural simply by adding *i* or *y* to the singular, instead of these endings the English plural ending *s* has been used; thus the Russian singular of *diak* has been changed in the plural form to *diaks,* instead of *diaki.* When the structure of the Russian noun in the plural form was quite different from that in the singular form, however, the Russian plural has been retained in order to avoid mutilation, as in the word *streltsy,* which has the singular form *strelets.* An index of Russian terms, with accents to indicate their correct pronunciation, has been added; page references designate the place where the explanation or translation of the term is given.

In addition to the aid which I received from Professor Kerner in the selection of the topic, I am under deep obligation to him for his helpful and stimulating guidance, as well as for his assistance in various ways.

I am also indebted for helpful suggestions to several friends.

G. V. L.

BERKELEY, CALIFORNIA.

---

[1] Univ. Calif. Publ. Hist., Vol. 31 (Berkeley, 1943).
[2] Full title: *The Urge to the Sea: The Course of Russian History—The Role of Rivers, Portages, Ostrogs, Monasteries, and Furs* (Berkeley, 1942).

CONTENTS

Contents

ILLUSTRATIONS

ABBREVIATIONS

A.A.E.	*Akty arkheograficheskoi ekspeditsii*
A.I.	*Akty istoricheskie*
Chteniia	*Chteniia v imperatorskom obshchestve istorii i drevnostei rossiiskikh pri moskovskom universitete*
D.A.I.	*Dopolneniia k aktam istoricheskim*
D.R.V.	*Drevniaia rossiiskaia vivliofika*
Ezh. soch.	*Ezhemesiachnyia sochinenia*
P.S.R.L.	*Polnoe sobranie russkikh letopisei*
P.S.Z.	*Polnoe sobranie zakonov rossiiskoi imperii*
R.I.B.	*Russkaia istoricheskaia biblioteka*
S.G.G.D.	*Sobranie gosudarstvennykh gramot i dogovorov*
Vremennik	*Vremennik imperatorskago moskovskago obshchestva istorii i drevnostei rossiiskikh*
Zh.M.N.P.	*Zhurnal ministerstva narodnago prosveshcheniia*

CHAPTER I

THE SIBERIAN PRIKAZ, AS A CENTRAL AGENCY OF THE SIBERIAN COLONIAL ADMINISTRATION

IN A STUDY of colonial administration the logical starting point is an inquiry into the origin, structure, and function of the agencies in the central government which guided and helped to determine the administrative development within the colony itself. In Moscow in the seventeenth century, the *Siberian Prikaz* was such an agency, created to deal with specific problems which arose as a result of the Russian expansion in Siberia. This office, which might be considered as the "Colonial Office for Siberia," was an organic part of the already existing administrative body of prikazes, and it cannot be comprehensively described without some explanation of the origin and nature of these institutions, which are comparable to modern ministries and departments.

THE ORIGIN OF THE PRIKAZES

The system of prikazes seems to have been fully developed by the end of the sixteenth century. Its origin, the various factors which influenced its particular features, and the exact time when it became crystallized are subjects of controversy and conjecture in Russian historical literature.[1] One can, however, trace the roots of this system as far as the appanage period of Russian history,[2] when, in the early principalities, certain offices in charge of the *dvoretskii* (major-domo), the *koniushii* (stable man), and the *kaznachei* (treasurer) were known as *prikazes.*[3]

The primary concern of these prikazes was to attend to the affairs of the household and fill the treasury of the prince whom they served. The officials of the prikazes were chosen from the

---

[1] N. P. Likhachev, *Razriadnye diaki XVI veka*, pp. 3–4, 26.

[2] A period of Russian history beginning with the death of Iaroslav (1054) and ending approximately in the first half of the fifteenth century is known as the appanage period. It is characterized by the splitting of Russia into a large number of separate principalities. The appanage period was followed by a period of unification of Russia under the leadership of Moscow.

[3] Likhachev, p. 4.

palace personnel which included *boiars*,[4] various retainers, free servants and *kholops* (serfs). In appointment to the higher posts, the preference naturally was given to the men of noble rank who were known then as *vvedennye* (commissioned, literally introduced) boiars.[5]

Gradually, with Moscow as a pivot, Russia emerged out of the chaos of the appanage period. By the time the formation of the Russian state was well under way, the prikazes of the Muscovite principality had acquired some degree of organization. Affairs demanding the attention of different officials increased in number and complexity. There were records to be kept and correspondence to be carried on. A staff of *diaks* (secretaries—the name is of the same origin as the English "deacon," meaning servant) and their assistants, the *pod'iacheis* (clerks, literally under-diaks), grew up around certain aristocratic boiars who acted as heads.[6] These clerical helpers, probably at first mere scribes, step by step gained considerable prestige. In the fifteenth century, documents were only occasionally attested by the signatures of the diaks. In the sixteenth century a state document without the signatures of the respective diaks was not regarded as valid.[7]

The importance of the office, known as the prikaz or the *izba*, was

---

[4] Before the coming of the Varangians the aristocratic landowners were known among the Russian Slavs as boiars. The same name was later applied to the prominent Russian and Norman members of the entourage of the Varangian princes who established themselves as the Russian rulers. Such boiars were mentioned in the treaty of Igor with the Greeks. They formed the senior *druzhina* (comitatus) of the princes, were consulted in all important matters, and became the nobility of the appanage period. Russian and foreign princes who lost their own possessions and entered the service of another prince were also included in this class. I. D. Beliaev, "Zhiteli moskovskago gosudarstva," *Vremennik*, III, 7–8, 17; *idem*, "Sluzhilye liudi v moskovskom gosudarstve," *Moskovskii sbornik*, I, 366; N. Pavlov-Silvanskii, *Gosudarevy sluzhilye liudi, proiskhozhdenie russkago dvorianstva*, pp. 2–3, 7, 13, 15, 51, 53, 146; V. O. Kliuchevskii, *Kurs russkoi istorii*, II, 94–95, 173–176; M. A. Diakonov, *Ocherki obshchestvennago i gosudarstvennago stroia drevnei Rusi*, pp. 74–89, 244–251, 268.

[5] Kliuchevskii, *op. cit.*, II, 422–423; Pavlov-Silvanskii, *op. cit.*, p. 30.

[6] The Code of Laws of 1497 thus illustrates the relative positions of the diaks and pod'iacheis:

"Collect one denga from the ruble for attaching the seal . . . , collect one altyn [six dengas] from the ruble as a fee for the diak who signed the charter, collect three dengas from the ruble for the pod'iachei who prepared the document. . . .

"Diaks must bring [certain documents] and give orders to pod'iacheis." *Sudebnik* (Code of Laws) of 1497. *A.I.*, I, 150–151.

[7] "Without the boiar's resolution and without the diak's signature the *otpusknaia gramota* (charter) is void." Sudebnik, 1497, *A.I.*, I, 153; Likhachev, p. 28.

enhanced as the diaks and their pod'iacheis became indispensable, trained specialists versed in the affairs of the state. Kliuchevskii has noticed that the provisions of the *Sudebnik* (Code of Laws) of 1497, recognized the prikazes not as the temporary offices of individual boiars, but as permanent departments of the state administration.[8] The Sudebnik required the boiars always to attend to official business in the presence of diaks and instructed the head of a prikaz to refer the cases beyond his jurisdiction to the sovereign himself.[9]

Owing to their origin in the palace offices, many prikazes retained their old household names and were chiefly occupied with the affairs of the prince's household. Such for instance, were the *Prikaz Bol'shogo Dvortsa* (Office of the Large Palace), or the *Koniushennyi Prikaz* (Office of Stables). The prikazes established later were named in accordance with the state functions they had to perform. The development of foreign relations resulted in the creation of the special *Posol'skaia Izba* or *Posol'skii Prikaz* (Office of Ambassadors, that is, Foreign Office). The need to keep the roads, which were infested with thieves and robbers, safe for merchants and other travelers, as well as to protect loyal subjects everywhere, led to the organization of the *Razboinichii Prikaz* (Office of Robberies, that is, Police Office). The expansion of the Muscovite state brought about the appearance of the *Kazanskii, Tverskoi,* and *Novgorodskii* prikazes (Offices of Kazan, Tver, and Novgorod) where the administration of the newly acquired territories was concentrated. In the creation of new offices no special effort was made either to separate the business of the new and old prikazes or to define their relationships. The new prikazes were simply added to the existing mosaic of governmental institutions. The overlapping of functions was a rule rather than an exception. Military affairs, for instance, were dealt with in about fifteen different prikazes.[10]

The number of prikazes, in spite of some consolidations was continually increasing. By the end of the sixteenth century there were over thirty of them, and about the middle of the seventeenth century, Kotoshikhin, a contemporary of the Tsar Aleksei Mikhailovich (1645–1676), counted forty-two.[11] The lack of definite plan-

[8] Kliuchevskii, *op cit.*, II, 431.
[9] Sudebnik, 1497, *A.I.*, I, 148.
[10] Kliuchevskii, *op. cit.*, II, 432–434, 436.
[11] *Ibid.*, II, 436; G. Kotoshikhin, *O Rossii v tsarstvovanie Aleksiia Mikhailovicha*, p. 131.

ning in the development of the governmental structure and the confusing overlapping of the functions of different prikazes hinders attempts at their systematic classification. Likhachev, author of a large monograph dealing with prikazes, and Kliuchevskii, the distinguished Russian historian, indicate two main categories: prikazes handling special types of government business throughout the state, such as the Posol'skii and the Razboinichii, and prikazes which had general charge of various administrative affairs, but within a limited territory, such as the Novgorodskii, or the Kazanskii.[12]

The History of the Siberian Prikaz

The Siberian Prikaz belongs to the latter group of the territorial prikazes. It did not come into existence simultaneously with the beginning of the conquest of Siberia. At first, Siberian affairs were directed from the Posol'skii Prikaz (Foreign Office), probably because in earlier times it had handled the diplomatic relations with the Siberian khans. The documents show that in 1594 the chief Russian official of the Siberian town, Surgut, was requested to forward the *iasak* (fur tribute) to the Prikaz of A. Shchelkalov, who at that time was the head of the Posol'skii Prikaz. In 1595 another official of Surgut was instructed to send certain papers to a diak of the *Posol'skii i Chetvertnoi Prikaz*. Then it was decided that the administration of Siberia should be handled by one of the territorial prikazes. In 1596 Siberian affairs were in charge of the *Novgorodskaia Chet'* (another name for the Novgorodskii Prikaz), known also as the *Chetvert' diaka Ivana Vakhrameeva*. From the Prikaz of Novgorod the administration of Siberia was transferred to the Prikaz of Kazan, or the *Kazanskii Dvorets*. In 1599 two official documents were sent to the Siberian town of Surgut, one signed by Nechai Fedorov, who was on the staff of the Kazanskii Dvorets, and another signed by the diak Ivan Fedorov (who, according to Likhachev, was the same man as Nechai Fedorov). Rozhkov called attention to the existence, in 1599, of the *Sibirskii stol* (Siberian table or desk) within the Kazanskii Dvorets. According to Ogloblin, in 1601 Siberia was definitely placed in charge of the *Kazanskii i Meshcherskii Dvorets*, under the diaks Nechai

---

[12] Kliuchevskii, *op. cit.*, II, 435; Likhachev, p. 3; K. A. Nevolin, "Obrazovanie upravleniia v Rossii ot Ioanna III do Petra Velikago," *Zh.M.N.P.*, Vol. XLI (1844), Nos. 1–3, pp. 30–31, 62.

Fedorov and Afanasii Vlas'ev. Finally, in 1637, as an outgrowth of this prikaz, a separate prikaz for Siberia, the Siberian Prikaz, was created.[13]

The name of the Siberian Prikaz as a subordinate department of the Kazanskii Dvorets appeared as early as 1614, when an official appointed to the Siberian town of Tara was reminded to send furs to the Siberian Prikaz of the Kazanskii Dvorets. At the end of the same document he was requested to address his reports to the Prikaz *Kazanskago i Meshcherskago Dvortsa i Sibirskago Prikazu* (Office of Siberia, at the Office of the Palace of Kazan and Meshchera).[14] Evidently the Siberian Prikaz grew, as it were, within the Kazanskii Dvorets, and even after it had been organized as an independent administrative office it retained for a while one common head with the Kazanskii Dvorets.[15] From 1637 to 1642 Boiar B. M. Lykov was in charge of both prikazes; from 1643 until 1645 Boiar N. I. Odoevskii headed both the Kazanskii Dvorets and the Siberian Prikaz; each prikaz, however, had a different staff of diaks. Later this connection was broken. Thus in 1686, for example, the head of the Siberian Prikaz was Boiar I. B. Repnin, while the head of the Kazanskii Dvorets was Boiar B. A. Golitsyn.[16] During the years 1661–1663 the Siberian Prikaz was temporarily united with the *Prikaz Bol'shogo Prikhoda* (Large Treasury Office). The same *okolnichii* (the rank next boiars in importance), assisted by the diaks G. Poroshin and L. Ermolaev, presided over both prikazes.[17] Again in 1704–1705 the diaks of the Siberian Prikaz had to bring their reports to the *Preobrazhenskii Prikaz* (Office of Criminal Investigation) because under F. I. Romodanovskii, the headship of two prikazes was once more combined, this time the

---

[13] Likhachev, appendix, pp. 95–98; N. N. Ogloblin, *Obozrenie stolbtsov i knig sibirskago prikaza, 1592–1768 g.g.* (cited hereafter as Ogloblin) I, 7; III, 209–210; IV, 123, 125–127; N. A. Rozhkov, *Russkaia istoriia*, Vol. IV, Part 1, p. 123; "Dva sibirskikh nakaza," *Chteniia*, Vol. CCXXIX (1909), Bk. 2, pt. 4, pp. 3, 7; V. K. Andrievich, *Istoriia Sibiri*, I, 113–114; P. N. Butsinskii, *Zaselenie Sibiri i byt eia pervykh nasel'nikov*, pp. 231–233; S. Prutchenko, *Sibirskiia okrainy*, I, 10; G. F. Mueller, "Sibirskaia istoriia," *Ezh. soch.*, XIX (1764), 523–527.

[14] Ogloblin, I, 7 n.; IV, 141–142.

[15] "The Siberian Prikaz: it is headed by the same boiar who is the head of the Kazanskii Dvorets. Two diaks are his associates. Within the jurisdiction of this prikaz are the Siberian kingdom and towns" (written about 1666–1667). Kotoshikhin, p. 104.

[16] *D.R.V.*, XX, 317–319, 395–397.

[17] Ogloblin, I, 6; IV, 69–70; *D.R.V.*, XX, 288.

Siberian and the Preobrazhenskii.[18] The Siberian Prikaz declined
in importance in 1711 when Prince Gagarin was appointed Gover-
nor General of Siberia, and the *Sibirskaia Kantseliariia* or the
Kantseliariia Sibirskoi Gubernii (the Siberian Office, or the Office
of the Gubernia of Siberia) took over the functions of the Prikaz.
In 1730 the Siberian Prikaz was re-established, although with fewer
powers than it had had in the seventeenth century, and it was
finally abolished in 1763 by the reforms of Catherine II.[19]

PERSONNEL OF THE SIBERIAN PRIKAZ

Throughout most of its existence the Siberian Prikaz had an organization similar to that of other prikazes, that is, it had a boiar as
its head, and two diaks. At one time instead of a boiar an okolnichii
was appointed, but he was raised to the rank of boiar before he
was out of office.[20] At another time instead of a boiar there was a
dumnyi diak (the highest kind of diak).[21] Sometimes an associate
from the court nobility was added to the office of the boiar. Boiar
Streshnev had first as his associate *Stolnik* (courtier of the table)
Fedorov and later Stolnik Iakovlev. Boiar Repnin had as his associate Okolnichii Musin-Pushkin. The number of diaks in the
Siberian Prikaz remained virtually constant: there were custom-
arily two of them, and only in 1660 were there three.[22]

The diaks represented, so to say, the nobility of the robe. Few
of them attained the rank of dumnyi diak, which was immediately
below that of okolnichii.[23] Among them was, for instance, Dumnyi

---

[18] *D.R.V.*, XX, 397.

[19] *Ibid.;* Ogloblin, I, 7; Prutchenko, I, 68–69; manifesto, 1763 *P.S.Z.*, XVI,
466; Andrievich, *op. cit.*, I, 115; Mueller, "Sibirskaia istoriia," *Ezh. soch.*, XIX
(1764), 527–528.

[20] Okolnichii Streshnev was raised to the rank of boiar in 1676. *D.R.V.*, XX,
396.

[21] *D.R.V.*, XX, 397; Ogloblin, IV, 9.

[22] *D.R.V.*, XX, 395–397.

[23] The Muscovite social structure was composed of the following ranks listed
in order of importance:
    1. Boiars (the highest nobility).
    2. Okolnichiis (courtiers of the immediate entourage of the tsar) and
       postelnichiis (courtiers of the bed).
    3. Dumnye diaks (state secretaries).
    4. Spalniks (courtiers of the bedchamber).
    5. Stolniks (courtiers of the table).
    6. Striaphiis (courtiers attending to food, clothing, and other household
       matters).
    7. Dvoriane Moskovskie (the nobles of Moscow).
    8. Diaks.

Diak A. A. Vinius, who had been the head of the Siberian Prikaz from 1697, holding an office usually filled by a boiar.[24] In discussing the social origin of diaks, Kotoshikhin remarks that they might be either nobles of Moscow, or provincial nobles, or *gosti* (members of the privileged upper class of merchants), or former *pod'iacheis* (clerks of the Prikazes). Most of them probably came from the last group. The diaks received salaries of from 80 to 150 rubles per year. The dumnye diaks during the reign of Mikhail Fedorovich drew salaries of 200 rubles per year; in 1686 their salaries were raised to 300 rubles, and in addition they received occasional bonuses.[25]

There seems to be a great deal of disagreement among historians about the importance of the different members of prikazes and their relations to each other. Likhachev is emphatic in his assertion that the boiars and their associates acted together as a board similar to the later "colleges" of Peter I. Other writers think that the boiar of a prikaz was the real "boss" of his prikaz, with other members of the staff occupying definitely inferior positions. Kavelin, while accepting the latter view for earlier times, concedes that the functioning of the prikazes in the seventeenth century was in many ways a preliminary step toward the subsequent colleges.[26]

In a meeting of the staff of the Siberian Prikaz, no doubt the voice of the boiar, with all the prestige of his noble origin and exalted rank, carried the greatest weight. It is nevertheless quite conceivable that the pompous importance of the aristocratic head of the Prikaz on many occasions had to yield to the diaks' knowl-

---

9. Zhiltsy (unit of the Moscow garrison composed of nobles).

10. Dvoriane gorodovye (provincial nobles).

11. Boiarskie deti (literally "sons of boiars"—a misleading name applied to petty nobility. The sons of boiars or as they are called in this study the "boiar sons" will be described in detail later, in chapter v).

Based on: Kotoshikhin, pp. 25–29, 31; *D.R.V.*, XX, 131–139, 142–147, 151–171, 198–201, 203–205, 221–222, 228–231; Diakonov, pp. 226–275; Pavlov-Silvanskii, *Feodalism v drevnei Rusi*, pp. 112–113; *idem, Gosudarevy sluzhilye liudi, passim.*

[24] *D.R.V.*, XX, 397.

[25] Kotoshikhin, pp. 28, 157–159; *D.R.V.*, XX, 150–157, 238.

Kliuchevskii (*Russkii rubl' XVI–XVIII v.*, pp. 35, 47, 51, 61) estimated the value of the Muscovite ruble as follows: in the second half of the sixteenth century, equal to 74 prewar rubles; in the "Time of Troubles," equal to 12 prewar rubles; in the second half of the seventeenth century, equal to 17 prewar rubles. (The prewar ruble was approximately equal to 50 cents—prewar here refers to the time prior to World War I.)

[26] Different points of view are listed by Likhachev, pp. 4–5, 11–19.

edge, experience, and ability to express their thoughts in writing.[27] As was stated above, the Sudebnik of 1497 required the presence of diaks during the performance of official business, and their signatures had to appear on accepted resolutions. In 1649 the *Ulozhenie* (Code) of the Tsar Aleksei Mikhailovich went further in this respect and gave the diaks the right to participate in making decisions. In order to prevent any irregular action of the boiar, the Ulozhenie demanded that records of attendance be kept and the absence of any member of the staff be duly accounted for.[28]

These regulations were in effect in the Siberian Prikaz even before the appearance of the Ulozhenie. Here official matters were attended to jointly by the boiar and his diaks; for instance, in 1637 the inventory of furs received by the Prikaz was submitted to the boiar Lykov and the diaks Shipulin and Patrikeev. Reports to the tsar were made from the staff as a body; for example, the report on furs in Mangazeia, was presented in 1635, jointly by the boiar Lykov and the diaks Panov and Peresonov. In the absence of any member of the staff the report contained an explanation such as "the diak Bolotnikov was ill" or "the boiar Cherkasskii was in the country." After the Ulozhenie went into effect the procedure already evolved in practice became fixed officially. In 1656 the appraisers of Siberian furs made their report not to a single official but to the boiar Trubetskoi and the diaks Protopopov and Ivanov. The report of 1686, about exacting money from the townsmen of Tiumen, was given to the tsar in the name of the boiar Repnin and the two diaks.[29] Apparently the diaks could sometimes use their own judgment and act on their own initiative. In 1594 certain officials appointed to assist the *voevoda* (the chief town official) in Surgut were told to write directly to the diak Nechai Fedorov of the Kazanskii i Meshcherskii Dvorets.[30] In 1648 the diak Proto-

---

[27] Kotoshikhin, himself a former pod'iachei, does not seem to entertain a very high opinion of the statesmanship of the Muscovite boiars: "The tsar honors many men by appointing them as boiars, not because of their wisdom, but because they belong to great families. Among these boiars there are men not able to read and write and not educated ... men who can only stroke their beards in silence [while attending the tsar's council]." Kotoshikhin, p. 27.

[28] "In every prikaz where are to be found a boiar, or okolnichii ... with ... associates. ... They have to attend to the business *vopche* (together). If one of them shall be absent on account of illness or an important engagement then the business is to be done by those present, and they all have to sign the decision. The name of the absentee should not be written [on the decision], but the reason for his absence must be stated." Ulozhenie, 1649, *P.S.Z.*, I, 21.

[29] Ogloblin, IV, 6, 9, 83.   [30] *Ibid.*, IV, 39.

popov alone acknowledged the furs received from the Enisei and Baikal regions.[31] The diaks also carried on correspondence with other prikazes, especially when some information was needed.[32] But their freedom of action was only within certain limits. In 1690 the diak Prokofiev took it upon himself alone to write instructions to the voevoda of Iakutsk. The latter, however, was asked to return this document, because it was issued without the sanction of the head of the Prikaz, the boiar Repnin.[33]

Subordinated to the boiar of the Siberian Prikaz and to his associates were the numerous pod'iacheis. They were divided into junior, intermediate, and senior grades. Halfway between the diaks and ordinary pod'iacheis were the so-called *pod'iacheis s pripis'iu* (pod'iacheis entitled to attest the documents and affix their signatures), who composed official *ukazy, gramoty i pamiati* (decrees, instructions, and memorials).[34] Ordinary pod'iacheis received from 3 to 40 rubles per year.[35] The salaries of the pod'iacheis s pripis'iu were much higher.[36] From senior pod'iachei and from pod'iachei s pripis'iu it was possible to be promoted to the rank of diak, and many pod'iacheis s pripis'iu were sent to Siberia, as associates of the local voevodas (such appointees had the standing of acting diaks).[37]

Organization of the Siberian Prikaz

These various officials handled Siberian affairs, which were distributed among the different *stols* (tables or desks accommodating one or several men) very much in the same fashion as the affairs of the state were scattered within the framework of prikazes. Some of the stols attended to specific activities concerning the whole of Siberia, while other stols dealt with a multitude of administrative detail, but within the limits of a definite geographic area. Included in the first group, for instance, were the *razriadnyi stol* (having charge of men in service) and the *denezhnyi stol* (having charge of money), both mentioned in documents pertaining to the period of 1668–1672. In the documents of 1686 the names of the *Tobolskii stol, Eniseiskii stol, Iakutskii stol* (same as *Lenskii stol*), and *Mangazeiskii stol* appear among the stols dealing with the regional administrative units of Siberia.[38]

[31] *Ibid.,* IV, 85.   [32] *Ibid.,* IV, 58.   [33] *Ibid.,* IV, 23.
[34] *D.R.V.,* XX, 153; Pavlov-Silvanskii, *Gosudarevy sluzhilye liudi,* p. 183.
[35] Ogloblin, III, 127–128; IV, 167.
[36] *D.R.V.,* XX, 153.   [37] *Ibid.*   [38] Ogloblin, IV, 48–49.

The subdivision of a prikaz into stols was common in Muscovite administrative practice. In this respect the Siberian Prikaz resembles other prikazes. It had, however, one interesting department which was without counterpart in other prikazes, the so-called *sobolinaia kazna* (sable treasury), where furs coming from Siberia were received, appraised, and disposed of. The sable treasury developed gradually. When Siberia was under the control of the Kazanskii i Meshcherskii Dvorets, there seems to have been no special department in charge of furs, although the receipt and disposal of furs was already in the hands of special types of officials, *golovas* (heads) and *tselovalniks* (literally sworn men), who acted as expert appraisers and were at that time entirely subordinate to the bureaucratic officials of the Dvorets.[39] When eventually a special fur department was organized, it was called at first *gosudareva kazna* (sovereign's treasury) and later became known as the sobolinaia kazna or the sable treasury. With the increase of business this sable treasury was divided into *palatas* (chambers). By the middle of the seventeenth century, there were in existence the *rostsennaia palata* (chamber of appraisal), the *kupetskaia palata* (merchants' chamber)—which should be distinguished from the *kupetskii stol* (merchants' table) of the Prikaz—the *kazennaia palata* (treasury chamber), called otherwise the *denezhnyi priem* (money receipts), the *skorniachaia palata* (chamber of furriers), and possibly some other palatas.[40]

A subsequent chapter will describe the part which the Siberian furs played in the revenues of the Muscovite state. Here it is sufficient to mention that the value and volume of fur shipments which had to pass through the sable treasury necessitated the employment of numerous fur experts, who were not to be found among the bureaucratic personnel of the Siberian Prikaz. These specialists had to be drafted from the businessmen of Moscow, furriers, dealers in cloth and leather, or men engaged in similar occupations. They were provided upon the request of the government by the *gostinnaia sotnia* (privileged merchants' hundred)— an organization similar to a guild—or by the *sukonnaia sotnia* (clothiers' hundred) which elected some of their members to serve in the sable treasury for one year without salary. The men elected, after some formalities, took a solemn oath to discharge their duties

---

[39] *Ibid.*, IV, 77.   [40] *Ibid.*, III, 150; IV, 77.

faithfully, the ceremony being performed in one of the famous Moscow cathedrals, and were then installed in an office which carried with it both honor and heavy responsibility.[41]

The social standing of the elected men determined their positions in the sable treasury. The most distinguished merchants assumed responsibility over different chambers of the treasury with the rank of *golova* (head). The rest of the elected men became *tselo-valniks* (sworn men) of different ranks, most important among them being the *kazennye tselovalniks* (sworn men of the treasury). The tselovalniks accepted, appraised, and sorted furs and other goods of the Siberian Prikaz, and disposed of them in various ways. They kept the records and performed all the work within the sable treasury. Only at the end of the seventeenth century did there appear among them the regular employees of the Prikaz—the pod'iacheis. At the beginning of their service the golovas received detailed instructions from the Siberian Prikaz proper, which office afterward was explicitly forbidden to interfere with their activi-ties, although it constantly supervised them. Energetic golovas and tselovalniks were occasionally rewarded with a silver cup, a piece of cloth, or some other goods. On the other hand, these elected officials were required to make up any deficit incurred through negligence or dishonesty, and when such losses were serious they could be punished by flogging.[42]

POLICIES OF THE SIBERIAN PRIKAZ IN SIBERIAN AFFAIRS

The care of furs by the almost autonomous sable treasury was only a part, although a very important part, of the business which went through the Siberian Prikaz. The development of the Siberian government, the guidance and supervision of Siberian officials, the organization and provisioning of the army of occupation, the ad-ministration of justice, the financial exploitation of Siberia, the colonization, the diplomatic relations with the peoples along the Siberian border, and many other problems occupied the attention of the Siberian Prikaz proper.

In formulating policies for its administrative agents in Siberia, the Prikaz needed a great deal of information about local condi-tions. This information was gathered from various sources, but

[41] Kotoshikhin, p. 157; Ogloblin, IV, 78–81.
[42] Ogloblin, IV, 77–84; Kotoshikhin, pp. 157–159.

chiefly from the *otpiski* (reports) of the local Siberian officials. According to Ogloblin, the archives of the Siberian Prikaz still contain from 20,000 to 30,000 such reports and replies to them from Moscow.[43] The government replies often contain such expressions as "and you did not write to us," or "you should write often," stressing the necessity of more complete and more frequent reports. Another important source of information for the Prikaz were the *chelobitnyia* (petitions) which were received from the serving men,[44] the settlers, and even the natives in Siberia. These documents, of which also several thousands are extant, either complained about certain existing evils of administration or pointed out some of the needs of the population.[45] In response to these petitions, the Prikaz sent to Siberia *syshchiks* (special investigators) who investigated the abuses of voevodas and other serving men, either in the territory of a certain town or in the whole of Siberia. Upon their return the investigators reported their findings to the Prikaz.[46] Finally, officials who completed their service in Siberia, messengers who brought furs or correspondence from Siberia, and merchants who returned from their business trips had to appear in the Siberian Prikaz and render accounts of Siberian affairs. Special books, *podnevnyia zapisi* (daily notes) were kept in the Siberian Prikaz where information concerning persons who had arrived from Siberia was duly recorded, as follows: the reason for their arrival from Siberia, news which they brought from their own town or *uezd* (geographic unit subordinated to a town), news of what they had seen or heard on the way, and comment of the Prikaz's officials as to how the statements obtained accorded with the material already on hand.[47]

Border affairs seemed to be of special interest to the Siberian Prikaz. Several inquiries concerning them are mentioned by Ogloblin. In 1628, for instance, the serving men from Tara were asked the details about measures taken to prevent the raids of the Kalmucks and about the building of an *ostrog* (fort or blockhouse) on the river Olga, a tributary of the Irtysh. Similar inquiries were also made in 1640 and 1641 about the same region and about its

---

[43] Ogloblin, III, 2.

[44] Throughout this study the term "serving men"—a literal translation of the Russian *sluzhilye liudi*—designates men employed in various types of military service.

[45] Ogloblin, III, 87.   [46] *Ibid.*, III, 180.   [47] *Ibid.*, IV, 100–101.

safety from the Kalmucks and Kirghiz. A great deal of interest was shown by the government in the situation in Dauria. In 1652 the cossacks from Irkutsk were questioned about the expedition of Khabarov. In 1680–1682 the serving men from Albazin gave a detailed report about the Amur basin. In 1686 men from Albazin had to give an account concerning the events which took place there in 1684. In 1701 Vladimir Atlasov submitted a report about the first expedition to Kamchatka. The Siberian Prikaz apparently was especially interested in information about the acquisition of new territories and the safety of frontiers. However, at the same time it also investigated very thoroughly the internal conditions of Siberia. Unrest among the natives, activities of the voevodas, the condition of crops, the prices of grain, the reasons for dissatisfaction among the agricultural settlers who were deserting the fields assigned to them, and other similar topics were given a large place in the statements made by the arrivals from Siberia.[48]

These continuous and persistent efforts of the Muscovite government to acquire a better knowledge of Siberia, and the careful attention with which it received every item of information are significant. They show that the government was aware of its ignorance of the Siberian colony, a fact which brought about a willingness to adopt policies sufficiently flexible to meet the particular needs of the Siberian administration. In his studies of the documents of the Siberian Prikaz, Ogloblin was greatly impressed by the extent to which the initiative and activity of the Siberian agents of the state had influenced the decisions of the Prikaz. Prutchenko, interested in the development of local administration in Siberia, has called attention to the fact that, while other prikazes carried out the policies of centralization and uniformity in the territories under their jurisdiction, the Siberian Prikaz allowed the Siberian administration to develop characteristics of its own.[49]

RELATIONS BETWEEN THE SIBERIAN PRIKAZ AND OTHER PRIKAZES

In several matters Siberian affairs brought the Siberian Prikaz in contact with other prikazes. The *Razriad* (Office of Military Affairs) provided the Siberian Prikaz with the voevodas, other officers, and troops for service in Siberia. The *Pomestnyi Prikaz*

---

[48] *Ibid.*, III, 35, 38; IV, 101–103.   [49] *Ibid.*, I, 11; IV, 3; Prutchenko, I, 11.

(Office of Estates) had charge of *pomest'ia* (estates) granted to the serving men to keep them in service. The *Posol'skii Prikaz* was involved in the diplomatic relations with the peoples along the Siberian frontier, and in matters concerning the furs which the Siberian Prikaz supplied to be used as gifts or bribes by the Russian diplomats. Questions concerning the exiled *Cherkasy* (Ukrainians) and the gifts of furs to Ukrainian officials and churchmen brought the Siberian Prikaz in contact with the *Malorossiiskii* (Little Russian, Ukrainian) *Prikaz*. There were also numerous dealings with the *Iamskoi Prikaz* (in charge of transportation), which supplied the means of transportation for the serving men going to Siberia. There was hardly a branch of the Muscovite administration which, for one reason or another, did not have official contacts with the Siberian Prikaz. With the development of extensive commercial activity through the sable treasury, the Siberian Prikaz was sometimes commissioned by the other prikazes to sell cloth, precious stones, and other goods which somehow came into their possession.[50]

Occasionally the Siberian Prikaz had to guard its authority against the encroachment or interference of other prikazes, some of which developed the practice of sending orders to the Siberian officials over the head of the Siberian Prikaz. To prevent confusion the tsar issued decrees in 1684 and 1695 prohibiting the Siberian voevodas from executing any of these orders. The decree of 1695 stated that if any money were spent by the local officials in order to satisfy the demands of other prikazes, without the approval of the Siberian Prikaz, the amount was to be exacted from these officials who, besides, would be subjected to the "anger and cruel punishment" of the tsar.[51]

Further conflicts between the Siberian Prikaz and other prikazes arose over the question of Siberian traffic. Travelers to Siberia, in order to pass the customhouse on the Siberian frontier and to obtain the state-controlled stage facilities, needed special *proiezzhiia i podorozhnyia gramoty* (passports and stage permits). Ordinarily the Siberian Prikaz handled all such documents and collected at the same time a special tax on goods to be imported to Siberia. To avoid the payment of this tax, merchants and other travelers applied to other prikazes, especially to the Iamskoi Prikaz, for

[50] Ogloblin, IV, 52–54, 74, 93.
[51] *Ibid.*, IV, 19; imennoi ukaz, 1695, P.S.Z., III, 206.

traveling papers and succeeded in getting them. To concentrate the control of the traffic to Siberia in the hands of the Siberian Prikaz alone, the government published an *imennoi ukaz* (decree of the tsar) in 1696, ordering a special seal for the Siberian Prikaz to be used on its documents. The customhouse in Verkhoturie received orders to recognize only the documents bearing this seal. Travelers with passports from other prikazes were to be detained, their documents were to be sent back to Moscow, and, if they were merchants trying to escape the payment of tax on their goods, the goods were to be "taken over for the great sovereign."[52]

Position of the Siberian Prikaz with Respect to the Boiarskaia Duma

In all cases involving conflicts with other prikazes, the Siberian Prikaz had to appeal to higher authority. In general, all matters of importance had to be referred to the tsar. The reports to the tsar usually contained the documents relating to the case, extracts from the existing regulations, and citations from precedents, either from the practice of the Siberian Prikaz or from the practice of other prikazes. Whenever a report called for a decision it bore the resolution of the tsar, probably adopted in conference with his councilors; if the report was presented only for information, it was marked simply "read in the palace."[53]

The Siberian Prikaz had to submit its reports not only to the tsar himself, but also to the *Boiarskaia Duma* (council of boiars). This institution was composed of boiars, okolnichiis, *dumskie dvoriane* (nobles of the council), and *dumnye diaks* (secretaries of the council).[54] The Ulozhenie of 1649, in all probability fixing a practice already in existence, definitely required the prikazes to submit all doubtful cases to the tsar and members of the Duma.[55] The reports to the Boiarskaia Duma occasionally were given in the absence of the tsar. Ogloblin, who studied several such reports,

[52] Imennoi ukaz, 1696, *P.S.Z.*, III, 266–268.
[53] Ogloblin, IV, 5–7.
[54] "The officials of the prikazes are ordered to decide various local and state affairs according to the Ulozhenie, but whenever questions arise which are beyond their authority, then they must ask boiars and *dumnye liudi* (councilors) or the tsar himself." Kotoshikhin, p. 136; Ogloblin, IV, 26.
[55] "The doubtful cases which the prikazes are not able to decide should be reported to the sovereign tsar ... Aleksei Mikhailovich ... and to his boiars, okolnichiis, and members of the Duma." Ulozhenie, 1649, *P.S.Z.*, I, 17; Prutchenko, I, 6–7.

hesitates to say whether the tsar attended only the most important sessions or whether his presence was purely a matter of chance.[56]

Another authority which assumed a certain control over the Siberian Prikaz was the *Raspravnaia Palata* (Chamber of Settlement or Adjustment), otherwise called *U Raspravnykh Del,* organized about the middle of the seventeenth century as a standing committee of the Duma. Professor Sergeevich, the author of *The Legal Antiquities of Russia,* has stressed in his work the difference between the ancient institution of Boiarskaia Duma and this new administrative body, the Raspravnaia Palata. The Boiarskaia Duma did not have a permanent membership. It held its meetings irregularly and only upon the wish of the tsar, and in his absence it acted only at a special order. This institution had not been subject to definite regulations. Its jurisdiction had not been confined to any special matter, and it discussed only business introduced at the wish of the tsar. On the other hand, the Raspravnaia Palata had a definite organization, held its meetings regularly, had its activity defined by the Ulozhenie and by decrees, and attended to the cases brought from different prikazes or to petitions of private individuals. One day a week was devoted, among other matters, to the reports from the Siberian Prikaz.[57]

The preparation of the Ulozhenie and the establishment of the Raspravnaia Palata were but steps in the administrative re-

[56] Ogloblin, IV, 8.

[57] V. I. Sergeevich, *Russkiia iuridicheskiia drevnosti,* Vol. II, Part 2, pp. 405–411, 413; Prutchenko, I, 7–8; Diakonov, pp. 448–449; Nevolin, p. 55.

"The boiars, okolnichiis, and councilors should hold their meetings in the chamber and by the sovereign's order they should decide all together on the various affairs." Ulozhenie, 1649, *P.S.Z.,* I, 17.

"Cases from the prikazes must be brought to the boiars in the Golden Chamber for deliberation and settlement; on Monday from the Razriad, Posol'skii Prikaz..., on Thursday from the Bol'shoi Dvorets, from the Siberian Prikaz..." Ukaz, 1669, *P.S.Z.,* I, 828.

"The great sovereign has ordered the boiars, okolnichiis, and councilors to report daily to the palace at one o'clock to attend to the business." Imennoi ukaz, 1676, *P.S.Z.,* II, 4.

"The *sudii* (judges or heads of prikazes) should bring cases which fall beyond their jurisdiction to the boiars... cases from the Siberian Prikaz should be brought on Tuesday." Imennoi ukaz, 1676, *P.S.Z.,* II, 72.

"Boiars, okolnichiis, and councilors must be seated in the chamber and attend to the contended cases and petitions from all prikazes and must decide... according to the decrees of the great sovereign and the Ulozhenie." Imennoi ukaz, 1680, *P.S.Z.,* II, 281.

"Boiars, okolnichiis, and councilors sitting in judgment *U Raspravnykh Del* in the Golden Chamber as associates of Prince Odoevskii should leave the chamber whenever there is a discussion concerning themselves or their relatives." Imennoi ukaz, 1681, *P.S.Z.,* II, 346.

organization of the Muscovite state toward greater efficiency and centralization. The Raspravnaia Palata became a unifying super-structure over the prikazes, which, accordingly, began losing some of their former importance. The decree of 1677, which transferred the appointment of the voevodas from the prikazes to the tsar himself[58] (meaning his council, or its executive committee, that is, the Raspravnaia Palata), was another step in this direction. The Siberian Prikaz now presented weekly reports to the Raspravnaia Palata instead of the former occasional reports to the tsar and his councilors, who had usually approved the measures of the Prikaz. The Raspravnaia Palata assumed a more dominating position and even censured the Siberian Prikaz. In 1697, for instance, it pointed out to the Prikaz that the merchants serving in the sable treasury had intentionally overappraised government furs. Thus the govern-ment could not dispose of its furs, whereas the merchants were doing a brisk business, successfully underselling government furs.[59]

In formulating the most important policies in respect to Siberia, the Siberian Prikaz was unquestionably influenced by the cream of the Muscovite political and social world, represented in the Boiar-skaia Duma. Here were to be found men who dreamed about fur-ther expansion in Siberia, about the sea route from Mangazeia (a town in Siberia) to India, and about the conquest of China.[60] It was here, around 1681, that plans were made to divide Russia into a number of large provinces, each in charge of a boiar appointed for life as a sort of viceroy. Siberia was designated as one such province. The ambitious originators of this scheme even obtained the consent of the Tsar Fedor Alekseevich, and the plan failed only through the stubborn resistance of the patriarch.[61]

This investigation of the origin, structure, and function of the Siberian "Colonial Office" seems to point to the conclusion that the Siberian Prikaz was not an innovation in Muscovite admin-

[58] Imennoi ukaz, 1677, *P.S.Z.*, II, 143.
[59] Nakaz to Tobolsk, 1697, *P.S.Z.*, III, 359.
[60] Who knows, it might be possible to find a road to the sea route from Man-gareia [Mangazeia] to India." Iu. Križanić, *Russkoe gosudarstvo v polovine XVII veka* (P. Bezsonov, ed.), Part I, p. 56.
"I have heard people saying that the tsar wishes to send the army to China. . . . The damned enemy [devil] would like to see the Russians attempt to conquer China. . . . In our time there are several men who submit their opinions about Siberia, and who advise the building of new ostrogs, and the expansion of power further and further." *Ibid.*, Part II, pp. 121–122; Prutchenko, I, 8–9.
[61] Kliuchevskii, *Kurs russkoi istorii*, III, 104–105.

istrative practice. It was one of several new prikazes added to the already existing system of these institutions. As the result of a common historical background, its organization was similar to that evolved by the older prikazes. Like the rest of them, the Siberian Prikaz had at its head a sort of board of directors, presided over by a nobleman of high rank, who had to maintain close coöperation with his colleagues—administrative experts of less distinguished origin.

Furthermore, because this "Colonial Office" of Siberia was not merely an administrative institution, but also the chief business office of the government fur enterprise, it had developed a special business department, managed by specialists, who were different from the ordinary type of government official. This was the feature which distinguished it from the other prikazes.

With the extension of Russian influence in Siberia, the Siberian Prikaz assumed a more and more important role. In 1637, about the time that the Russians tapped the wealth of furs on the Lena River, it was established as a separate prikaz. The former "Siberian stol," which at first was shifted from one prikaz to another, evolved into one of the largest and most important government offices. As such it was able to assert itself among the other prikazes, and its decisions could be overruled only by the tsar. With the appearance, however, of the Raspravnaia Palata, the Siberian Prikaz had to recognize the authority of this administrative superstructure over the prikazes.

CHAPTER II

THE FEUDAL BACKGROUND OF SIBERIAN ADMINISTRATION

T HE PRECEDING CHAPTER traced the origin and gave a description of what might be called the "Siberian Colonial Office." The subsequent chapters will discuss the colonial administration as it operated in Siberia. As a preliminary step, the present chapter offers a survey of the historical antecedents of the local Siberian administrative system. The purpose of such a survey is to bring out the influence of the old administrative institutions and practices within this system as distinct from the new administrative developments, whether created by the deliberate policies of the Muscovite government, or evolved as a product of local circumstances.

THE SYSTEM OF "KORMLENIE"

Lack of proper historical perspective decreases the value of several works devoted to the early history of Siberia whenever a question of Russian colonial administration enters into the discussion. Much energy has been wasted, for instance, on the condemnation of the early Siberian officials, who, in addition to the government revenues, were accustomed to impose special tributes on the population for personal benefit—a practice which often has been interpreted as clear evidence of administrative corruption. This severe judgment would have been modified, no doubt, had the writers taken into consideration the extent to which the average administrator of the seventeenth century was still entangled in the feudal trappings of the past, among which *kormlenie* (literally, feeding), had held a most prominent place.

This system had existed in the appanage period of Russian history and lasted well into the second half of the sixteenth century. Because feudalism developed differently in Russia and in western Europe, and because Russian feudal institutions are not widely known, a brief explanation of the system of kormlenie may be justified.[1] The nature of this system is suggested by its name—

---

[1] An extensive and authoritative explanation of the nature of kormlenie is given in an article by V. O. Kliuchevskii, "Po povodu zametki Golovacheva," *Russkii arkhiv*, 1889, No. 2, pp. 138–145.

feeding. The ancient Russian code of laws, the *Russkaia Pravda* (Russian Law),[2] for example, declared that a certain official was to receive from the community where he performed his duties various items of subsistence, including two chickens every day, some cheese on Wednesdays and Fridays, and seven loaves of bread every week.[3] This was the original "feeding." The more important the official, the greater and more variable was the amount of feeding, because not only he but also his servants and horses had to be taken care of. Also, a large and wealthy community could furnish feeding far in excess of the immediate needs of an official. The early princes found that the system of kormlenie offered an excellent opportunity to reward faithful nobles for their military and court service. The boiars were given the larger towns, and the less important nobles obtained the smaller towns or rural districts. The holders of towns were called *namestniks* (prince's lieutenants) and the holders of rural districts were known as *volostels* (a name derived from *volost*, a rural district). These nobles, collectively known as *kormlenshchiks,* were supposed to protect their holdings and to maintain law and order within them.[4] In return, the towns and villages were to supply them with feeding, which was enlarged beyond mere food to include "gifts" in the form of produce and money, as well as various taxes and dues. Important sources of a kormlenshchik's income were court dues and fees, marriage taxes, and sometimes customs taxes. Later, the Muscovite government regarded these sources of income as its own prerogative, but the Siberian officials, following the usages set by the kormlenshchiks before them, continued to collect their own taxes in addition to those of the government, and expected the administered population to "remember" them with gifts on holidays and special occasions.[5]

Within their holdings the namestniks and volostels appointed a number of officials whom they picked from their own household retainers, either free servitors or serfs. Some of the namestniks were important nobles with petty armies of their own. During the

---

[2] The *Russkaia Pravda* is commonly translated as the "Russian Truth." In the opinion of the author the accurate meaning of this title is as given above.
[3] The Russkaia Pravda, L. Maksimovich, comp., *Ukazatel' rossiiskikh zakonov,* pp. 2–3.
[4] Kliuchevskii, "Po povodu zametki," pp. 138–145; B. Chicherin, *Oblastnyia uchrezhdeniia Rossii v XVII veke,* pp. 4–5; V. O. Kliuchevskii, *Kurs russkoi istorii,* II, 425–428.
[5] Kliuchevskii, *Kurs russkoi istorii,* II, 426–428; Chicherin, pp. 9–12; M. N. Pokrovskii, *Russkaia istoriia s drevneishikh vremen,* II, 249.

appanage period the bonds which attached them to their princes were rather loose; they were free to leave their masters and seek service under other princes if they so desired. With relative independence in the administration of their holdings, they might have become feudal lords of the west-European pattern. Under the system of kormlenie it would seem that the control over the towns and volosts granted to the kormlenshchiks might easily have slipped out of the hands of the princes. However, such a situation did not arise owing to the circumstances involved in the assignment of kormlenie. It often happened that the same town was granted simultaneously to two namestniks each with a rival set of officials. In many places the kormlenshchik received only a part of the revenues from his holding, the other part being retained by the prince; in such places the prince maintained his own agents side by side with those of the namestnik.[6] Furthermore, kormlenie was regarded as a temporary reward, and, after improving his fortune, the kormlenshchik was expected to return to the capital and resume active service for the prince, with a possibility of getting another kormlenie in the future. Kormlenie was seldom given for life and rarely became hereditary.[7] During the appanage period, the princes made arrangements among themselves whereby they could jointly exploit the larger and wealthier towns. It was not unusual to find in the same town an alternation of namestniks sent by different princes, or even to find there namestniks of different princes at the same time. Quite naturally, a stronger prince had a greater opportunity to exploit the town in the interests of his namestniks than a less important prince.[8]

The system of kormlenie could flourish when the prince had no administrative machinery at his disposal and when he could not appear everywhere in person to collect his revenues, which were usually in the form of bulky produce. Under such conditions the distribution of certain localities among the namestniks and volostels offered definite advantages to the rulers.[9] During the Musco-

---

[6] Chicherin, pp. 7, 12; Kliuchevskii, *Kurs russkoi istorii,* II, 428.

[7] Kliuchevskii, *Kurs russkoi istorii,* II, 429.

[8] "I shall send my namestnik to the town . . . , and you will send yours." Treaty of Prince Dimitrii Ioannovich . . . with his brothers, 1388, *S.G.G.D.,* I, 57. "We will not hold court without your namestnik, and you shall not hold court without our namestnik." Treaty of Prince Vasilii Dmitrievich with his brothers, 1389, *ibid.,* I, 63; also the will of Ivan III, 1504, *ibid.,* I, 394; instructions to the namestnik of Kostroma, 1499, *A.I.,* I, 164; Chicherin, p. 7.

[9] Pokrovskii, II, 79–80.

vite period, however, especially after the middle of the fifteenth
century, the Muscovite princes began to feel the disadvantages of
this arrangement. By this time the growing Muscovite state, which
had absorbed one principality after another, had developed within
itself a strong feudal aristocracy. This aristocracy was composed
of the old Muscovite boiars, of boiars who had formerly served
other princes and had been induced to abandon their masters for
the prince of Moscow, and of princes who had by then lost their
possessions. As the price of their loyalty, the Muscovite princes had
to grant them lands, privileges, and appointments as kormlenshchiks. Such a policy facilitated the consolidation of the state, but
at the same time weakened its internal structure. It created a strong
political power whose interests often conflicted with the interests
of the central authority which the Muscovite princes tried to
develop. The Muscovite rulers became aware of this and sought to
remedy the situation by placing restrictions on kormlenie. In doing
so they were also prompted by the growing and sometimes violent
dissatisfaction of the population with the rule of the namestniks
and volostels.[10]

After about the last quarter of the fifteenth century, the Muscovite government, usually in response to local petitions, granted
special protective charters to several communities.[11] These charters,

[10] Charter to Belöozero, 1488, *A.A.E.*, I, 92–95; charter to fishermen of
Pereiaslavl', 1555, *ibid.*, I, 262; Pokrovskii, II, 79; Kliuchevskii, *Kurs russkoi
istorii*, II, 445–446.

[11] A typical charter illustrating the new tendencies in the government and
throwing a light on the operation of the system of kormlenie is quoted below:
"The grand prince Ivan Vasilievich has granted a favor to his people in
Belöozero.... Namestniks appointed there must observe this charter. Upon
their arrival they must be satisfied with whatever donations the people may
bring to them. [Next the document contains specific instructions as to how
much food and money the people should bring to the namestniks and their
officials on various occasions.] The namestnik should employ only two *tiuns*
(deputy justices) and ten *dovodchiks* (prosecutors).... While making a cir-
cuit ... the dovodchik shall not collect any dues, but he shall receive them in
the town from the *sotskii* (hundreder, an official elected by the people). The
dovodchiks shall not trespass upon each other's districts [this was to avoid
the duplication of fees]. "They shall not dine where they spent the night, and
shall not spend a night in a place where they had dinner ... [this was to decrease the cost of a visit]. The regular levies for the namestnik and for his
officials are to be collected by the sotskii who will deliver them in the town to
these officials.... The namestniks are to receive the following taxes and court
dues [a detailed enumeration follows]. The namestniks and their tiuns shall
not hold court in the absence of the sotskii and good men." Charter to Belöozero,
1488, *A.A.E.*, I, 92–94; see also similar charters to Mariinskii district, 1506,
A.A.E., I, 116–117, and to Kamenskii district, 1509, *A.A.E.*, I, 120–122, and
others.

apparently directed against excessive demands and extortions, defined the obligations of the population, and incidentally restrained the administrative activities of the kormlenshchiks and their agents. In addition to charters which operated only within a given locality, the Muscovite government limited the administrative importance of the kormlenshchiks by certain articles in the codes of laws which were compiled in 1497 and 1550, whereby some administrative and judicial matters formerly handled by the namestniks were transferred to the *Boiarskaia Duma* (Boiars' Council) in Moscow. Furthermore, the period for which kormlenie was granted was reduced to one year. In 1552 Ivan IV announced his intention of abolishing the system of kormlenie entirely, and three years later a law was issued to this effect. For some reason it was not enforced, and for a time towns and volosts were still given away on the basis of kormlenie, but from now on the communities were permitted to rid themselves of the namestniks and volostels upon request, and many of them took advantage of this opportunity.[12]

After the middle of the sixteenth century the system of kormlenie rapidly declined, and by the time the Muscovite government launched the conquest and administrative organization of Siberia it had practically ceased to exist. Nevertheless, it left behind a host of administrative habits and methods developed by centuries of political experience, which could not be eradicated through a change of administrative structure. Therefore, it is not surprising that the Siberian officials, although representing the new "administration by the voevodas," which will be described later on, still firmly adhered to such views of their duties and privileges as were shaped for them by their predecessors, the kormlenshchiks. The government, on its part, incorporated into the colonial administration many features which were the negative results of its experience with the system of kormlenie. The short terms of office in Siberia were analogous to the abbreviated period to which the holding of a kormlenie was reduced in the time of Ivan IV. Steps were taken to prevent the concentration of too large powers in the hands of any single official. Remembering the exorbitant demands of the kormlenshchiks upon the people in their charge, the government pro-

---

[12] Chicherin, pp. 38, 44; Kliuchevskii, *Kurs russkoi istorii*, II, 447–448, 463–464; N. A. Rozhkov, *Russkaia istoriia*, Vol. IV, Part 1, p. 113; Nikon Chronicle, 7064 (1556), *P.S.R.L.*, XII, 267–268.

hibited the oppression of the Siberian natives, and if the latter "voluntarily" brought gifts to the voevodas,[13] such gifts were to be deposited in the tsar's treasury. In limiting the greediness of the voevodas by means of instructions, the government followed a method similar to the one which it used in granting charters to the population specifying its financial obligations to the namestniks. The amount of money and property (especially in furs) which the Siberian voevodas were allowed to accumulate for themselves while in office was limited. Yet, by recognizing the possibility of a private income for their agents, the government tacitly admitted the existence of practices not very different from the old levies of the kormlenshchiks.

Administrative Experimentation in the Sixteenth Century

As has already been indicated, one of the primary motives involved in the restriction and eventual elimination of the system of kormlenie was the desire of the Muscovite rulers to weaken the feudal boiar aristocracy—a policy clearly manifested throughout the reign of Ivan IV. However, after the boiars had faded from the political picture the government faced the problem of finding other social elements which would fill the position of the kormlenshchiks in the administrative organization of the state. A partial solution of this problem was the utilization of the democratic elective officials.

The elective officials had existed in Russian communities for a long time, side by side with the kormlenshchiks. There were *starostas* (elders) in towns and suburban districts, and *sotskiis* (hundreders) in rural districts. What their functions were, the documents of the appanage period do not make clear. Probably they handled purely local affairs, including some police duties.[14] When the government began to curtail the activities of the kormlenshchiks, it imposed the collection of levies upon the elected officials.[15] Likewise, in the code of 1497, the government prescribed that the namestniks should hold their court in the presence of these officials. Their attendance at the court during trials was insisted upon in conformity with the ancient Russian custom which re-

---

[13] The chief town officials, who were appointed instead of namestniks.
[14] Kliuchevskii, *Kurs russkoi istorii*, II, 448–449.
[15] Charter to Belöozero, 1488, *A.A.E.*, I, 92; charter to the Kamenskii district, 1509, *A.A.E.*, I, 121.

quired the presence of witnesses to make any legal act valid.[16] Another code of laws, prepared in 1550, stipulated again that no case should be tried by the namestniks, unless the starostas and the tselovalniks elected by the people were present. Furthermore, if the community did not have such officials before 1550, they had to be elected to fulfill the requirement. At the court they were "to uphold justice according to the sacred oath and without any malice," which meant that they were to see that no injustice befell their electors at the hands of a namestnik.[17] A further field for the activities of the elected officials was opened when the government created a special rural administration to combat widespread banditry. As early as 1539 certain rural districts were allowed to elect special officers, some from the gentry and some from the population at large, whose duty was to apprehend and prosecute highwaymen. This administration by the *gubnye starostas* (criminal judges, literally elders) appeared later in many places, and, by the code of laws of 1550, was made independent of the namestniks and their agents.[18]

With the decline of the system of kormlenie, the government not only employed the elected officials as judicial and police functionaries, but also made extensive use of them in the financial administration. When, in response to the complaints of the population, the government removed the kormlenshchiks from certain communities, it imposed upon these communities as compensation for this favor the yearly payment of a lump sum, known as *obrok,* which took the place of various specified dues formerly payable to the kormlenshchiks. Such communities were granted a degree of self-government, and the fulfillment of their financial obligations to the state naturally was in the hands of the local officials elected by the people. Among the local officials it is necessary to note the *izliublennye golovas* (literally, most respected heads), who held superior positions, as government financial agents, and their assistants chosen from tselovalniks, already mentioned in this study. Some documents speak of *izliublennye starostas* (most respected

---

[16] Sudebnik (Code of Laws), 1497, *A.I.*, I, 153; Kliuchevskii, *Kurs russkoi istorii*, II, 449.

[17] Sudebnik, 1550, *A.I.*, I, 238–240; Kliuchevskii, *Kurs russkoi istorii*, II, 450–451.

[18] Charter to Belöozero, 1539, *A.A.E.*, I, 164; charter to Kargopol, 1539, *D.A.I.*, I, 32–33; Sudebnik, 1550, *A.I.*, I, 235–236; Kliuchevskii, *Kurs russkoi istorii*, II, 453–454; see also fn. 19 following.

elders) instead of golovas, both terms indicating the same type of officials.[19] Later golovas and tselovalniks played an important part in the financial administration of Siberia.[20]

The elected financial agents of the government were to be found also in the communities which still retained the namestniks. The charter to Belöozero (1488) mentions elective officials who acted as revenue collectors for the namestniks. Although in 1551 there were still namestniks in this town with some administrative and judicial functions, the whole financial administration was managed by the elective officials, who collected customs dues, sales' taxes, and property taxes, and who paid the namestniks approximately one half of the revenues, the other half going to the tsar's treasury. A similar arrangement existed in 1556 in Novgorod where, alongside the namestniks, the government maintained its own bureaucratic officials, the *diaks*,[21] whose functions as town magistrates will be explained below. Neither the namestniks nor the diaks in Novgorod had much to do with the actual procedure of the revenue collection, which was handled by the elective officials. It is worth noting that not all these elective officials were local men. For instance, in Belöozero in 1551 the financial administration was under the charge of two chief officials elected in Moscow, who were assisted by twenty other men elected in Belöozero. This practice of placing

---

[19] "We, Ivan Vasilievich, the Tsar and Grand Prince of all the Russias, thus favor the peasants of the Ustiug uezd.... Until now we have assigned the towns and volosts to our boiars, princes, and boiar sons.... There have been many complaints and petitions from the peasants that, in spite of our orders, the namestniks and volostels ... oppressed them and ruined them. On the other hand, the namestniks and volostels ... have brought the complaints that the townsmen and villagers refuse to attend their courts and pay their dues. The peasants even beat them....

"As a favor to the people, we removed the namestniks and volostels from the towns and volosts. We ordered our taxes to be imposed on townsmen and villagers in place of what they used to pay to the namestniks and volostels.... We command that the population at large elect the izliublennye starostas. These men shall act as administrators, collect what revenues were formerly paid to the namestniks and volostels and deliver them on time to us.... They are to follow the Sudebnik and this charter in their work....

"The cases of robbers shall be in charge of the gubnye starostas, who have their instructions from the government.... To attend the court of the gubnye starostas, the people are to elect the tselovalniks and to keep the records, they are to employ the *zemskii diak* [community clerk].... If these elected officers, starostas and tselovalniks judge partially, ... take bribes, ... neglect their duties, ... they are to be punished by death and their property is to be confiscated." Charter to Ustiug uezd, 1555, *A.A.E.*, I, 264–267; see also charters to Vaga, 1552, *A.A.E.*, I, 231–239; to Pereiaslavl, 1555, *A.A.E.*, I, 261–264.

[20] See chapter vii, *infra*.

[21] See *supra*, p. 2.

men brought from the outside at the head of the staff later prevailed in Siberia, where most of the financial administrators were drawn from among the local men, but the higher posts were occupied by men elected in towns of European Russia. In general, the financial administration in Belöozero and Novgorod, as it operated in the middle of the sixteenth century, bears a marked resemblance to the financial administration of Siberia in the seventeenth century; analogies may easily be traced in comparing the types of officials, the scopes of their activities, and their relations to other government agents.[22]

In speaking of the origin and precedents of the Siberian administration one cannot leave out the experimentation of the Muscovite government with the so-called *prikaznye liudi* (men under orders, men given a commission). These officials were sent from Moscow prikazes to many cities which still retained namestniks. Acting under directions from the central government, the prikaznye liudi assumed a large part of the administrative functions formerly handled by the namestniks who were reduced thereupon to a more or less passive role as mere recipients of a share of local revenues, the bulk of which now went to the state. A reference was made above to the two diaks appointed as prikaznye liudi to Novgorod. These diaks supervised transportation, recruited men for military service, paid salaries to the army, directed the financial agents elected by the population, and not infrequently decided judicial cases. During the interval between the departure of the retired namestniks and the arrival of the new ones, the entire administration was in the hands of the diaks.[23] Whereas the diaks were appointed to the larger cities such as Novgorod and Pskov, the government supplied the smaller towns with prikaznye liudi of lesser importance called *gorodovye prikashchiks* (town commissioners) who administered their respective towns according to the instructions received from Moscow.[24] The diaks, as associates of the chief town officials, the voevodas, later became an integral part of the Siberian administration. As will be shown, their rela-

[22] Charter to Belöozero, 1488, *A.A.E.*, I, 92–94; customs instructions to Belöozero, 1551, *A.A.E.*, I, 222–226; instructions to Novgorod, 1556, *D.A.I.*, I, 145–146.

[23] Instructions to Novgorod, 1555–1556, *D.A.I.*, I, 119, 128, 136, 139–144, 155.

[24] Instructions of Vasilii Ioannovich, 1533, *A.A.E.*, I, 148–149; instructions of Ioann Vasilievich, 1536, *A.A.E.*, I, 154; the tsar's instructions, 1582, *A.A.E.*, I, 376; instructions of ... Godunov, 1588, *A.A.E.*, I, 407.

tion to the voevodas in the seventeenth century resembles, in many respects, their relation to the namestniks in the sixteenth century. The diaks represented, in both instances, the bureaucratic element of the central government placed alongside the noble office holders. Likewise, the prikaznye liudi who managed the Siberian ostrogs corresponded to the gorodovye prikashchiks found earlier in European Russia.

In the second half of the sixteenth century, as a result of experimentation, innovations, and partial reforms, the provincial administration of the Muscovite state consisted of a diversity of old decaying forms closely interwoven with the emerging new types. In spite of the governmental program of 1552, which aimed at the abolition of kormlenie, there were still a few namestniks and volostels. Certain communities had local self-government. Many towns had the Muscovite prikaznye liudi as their administrators. Competing types of administration often occurred side by side and in various relationships with one another. None of them presented as yet a satisfactory administrative organization. Kormlenie, based on the feudal conception of the state's surrendering governmental functions to private individuals for their profit, had apparently outlived itself. Self-government was not consistent with the general policy of Moscow which tried to uphold the supreme authority of the central government. The bureaucratic government was still in an embryonic stage, handicapped by the social traditions which prevented the able men of non-noble origin from holding responsible positions of higher rank.[25]

During this transitional period, the social elements appearing conspicuously within the various forms of administrative organization were the old feudal nobility, the town bourgeoisie, and the Muscovite bureaucrats. Meanwhile, the reign of Ivan IV was particularly marked by the rise of less distinguished nobles, who held their landed estates, not on a hereditary basis like the grand nobles of the boiar class, but in exchange for almost constant military service. The members of this group, which was also essentially feudal, were known as *sluzhilye dvoriane* (serving nobles) or *pomeshchiks* (landowners—from the word *pomest'e*, an estate). These petty vassals supported the tsar in his struggle with the old boiar nobility, a struggle which culminated in wholesale "purges" of

---

[25] Chicherin, pp. 51–52; Rozhkov, Vol. IV, Part 1, p. 120; Part 2, p. 69.

boiar opposition.[26] While the tsar was liquidating the political power of the great feudal lords, the smaller nobility stepped into the arena and acquired a considerable political significance. The general administrative confusion and constant use of military force during the wars and insurrections of the sixteenth and seventeenth centuries quite naturally brought the class which furnished officers for the army to an active participation in provincial and colonial administration.

INTRODUCTION OF ADMINISTRATION BY VOEVODAS

From this class the government appointed the voevodas, at first in the frontier towns and later in the rest of the towns as well. Although the administration by the voevodas originated in the second half of the sixteenth century, the term "voevoda" was long in existence. It was used to designate the commanding officers in the army. With the end of hostilities, the voevodas surrendered their office which, as a rule, lasted no longer than the military emergency.[27] The necessity of keeping constant watch in certain strategic localities even in time of peace tended to prolong the service of the voevodas there. Apparently one of the first appointments of a town voevoda was in Murom, situated near the Kasimov Tatars.[28] The voevodas, in addition to their military duties, soon acquired authority over the civil government. Thus, immediately after the conquest of Kazan, Astrakhan, Polotsk, and the Siberian Khanate, the government found it expedient to place voevodas in the acquired territories as military governors, but also with judicial, financial, and police functions.[29] The idea of namestniks, however, was not completely discarded, and in 1555 in Kazan and Sviiazhsk administrative offices were held by both voevodas and namestniks.[30] In Novgorod, in 1555, the namestnik Paletskii, because there was war with Sweden, was appointed also as the voevoda.[31] There is evidence to show that after 1555 Novgorod was administered by the voevodas and diaks, who collected certain fees for the local namestnik.[32]

---

[26] Pokrovskii, II, 96–125 *passim*, especially pp. 112–115.

[27] *D.R.V.*, XX, 202–203, 218–219.

[28] Instructions to Murom, 1547, *S.G.G.D.*, II, 44.

[29] Instructions to Kazan, 1553 and 1555, *A.A.E.*, I, 239, 261; instructions to Polotsk, 1563, *A.I.*, I, 321–325; instructions of Fedor Ioannovich, 1587, *R.I.B.*, II, 45; Chicherin, pp. 52–53.

[30] Documents of Archbishop Gurii, 1555, *A.A.E.*, I, 260.

[31] Instructions to Novgorod, 1555, *D.A.I.*, I, 134.

[32] Charter to the Vvedenskii monastery, 1597, *D.A.I.*, I, 233–235.

It was perhaps along the southern frontier that the administration by voevodas was first firmly rooted. At least this was the assertion made by the representatives of the merchant class, who rose in defense of their former liberties,[33] at the meeting of the *Sobor* of Azov.[34] Certain documents mention the presence of voevodas on the southern frontier in 1571.[35] In 1572 the towns of Donkovo, Epifan, Dedilov, and Kropivna were apparently administered by voevodas.[36] The decision of the Boiarskaia Duma in 1577 states definitely that Putivl and Rylsk had both voevodas and namestniks, Orel and Karachev had only voevodas, while Riazhsk, Donkovo, Epifan, Dedilov, Novosil, and Mtsensk had voevodas or other miltary officers in charge.[37] In 1586–1587 voevodas were sent to found the towns of Voronezh and Livny and to administer them.[38] But those were not the only towns ruled by the voevodas at that time. In 1581 there were also voevodas in Nizhnii Novgorod situated in more or less central Russia, and after 1587 the newly built town of Arkhangelsk (Archangel), commanding the entrance of the North Dvina into the White Sea, was administered by voevodas.[39]

As a result of the successful operation of the administration by voevodas elsewhere, these officials were introduced in Siberia from the beginning of the conquest. Every step of the Russian advance there was marked by the building of fortified towns. These towns were, for the most part, built in the territories of hostile native tribes. Constant military vigilance was required to keep these tribes peaceful and obedient. Such circumstances necessitated a strong semi-military government, which was represented by the voevodas.

During the period immediately preceding and following the accession to the throne of Mikhail Fedorovich Romanov, the unsettled situation in Russia hastened the disappearance of any ad-

---

[33] "Under previous tsars, the towns had been in charge of gubnye starostas, and the townsmen had held their own court. The voevodas had then been sent by the tsars *only to frontier towns* [italics mine] to protect them against the Turkish, Crimean, and Nogai Tatars." Decisions of the Sobor, 1642, *S.G.G.D.*, III, 395.

[34] The Sobor of Azov was an assembly of clergy, nobility, and merchants, called in 1642 to decide the fate of Azov which had fallen into the hands of cossacks.

[35] The decree of the tsar, 1571, Akademiia nauk, *Akty moskovskago gosudarstva*, I, 1, 3.

[36] Decision of the Boiars, 1572, *Ibid.*, I, 18.

[37] Instructions to Enikeev, 1577, *ibid.*, I, 20.

[38] Decision of the Boiars, 1586–1587, *ibid.*, I, 59.

[39] Instructions to Saburov, 1581, *A.I.*, I, 400–402; instructions to Nashchekin and Volokhov, 1583, *A.A.E.*, I, 380; *D.R.V.*, XVIII, 15.

ministration other than military.[40] The introduction of voevodas
was, however, a gradual process.[41] Wherever some other type of
administration had existed before the appearance of the voevodas,
the old officials were allowed to remain, although their offices were
either overshadowed or absorbed by those of the voevodas' administration. This, for instance, was the procedure with respect to the
namestniks. They were often found in the same town with the voevodas, or, sometimes, the chief voevoda assumed also the rank of
namestnik. In either case the office of namestnik lost its administrative importance, and the word namestnik ceased to have any
meaning but that of an honorary title.[42] In towns which were administered by prikaznye liudi, the ground was already prepared
for the introduction of voevodas. Unlike the kormlenshchiks, both
the prikaznye liudi and the voevodas were subordinated to the
Muscovite prikazes and received orders from them. The main difference between these two types of officials was in their relative
importance. The voevodas were chosen from men of higher social
standing and had greater authority. They became the chief officials,
and the prikaznye liudi were attached to them as associates or
assistants.[43] In those towns which had a degree of self-government,
the local officials were also incorporated into a new administration
by voevodas. The popularly elected golovas and tselovalniks were
retained to handle, under the supervision of the voevodas, various
obligations of the population, especially those which involved the
payment of duties and taxes.[44]

From the point of view of the Muscovite government, the system
of administration by the voevodas offered many advantages. Semi-
military in character, it welded the state shattered by the "Time of
Troubles," holding the restless elements of the population in a
much stronger grip than had ever before existed. It brought about
the consolidation of territorial administrative units, for the voevodas managed not only towns, but the surrounding *uezds* (rural
districts) as well. The new system was a great step toward centralization because it effectively checked the separatist leanings of the

[40] Kliuchevskii, *Kurs russkoi istorii*, III, 189; Chicherin, p. 53.
[41] Pokrovskii, II, 258.
[42] Chicherin, pp. 54, 57; memorial, 1680, *S.G.G.D.*, IV, 372–373.
[43] Chicherin, pp. 53–54.
[44] *D.R.V.*, XVIII, 19; Kliuchevskii, *Kurs russkoi istorii*, III, 192–195; Chicherin, pp. 53–55.

high feudal nobility and suppressed the rise of local self-government which might have developed a tendency to serve local interests rather than those of the state.[45]

The administration by the voevodas in Siberia will be fully described in the chapters to follow. For the present it is sufficient to note that, as a result of previous administrative experimentation, the Muscovite government found it expedient to employ for its service there various social elements: the new military serving nobility, the muscovite bureaucrats, and the town bourgeoisie. The nobles held positions as voevodas and their subordinate military officers, the bureaucrats filled the positions of diaks and pod'iacheis, while the townsmen served as heads and sworn men. Furthermore, because the government in Moscow was fully aware of the vitality and persistence of feudal traditions, the organization of the administrative structure in Siberia was characterized by a lack of concentrated authority in the hands of individual administrators. As to the Siberian administrators themselves, they preserved the same attitude toward their office as had the former kormlenshchiks, regarding it as a means of filling their personal treasury rather than as a duty to the state and the governed population.

[45] Kliuchevskii, *Kurs russkoi istorii*, III, 190; Rozhkov, Vol. IV, Part 2, p. 70.

CHAPTER III

TERRITORIAL ORGANIZATION
OF SIBERIA

T HE SIBERIAN COLONY of Russia never knew any administration
except that by the voevodas. In the process of conquest, Russian
military detachments moved into the territories occupied by
the Siberian natives, established fortified towns, and enabled the
Russian colonists to settle there in safety. The towns became centers
for the collection of the fur tribute from the natives, markets for
the fur trade, and nuclei for further expansion. The voevodas, who
commanded the troops, were in charge of building and defending
the towns. In addition to their military duties, they performed
several functions which ordinarily fall within the domain of civil
officials, because the frontier conditions favored semi-military
administration.

With the development of the Russian expansion in Siberia, questions arose concerning the comparative importance of the voevodas
of different towns, and their relations to each other. The interests
of the state required the coördination of the activities of its agents.
Some sort of administrative order was necessary to prevent rivalry
among the voevodas and to secure unity of action. This problem
might have been solved by establishing in Siberia an office comparable to that of the viceroy found in some colonies of the west
European countries. But an ambitious and influential noble with
vast powers, an army, and the wealth of Siberia at his disposal
could easily have become a source of worry to the central government. With a fresh memory of the past struggle with the appanage
princes and feudal nobles, the Muscovite rulers would not consider
such a scheme. Instead the government allowed a slow and gradual
accumulation of power in the hands of the voevodas of certain
important towns. With the growth of these towns, there evolved
the administrative hierarchy and territorial organization to be
described in this chapter, which will be followed later by the
description of the government apparatus set up within single
towns. Tobolsk, Tomsk, Iakutsk, and Eniseisk are the towns
deserving special notice.

THE RISE OF THE PRINCIPAL TOWNS

Tobolsk.—The first important Russian town in Siberia was Tiumen, which was occupied in 1586 and which served as the initial stepping stone for Russian expansion. In a very few years, however, it was completely overshadowed by Tobolsk,[1] situated on the main route connecting Siberia with European Russia and having the advantage over Tiumen of a more central location with respect to the Ob'–Irtysh river system. There are indications that Tobolsk, as early as 1594, had become not only the distributing center for supplies brought from European Russia to the sundry newly built towns, but also a depositary for furs en route to Moscow from these towns.[2] In the foundation of new fortified settlements Tobolsk also assumed an active role. In 1600, by orders of the Tsar, the voevodas of Tobolsk sent officers and men to build an ostrog in Mangazeia;[3] in 1601, an expedition from Tobolsk founded the town of Tomsk.[4] By 1601–1602 the towns Tara, Surgut, Berezov, Narym, Ketsk, Mangazeia, and Tomsk were said to belong to the *razriad*[5] of Tobolsk: in other words they were placed in a position subordinate to Tobolsk which became their principal town.[6] In 1607 the government issued a special seal to be used exclusively by the voevodas of Tobolsk in their official correspondence, while the voevodas in other towns continued to use their personal seals until 1625–1635.[7] The prestige

---

[1] S. Prutchenko, *Sibirskiia okrainy*, I, 13.

[2] N. N. Ogloblin, *Obozrenie stolbtsov* (cited hereafter as Ogloblin), III, 210, 212; IV, 123.

[3] *D.R.V.*, III, 114–115.

[4] *Ibid.*, III, 117–118.

[5] The term *razriad* was applied in Moscow to the Prikaz or Office of Military Affairs (see *supra*, p. 13). Originally the term indicated the management of military or "serving" men. In the seventeenth century it acquired a special meaning. It began to be used to denote a grouping of several towns wherein one of them, called a "principal" town, acted as a sort of administrative center for the rest, known as *pripisnye* (literally assigned) towns. The voevoda of the principal town acted as the head of the razriad. Such an organization of towns was introduced for reasons of military convenience, and, to a certain extent, the razriads might be considered as predecessors of the gubernias introduced by Peter the Great. In European Russia in the reign of Mikhail Fedorovich the razriads of Riazan and Ukraine were established. Tsar Aleksei Mikhailovich added to them the razriads of Novgorod, Sevsk or Seversk, Belgorod, Tambov, and Kazan. (V. O. Kliuchevskii, *Kurs russkoi istorii*, III, 195; B. Chicherin, *Oblastnyia uchrezhdeniia*, p. 61.)

[6] *D.R.V.*, III, 117–118.

[7] V. K. Andrievich, *Istoriia Sibiri*, I, 113, 115; I. V. Shcheglov, *Khronologicheskii perechen' vazhneishikh dannykh iz istorii Sibiri (1032–1882)*, p. 83; P. N. Butsinskii, *Zaselenie Sibiri i byt eia pervykh nasel'nikov*, p. 233.

of Tobolsk was greatly enhanced when it became the center of the religious administration of Siberia. In 1621 the first Siberian archbishop arrived in Tobolsk, and in 1668 Tobolsk was made the seat of the Siberian metropolitan who occupied the fourth rank in the religious hierarchy of Russia.[8] In 1696, Tobolsk only, of all Siberian towns, was granted the seal of the Siberian Kingdom (*tsarstvo*); this seal, like that of the Siberian Prikaz, if attached to goods made them exempt from customs duties at the Siberian frontier customhouses of Nerchinsk and Verkhoturie.[9]

By these means the preëminence of Tobolsk was firmly established. Following the first quarter of the seventeenth century, the government organized new administrative units, *razriads*, in Siberia, but Tobolsk, surpassing other principal towns in size, wealth, population, and number of officials, retained its position as the most important town in Siberia.[10] In these days every appointment was made with a strict regard to the position of the officeholder on the complicated ladder of the Muscovite nobility, and the chief voevodas of Tobolsk invariably came from the most distinguished families (usually they were boiars).[11] Once, in 1599–1600, a relative of the Tsar Boris Godunov,[12] was appointed as its chief voevoda.[13] It is not surprising therefore that the contemporary writers often referred to Tobolsk as the chief town of Siberia.[14]

Tomsk.—Until 1627 there was only one razriad in Siberia. As soon as the Russians resumed their eastward movement, which had been checked temporarily by the "Time of Troubles," and began to establish new towns and ostrogs in the basin of the river Enisei, Moscow decided to divide Siberia into two administrative units. This was accomplished in 1628–1629. Tomsk, situated halfway between the Enisei and the Irtysh, was chosen as the center or the principal town of the new razriad of Tomsk. The towns of Narym, Ketsk, Eniseisk, Krasnoiarsk, and Kuznetsk were assigned to the

[8] Shcheglov, p. 79; Prutchenko, I, 14; P. A. Slovtsov, *Istoricheskoe obozrenie Sibiri*, I, 30.

[9] Slovtsov, I, 163.

[10] Prutchenko, I, 13; Slovtsov, I, 34.

[11] *D.R.V.*, III, 104–288, *passim*.

[12] Okolnichii Saburov.

[13] *D.R.V.*, III, 113; Andrievich, *op. cit.*, I, 117.

[14] "The chief town in Siberia is called Tobolesk [*sic*]," G. O. Kotoshikhin, *O Rossii v tsarstvovanie Aleksiia Mikhailovicha*, p. 76; "Tobolinum [est] metropolis, ubi residet episcopus metropolitanus et praetorum primas, qui reliquis Sibiriae praetoribus imperat," *Historia de Sibiria*, written about 1680, A. A. Titov, ed., *Sibir' v XVII veke*, p. 125.

jurisdiction of Tomsk, while Verkhoturie, Pelym, Turinsk, Tiumen, Tara, Surgut, and Mangazeia remained within the razriad of Tobolsk.[15] This change chagrined the voevodas of Tobolsk, who saw a diminution of their own importance and who, for a while, continued to claim certain territories of the new razriad.[16]

To the north of the new principal town lay the chief route of communication between western and eastern Siberia, by way of Ketsk and the Makovskii ostrog.[17] South of Tomsk was the Russian southern frontier, constantly threatened in this region by strong and hostile tribes of Kirghiz. Thus Tomsk by its strategic position protected the Ketsk-Makovskii route and at the same time served as a base for further expansion. From Tomsk, serving men were sent to reinforce expeditions undertaken by other towns.[18] The establishment of the razriad of Tomsk made quick concerted action in this region possible, since it was no longer necessary first to consult Tobolsk in military affairs.

Iakutsk.—The decade following the organization of the razriad of Tomsk was marked by the Russian penetration into the Lena River basin, especially from the towns of Mangazeia (subordinated to Tobolsk) and Eniseisk (subordinated to Tomsk). Both towns claimed the Lena territory as their own. The Siberian Prikaz received the disconcerting news that the serving men of the rival towns fought each other, being less interested in the revenues of the state than in the acquisition of furs for themselves. Furthermore these serving men mercilessly mistreated and robbed the natives. In addition to the consternation the conduct of the serving men caused,[19] there was also great alarm about the activities of private traders and trappers who annihilated valuable fur-bearing animals and rivaled the serving men in terrorizing the

[15] *D.R.V.*, III, 148–149; Ogloblin, I, 26; Slovtsov, I, 33.

[16] Ogloblin, III, 237–238.

[17] Instructions to Iakutsk, 1658, *D.A.I.*, IV, 100; documents dealing with the shipments to Iakutsk, 1676–1680, *D.A.I.*, VII, 130, and other documents; R. J. Kerner, *The Urge to the Sea: the Course of Russian History (the Rôle of Rivers, Portages, Ostrogs, Monasteries, and Furs)*, p. 73.

[18] Instructions to Tomsk, 1664, *D.A.I.*, IV, 325–326; J. E. Fischer, *Sibirskaia istoriia*, pp. 376–381.

[19] "According to reports from Siberia ... the voevodas of Tobolsk, of Mangazeia, and of the Eniseiskii ostrog started sending men to the great river Lena.... The serving men collect a little fur tribute for the state, and a great deal for themselves.... [The serving men] fight and kill private hunters, as well as each other; they oppress the natives and drive them away." Instructions to Golovin, 1638, *R.I.B.*, II, 966–967.

native population. The Muscovite government decided to put an end to wasteful plundering and to save the enormous wealth of the Lena furs for the state by organizing the Lena territory.[20] According to government instructions, several ostrogs were built along the Lena and its tributaries. Because of its convenient location, one of them, Iakutsk, became the adminstrative center. In 1638, voevodas were sent to Iakutsk *svoim stolom* (with an administration of their own, that is, independent of the existing razriads).[21] While Tomsk and Tobolsk had several towns within their razriads, the territory subordinated to Iakutsk contained only small ostrogs and fur posts. Probably for this reason it was not called a razriad at first, although it formed a separate administrative unit.[22] Ilimsk, in 1649, was the first important ostrog, with a voevoda in charge, to become dependent on Iakutsk.[23]

After the establishment of the voevoda in Iakutsk, the former rivals, Mangazeia and Eniseisk, were prohibited from sending their men to the Lena, and furs collected in the basin of this river were brought to Iakutsk for shipment to Russia. The voevodas of Iakutsk assumed direction of the armed conflicts with the Lena natives. Iakutsk was made a storehouse and distributing center of food and military supplies for its subordinate ostrogs and became a base for the exploration and conquest of eastern Siberia.[24]

Eniseisk.—The next important change in the administrative structure of Siberia came in 1676–1677 with the organization of the razriad of Eniseisk, with Eniseisk, formerly a town within the jurisdiction of Tomsk, as the principal town.[25] As has already been indicated, Eniseisk, before the establishment of the voevodas in Iakutsk, had taken a leading part in the exploration of the Lena region. The men from Eniseisk had built the ostrog of Ilimsk there,

---

[20] It may be noted that the Siberian Prikaz was separated from the Kazanskii Dvorets in 1637 (see *supra,* p. 5). Significant changes both in the central government and in colonial administration followed the receipt of information about the wealth of Lena furs.

[21] Fischer, pp. 352–363; *D.R.V.*, III, 161; Slovtsov, I, 40–42; Ogloblin, IV, 160.

[22] Under 1645 the books of the Siberian Prikaz mention separately furs received from the razriad of Tobolsk, from the razriad of Tomsk, and furs "from the great river Lena." Ogloblin, IV, 160. S. V. Bakhrushin refers to the razriad of Iakutsk as "Lenskii razriad" ("Istoricheskie sud'by Iakutii," *Iakutiia. Sbornik statei,* p. 279).

[23] Slovtsov, I, 42.

[24] V. I. Ogorodnikov, *Ocherki istorii Sibiri do nachala XIX veka,* Vol. II, Part 2, pp. 49, 53.

[25] *D.R.V.*, III, 223; Prutchenko, I, 13; Slovtsov, I, 115.

commanding the connection between the rivers Enisei and Lena. Eniseisk was especially active in spreading Russian influence through southeastern Siberia. During the years 1627–1654, the valley of the Angara River had been conquered, chiefly by men from Eniseisk. Out of several ostrogs and *zimov'es* (winter camps or quarters) founded there, one, Irkutsk, later became a very important town.[26] Between 1644 and 1666, the agents who were sent from Eniseisk set up a number of ostrogs in the trans-Baikal region.[27] When, in 1656, the Muscovite government planned to establish an independent voevoda (similar to the one in Iakutsk) on the Amur River, it sent there the former voevoda of Eniseisk, who had to rely on Eniseisk for assistance during his commission.[28] In 1663–1664 Eniseisk gave military aid to Krasnoiarsk,[29] which later became subordinated to Eniseisk. For a long time Eniseisk supplied the Lena, the Angara, and the Baikal regions with men, arms, and food.[30] Eventually, the Muscovite government became aware of the significance of Eniseisk and made it the principal town of the new razriad. Within this razriad were included the Daurskii, Nerchinskii, Irkutskii, Albazinskii, Selenginskii, Amurskii, and Baikalskii ostrogs.[31]

A survey of the gradual rise of certain Siberian towns to a position of administrative importance shows that the administrative organization of Siberia, as it developed during the greater part of the seventeenth century, owed its origin to the military circumstances of the conquest, which in turn was motivated by the desire to exploit the fur riches of Siberia. In 1687, however, an administrative change which involved other than military factors took place. The government maintained the chief border customhouse in the town of Verkhoturie, the crossing point from Europe to Asia. Here the customs officials were supposed to prevent the smuggling of contraband goods by the Siberian voevodas, when the latter passed across the frontier. The officials of Verkhoturie could not exercise their functions efficiently so long as they were under the jurisdiction of the voevodas of Tobolsk. Consequently the government re-

---

[26] Ogorodnikov, *op. cit.*, II, 63–66.

[27] *Ibid.*, II, 69–73.

[28] *Ibid.*, II, 99; report of Pashkov, 1661, *D.A.I.*, IV, 260.

[29] Report from Krasnoiarsk, 1663–1664, *D.A.I.*, IV, 318–319; Ogloblin, III, 36.

[30] Instructions to Ilimsk, 1659, *D.A.I.*, IV, 158; instructions to Eniseisk, 1663, *D.A.I.*, IV, 320.

[31] Slovtsov, I, 115.

moved Verkhoturie, Pelym, and Turinsk from the razriad of Tobolsk and organized them into a small separate razriad with Verkhoturie as the principal town.[32] This razriad existed, however, only until 1693.[33] Thus, as a result of various administrative changes, at the end of the seventeenth century Siberia was composed of four razriads: Tobolskii, Tomskii, Iakutskii (the name of the Iakutskii razriad first appears in documents dated 1697[34] but probably was in use before that time), and Eniseiskii.

SIBERIAN RAZRIADS

The razriads organized in Siberia were regarded by the central government as more or less independent of each other, and within the Siberian Prikaz the business of each of the razriads was dealt with separately.[35] Nevertheless, the Prikaz expected coöperation among the heads of the various razriads and used the voevodas of Tobolsk as their intermediary agents in dealing with the more remote principal towns. It was easier to send men, arms, and food to other towns of Siberia from Tobolsk than from Moscow. For that reason, the government made it a depot of men and supplies, a sort of sifting place for sundry colonists, especially exiles,[36] and used it to obtain information about the rest of Siberia. The voevodas of Tobolsk were commissioned also to render assistance to other razriads whenever it seemed necessary.[37]

---

[32] Instructions to Verkhoturie, 1687, *A.I.*, V, 285; *D.R.V.*, III, 270.

[33] *D.R.V.*, III, 280.

[34] Ogloblin, II, 144.

[35] *Ibid.*, I, 37, 118, 219, 233 ff.; IV, 48, 49.

[36] *Ibid.*, I, 133.

[37] "To the boiar and voevoda Prince Aleksei Andreevich [Golitsyn]: Write to the town of Tomsk ... the news, and about various affairs of the great sovereign and keep up the correspondence, as before, in order that the affairs of the great sovereign and all news may be known to both the Tobolskii and the Tomskii razriads. If the voevodas of Tomsk, ... [or] the voevodas of ostrogs within the Tomskii razriad should write to Tobolsk and to the towns and ostrogs of the Tobolskii razriad asking for men, or arms, or military supplies [there follows enumeration of supplies], then ... the boiar [Golitsyn] and his associates must send the requested aid immediately.... [Tobolsk] is not to bicker with the Tomskii razriad, lest such disputes bring about disaster to the Siberian towns and ostrogs, ... deficit to the treasury, ... or harm to the population.

"Should the serving men ... of Tomsk and of the Tomskii razriad not receive the money and grain which is due to them ... the voevodas of Tomsk should write about it to Tobolsk ... [and] the amount making up the shortage must be sent from Tobolsk.... Because of the fact that Tomsk and the ostrogs of the Tomskii razriad are at a great distance from Moscow, the time it would require for the voevodas of Tomsk and of the Tomskii razriad to write to Moscow about grain and money salaries would cause great suffering to the

These circumstances raised Tobolsk above the principal towns of other razriads and brought additional importance and responsibilities to the voevodas of Tobolsk; nevertheless, these voevodas were not given an opportunity to acquire complete administrative control over the other razriads. The government in Moscow adhered to the policy of managing the razriads itself, and the voevodas of other principal towns, jealous of their own authority, were always ready to challenge the right of the voevoda of Tobolsk to act as their superior. The case of Veliaminov, a voevoda of Tomsk, may serve as an illustration. In 1671, he left office without rendering the required account of his service to his successor. The central government sent him orders to appear before the voevoda of Tobolsk and answer the accusations of the population of Tomsk. Veliaminov came to Tobolsk and stayed there for two years, but steadily denied the right of the voevoda of Tobolsk to try him. The latter could do nothing about the matter, and in the end had to allow Veliaminov to depart for Moscow.[38]

Some writers have had a tendency to regard Tobolsk of the seventeenth century as a sort of colonial capital. Among them might be mentioned V. K. Andrievich and Professor F. A. Golder.[39] The evidence does not seem to support this view of the administrative position of Tobolsk. The Veliaminov incident, occurring in 1671—when according to the assertions of Andrievich and Golder, Tobolsk definitely governed the rest of Siberia—gives support to the more cautious view accepted in this study. The voevoda of Tobolsk, on this occasion, plainly demonstrated insufficient power to carry out orders from Moscow in dealing with the voevoda of Tomsk. Possibly both writers examined material concerning the relations between Tobolsk and the assigned towns of its own razriad, and assumed that similar relations existed between Tobolsk and the rest of the Siberian towns.

---

serving men. Tobolsk and the towns and the ostrogs of the Tobolskii razriad are nearer to Moscow and are easier to reach. The voevoda of Tobolsk and his associates writing to the great sovereign can always get immediate aid." Instructions to Tobolsk, 1664, *D.A.I.*, IV, 350–351. Compare with the instructions to Tobolsk, 1697, *P.S.Z.*, III, 347.

[38] *D.R.V.*, III, 210.

[39] Andrievich, *op. cit.*, I, 117; F. A. Golder, *Russian Expansion on the Pacific, 1641–1850*, p. 19. It might be noted that neither Andrievich nor Golder makes any reference to the source of the information which led to this conclusion; possibly the source was Slovtsov, I, 67.

Bakhrushin, also, once casually remarked that the chief voevoda of Tobolsk was regarded by other Siberian voevodas as the supreme ruler of Siberia. As an illustration he related a story of how in 1631 the voevoda of Verkhoturie gave a big dinner in honor of the newly appointed voevodas who, on their way to Siberia, passed through his town. During the dinner some local "boiar sons" became intoxicated and caused a considerable scandal by paying the "royal homage" to the chief voevoda of Tobolsk. The whole incident seems too insignificant to furnish a basis for conclusions about the role played by the voevodas of Tobolsk. Moreover, immediately after this story Bakhrushin told another one which points in quite a different direction. In 1639, when another group of newly appointed voevodas stopped in Verkhoturie, the diak of Mangazeia used the occasion for calling the attention not of the chief voevoda of Tobolsk alone but of the whole gathering of the voevodas to the unlawful activities of the voevoda of Mangazeia. This second story seems to place the voevoda of Tobolsk as "the first among equals" among the Siberian voevodas rather than as their supreme ruler.[40]

A mind which tended toward logical systematization would be inclined, at a first glance, to represent the Siberian administrative structure as a sort of well-organized pyramid with Tobolsk at its peak. It is so simple to place below Tobolsk the upper story of the other principal towns, supported by the next story of assigned towns and to have the whole supported by a base formed of small ostrogs and zimov'es. Such was apparently Professor Golder's conception of the Siberian administrative scheme.[41] To be acceptable, however, this scheme needs certain modifications. To begin with, the top of the pyramid was somewhat flat, with Tobolsk not a peak but an elevated part in the row of other principal towns. Going down the pyramid, there are good reasons for placing the assigned towns under their respective principal towns, but with the understanding that neither Tobolsk nor any other principal town had complete charge of the secondary or so-called *pripisnye* towns of their razriads. The smaller towns were not exactly "subject to orders of their superiors in Tobolsk and Tomsk," because of the participation of Moscow in the local affairs of individual towns and

[40] S. V. Bakhrushin, *Ocherki po istorii kolonizatsii Sibiri v XVI i XVII v. v.*, p. 105.
[41] Golder, p. 18.

because of the extent to which the Muscovite government reduced the sphere of influence and control of the principal towns.

In spite of interference by Moscow in the administration of the assigned towns, the voevodas of a principal town still exercised a great deal of authority over other voevodas of their razriad. The voevodas of the principal town could admonish other voevodas, could request them to carry out certain orders, and could demand information concerning administrative affairs of the assigned town.[42] On some occasions the voevodas of the principal town commissioned special investigators to the assigned towns. Thus in 1620 a voevoda of Tobolsk sent special officers to find out the reasons for the lack of military activity on the part of the Ketsk voevoda.[43] In 1631 in the district of Tara similar officers investigated the natives' failure to pay their *iasak* (fur tribute).[44] In 1697 the voevoda of Tobolsk received instructions from Moscow to make a survey of the towns of the Tobolsk razriad to determine whether the local voevodas were engaged in distilling and selling hard liquors for personal profit.[45] There were also occasions when agents from the principal town took charge of some local administrative functions. In 1620–1623 the voevodas of Tobolsk sent their men to Verkhoturie to collect local grain and revenues from the sale of wine.[46]

The closest relationship and the greatest degree of subordination between the assigned and the principal towns were established in military matters. The voevodas of the assigned towns depended on their principal town rather than on Moscow for the reinforcement of garrisons and the allotment of food and military supplies.[47] The voevodas of the assigned towns were continuously reminded both by the Muscovite government and by the heads of the razriads to report to the principal town all alarming news about unrest among the conquered natives or menace of raids from the hostile frontier tribes. In addition, the assigned towns had to supply complete in-

---

[42] Butsinskii, *op. cit.*, p. 233.

[43] Fischer, pp. 276–277.

[44] Instructions to Tara, 1631, *P.S.Z.*, III, 557, 572; Ogloblin, III, 90.

[45] Instructions to Tobolsk, 1697, *P.S.Z.*, III, 347.

[46] Instructions to Verkhoturie, 1623, *A.I.*, III, 187–188; instructions to Verkhoturie, 1648–1649, *A.I.*, IV, 56, 119.

[47] Instructions to Tobolsk, 1599, Ogloblin, IV, 132; report from Tobolsk, 1659, *D.A.I.*, IV, 185–186; instructions to Tobolsk, 1660, *D.A.I.*, IV, 189; instructions to Tomsk, 1664, *D.A.I.*, IV, 325; instructions to Tobolsk, 1697, *P.S.Z.*, 340–341, 345, 353; communication from Eniseisk to Tomsk, 1652, *D.A.I.*, III, 343–344.

formation concerning their own preparedness, especially in regard to the quantity and condition of available food and ammunition.[48]

Since the razriad was originally a unit of the military administration, and Moscow was too distant to be of any use in military emergencies, the military orders of the heads of the razriads were to be strictly obeyed, even if adherence to such orders at times led to unfortunate consequences. In 1634, for example, the voevoda of Tiumen preferred devastation of his uezd by the Kalmucks to any action without the sanction of the voevoda of Tobolsk. In 1636 the Muscovite government received a petition from the local serving men asking permission for the voevoda of Tiumen to act without waiting for orders from Tobolsk in case of another raid. The petition pointed out that "while the voevodas confer with each other, the Kalmucks and the rebels among the local Tatars kill and capture the Russians and the loyal natives and plunder their villages. By the time the troops are ready the raiders have disappeared." This petition was supported by another from the Russian peasants. The Muscovite government sternly refused both petitions and reminded the voevoda of Tiumen once more of the necessity of military coöperation with Tobolsk.[49]

Except in military affairs, the ties connecting the assigned towns with Moscow apparently were stronger than those attaching them to the principal towns. Because the central government was always reluctant to give up its direct contact with individual towns, the authority over the voevodas of the assigned towns was never absorbed by the voevodas of the principal towns.[50] During the "Time of Troubles," the rival pretenders to the throne appealed for support to all the Siberian voevodas, over the head of the principal town, Tobolsk.[51] Later, in the time of the first Romanovs, the Muscovite government coontinued to write to all the Siberian towns about matters concerning the state as a whole.[52]

The Siberian Prikaz carried on a very extensive correspondence

[48] Instructions to Tiumen, 1616, *R.I.B.*, II, 341; instructions to Surgut, 1594 and 1597, Ogloblin, III, 210, 212; instructions to Tobolsk, 1601–1602, *ibid.*, IV, 139; instructions to Kuznetsk, 1625, *A.I.*, III, 220–221; instructions to Tobolsk, 1697, *P.S.Z.*, III, 345.

[49] Butsinskii, *op. cit.*, pp. 233–234; instructions to Tiumen, 1636, *R.I.B.*, II, 544–547.

[50] Prutchenko, I, 14.

[51] Messages of Maria and Fedor Godunov, of the patriarch Iov, of Pseudo-Dmitrii, of Vasilii Shuiskii, 1605–1609, *S.G.G.D.*, II, 83, 84, 89, 90, 150, 185.

[52] Message of Tsar Aleksei Mikhailovich, 1650, *S.G.G.D.*, III, 458–461.

with Siberia, as we saw in an earlier chapter.[53] Every assigned town
had to send reports on all phases of the local administration to
Moscow. In their relations with each other and with their principal
towns, the assigned towns, likewise, were required to exchange
information about "the affairs of the sovereign" as well as "various
news."[54] The character of the communications sent to Moscow or to
the principal towns, however, was dependent upon their recipient.
The voevodas of the assigned towns were instructed to write to
Moscow for advice in all matters of primary importance, and to
consult the voevodas of the principal towns, unless under circumstances of military urgency, only in matters of secondary
importance.[55]

For their administrative guidance the voevodas of the assigned
towns received instructions both from Moscow and from the principal town of their razriad. The Muscovite instructions were prepared in the Siberian Prikaz on the basis of reports and other
valuable information from Siberia and were expected to cover
every local administrative contingency known to the Prikaz. These
instructions were delivered to each voevoda upon his acceptance of
the office. In comparison with these, the instructions from the principal town were far less significant. For the most part, the voevodas
of the principal town repeated the already familiar orders of the
Siberian Prikaz and insisted that they be carried out. If the voevodas of the assigned towns asked for advice, the answer of the
principal town was usually based on previous instructions from
Moscow.[56]

In establishing razriads the Muscovite government attempted to
set up local administrative centers which could handle minor
details of the administration or take the initiative in those matters
which required immediate action. In practice such a scheme did not

[53] See *supra*, pp. 11–13.
[54] Documents of Tiumen, Tara, Berezov, Surgut, Pelym, and Verkhoturie,
1601, Ogloblin, III, 2; IV, 139; instructions to Kuznetsk, 1625, *A.I.*, III, 221;
instructions to Tiumen and Tara, 1633 and 1699, *P.S.Z.*, III, 535–536, 569.
[55] "Write to ... Tobolsk ... and about important matters write to the sovereign in Moscow." Instructions to Kuznetsk, 1625, *A.I.*, III, 221.
"About important matters write to the great sovereign ... and write about
the same matters to Tobolsk also." Instructions to Tara, 1633, *P.S.Z.*, III, 569.
"About important matters write to Moscow ... and about small affairs write
to Tobolsk." Instructions to Tiumen, 1699, *P.S.Z.*, III, 535–536; see similar
instructions to Surgut, 1623, Ogloblin, IV, 129.
[56] Instructions to Tobolsk, 1660, *D.A.I.*, IV, 158; instructions to Tomsk,
1664, *D.A.I.*, IV, 326; instructions to Tobolsk, 1697, *P.S.Z.*, III, 345.

function without complications since the Muscovite government failed to define the division of authority, except by such vague terms as "important matters" and "unimportant matters."[57] The voevodas of assigned towns, who were appointed and rewarded for service by Moscow and could appeal to Moscow over the heads of the voevodas of their principal towns, were not always willing to recognize the authority of the latter.

In 1610 the voevodas of Surgut in their report to Moscow contended that the demand of the voevodas of Tobolsk that they be written to for instructions was a "reflection upon the honor" of the voevodas of Surgut. The same report expressed doubts as to whether the correspondence from Surgut was reaching Moscow since the voevodas of Tobolsk "open the mail." The Siberian Prikaz had to pacify the complaints with the advice "to do just as all voevodas of Siberian towns do."[58] In 1641 the voevoda of Ketsk refused to send financial information to Tomsk, and issued passports without consulting Tomsk officials. The voevoda of Tomsk complained to Moscow and received instructions to send a trustworthy man to Ketsk, at the expense of the voevoda of Ketsk, in order to get the account books.[59] On another occasion the Muscovite government had to reprimand the voevoda of Tiumen who disregarded the instructions from Tobolsk.[60] In general, the voevodas of the principal towns lacked the means to enforce their demands upon the voevodas of the assigned towns. In 1669 a voevoda of Tiumen was removed from his office by order of the voevoda of Tobolsk. This action, however, was considered unlawful.[61] The only recourse in the case of a recalcitrant voevoda was a threat to report his misdeeds to Moscow.[62]

As a conclusion to this chapter, the distribution of authority within the Siberian colonial administration may be illustrated by the diagram shown on the following page.

In this diagram the arrows radiating from Moscow to all Siberian

---

[57] See *supra*, p. 44, n. 55.
[58] Ogloblin, III, 215.
[59] *Ibid.*, III, 36.
[60] "In the future write about such matters to Tobolesk [*sic*] to our boiar and voevoda ... Khilkov, and you are to do whatever our boiar and voevoda tells you." Instructions to Tiumen, 1661, *D.A.I.*, IV, 232–233.
[61] *D.R.V.*, III, 202; Chicherin, pp. 352–353.
[62] Communications from Tobolsk to Verkhoturie, 1652, *A.I.*, IV, 171; and 1685, *A.I.*, V, 185.

towns indicate its direct control over both the principal and the assigned towns. Tobolsk is placed in such a way as to show its priority among the principal towns. The broken lines from Tobolsk

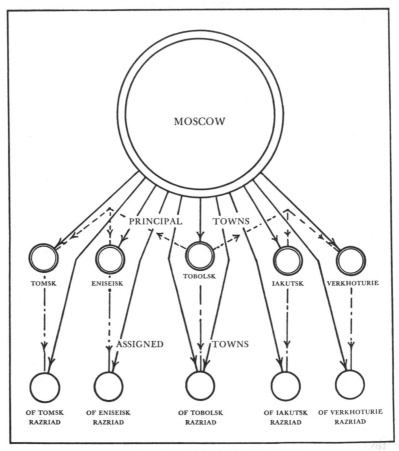

ADMINISTRATIVE HIERARCHY OF SIBERIAN TOWNS

to the other principal towns indicate that it had but little authority over them. The lines leading from the principal to the assigned towns indicate the subordinate position of the latter. The domination of the principal towns over the towns of their respective razriads, however, is limited, because the assigned towns often received orders directly from Moscow over the head of the principal towns.

CHAPTER IV

SIBERIAN OFFICIALS

EACH SIBERIAN TOWN controlled a large area of territory which, by analogy with the territorial organization in European Russia, was called an *uezd*. Unlike their Russian counterparts, the Siberian uezds, especially in the early period of occupation, lacked clearly defined boundaries—a situation which led to conflicts among the local officials when they collected furs from the natives.[1] Within the uezds there were smaller administrative units, *volosts,* representing either groups of native settlements organized under their chiefs,[2] or, with the arrival of the Russian colonists, groups of Russian villages. Probably as a result of unsatisfactory experiences with the namestniks and volostels in European Russia, the town and its uezd in Siberia did not have separate officials, but both were administered by the voevodas, who will be described in this chapter.

VOEVODAS

Voevodas were the most important officials in Siberia; they were always appointed from Moscow, and since the position of voevoda offered many lucrative possibilities, the government never had any difficulty in filling the vacancies. Among the Muscovite nobility there were always a number of candidates eager to obtain an appointment. The office seekers made out petitions, sometimes but not always specifying the desired town, and presented them to the *Razriad*[3] (Office of Military Affairs), because the service of the voevoda required military qualifications and the Razriad was in charge of all serving men. A good military record and wounds

---

[1] J. E. Fischer, *Sibirskaia istoriia,* p. 481; G. F. Mueller, *Opisanie Sibirskago tsarstva i vsekh proisshedshikh v nem del ot nachala a osoblivo ot pokoreniia ego rossiiskoi derzhave po sii vremena,* p. 322; P. N. Butsinskii, *Mangazeia i mangazeiskii uezd,* pp. 18, 24; P. A. Slovtsov, *Istoricheskoe obozrenie Sibiri,* I, 43.

[2] "From the town of Tobolsk volosts up the Irtysh River ... are assigned to the new town at Ialov, which town is to be built on the Tara River: volost Kurdak under the chief Kankul with a population of 350 men,..., volost Sorgash with a population of 80 men ... volost Otuz having a population of 15 men ... volost Tavu having 10 men ... volost Uruz having 6 men,... volost Tokuz where there are 3 men ... volost Aialy where they have 500 men." Mueller, *Opisanie,* pp. 207–216.

[3] The Razriad (Office of Military Affairs) should not be confused with razriads—administrative territorial units.

received in action counted in favor of a candidate, but to bring about the desired results the petitions had to be accompanied by bribes, the diaks of the Office having a regular scale of rates for the different towns. The Razriad prepared a list of prospective voevodas, and the names were submitted to the tsar for approval. After that, the list was sent to the Siberian Prikaz, which announced the appointments. Usually all the voevodas within the same razriad[4] were replaced simultaneously; sometimes the change affected all the Siberian voevodas.[5]

Before the newly appointed voevodas started their journey to Siberia, the Siberian Prikaz had to enter into negotiations with other prikazes, concerning certain privileges and exemptions which were enjoyed by the Siberian voevodas. The status of the Siberian voevodas was that of voevodas in active military service. During their stay in Siberia their estates, whether inherited or granted for service, were exempt from taxation and guaranteed to remain intact. The peasants at home who leased the land from the voevodas and were dependent on them, as well as their *dvorovye liudi* (household serfs) were not to be tried in courts, except on charges of thievery and robbery. Lawsuits against the voevodas themselves had to wait until their return.[6]

Upon their departure the voevodas received their traveling expenses in advance, as well as salary in food and money. The money usually came from various sources. In 1613, the voevoda of Pelym was supposed to get his salary from the towns of Ustiug and Tot'ma but for certain reasons he could not get it there and was paid from the treasury of Verkhoturie.[7] In 1628 the voevoda Trubetskoi was paid from the two Muscovite prikazes, Galitskaia Chet and Ustiuzhskaia Chet.[8] The voevodas and the diak appointed to Iakutsk in 1639–1641 received their salaries for three years from the Vladimirskaia, Galitskaia, and Ustiuzhskaia Chets: one voevoda 700 rubles, another 500 rubles, and the diak 400 rubles.[9] In 1648 the

---

[4] A Siberian administrative unit, described in the preceding chapter.

[5] Decree, 1676, *P.S.Z.*, II, 76; decree, 1677, *P.S.Z.*, II, 143; B. Chicherin, *Oblastnyia uchrezhdeniia* ... , pp. 83, 85; N. N. Ogloblin, *Obozrenie stolbtsov* (cited hereafter as Ogloblin), III, 26–27, 31; IV, 52.

[6] Ogloblin, III, 24–27; decree, 1683, *P.S.Z.*, II, 549; Chicherin, pp. 84–85; Ulozhenie, 1649, *P.S.Z.*, I, 39.

[7] Instructions to Verkhoturie, 1613, *A.I.*, II, 407.

[8] Ogloblin, III, 24.

[9] "Otnosheniia voevod i diakov," *Chteniia*, Vol. CCXXXIII (1910), Bk. 2, pt. 5, p. 15.

WINTER TRAVEL IN THE SEVENTEENTH CENTURY

voevoda Frantsbekov, appointed to Iakutsk, received 370 rubles
from the Siberian Prikaz in addition to the 330 rubles given to him
from the prikazes Galitskaia Chet and Vladimirskaia Chet.[10] In
1655 the Siberian Prikaz sent an order to the voevoda of Eniseisk
to pay his predecessor, who was now transferred to the Amur
River.[11]

As a result of arrangements between the Siberian Prikaz and
the Iamskoi Prikaz, the voevodas were provided with means of
transportation. A great many horsecarts, when they went by land,
or boats, when they went by water, were required to take care of
the voevodas, who brought their families, servants, and abundant
supplies. In 1635 the voevoda of Mangazeia was accompanied on his
journey by his personal priest and thirty-two household retainers,
while his baggage contained 200 buckets of wine, 35 pounds of
honey, 35 pounds of butter, 6 buckets of vegetable oil, 150 hams,
besides flour, grits, and other food. In 1643 the voevoda of Tiumen
took a retinue of forty men to Siberia. The voevodas of Tobolsk
were usually accompanied by from sixty to seventy relatives and
servants. Concealed, within the train of the voevodas, were goods
and wine for their private trading, although this was forbidden.
To stop the smuggling of saleable articles, the Prikaz issued regulations concerning the amount of food and other supplies the voevodas should take or buy on their way.[12] The baggage of the
voevodas was examined at the border, and whatever they had in
excess of these regulations was confiscated.[13] By 1678 the government prepared norms specifying the number of horsecarts which
were allotted at governmental expense to the voevodas and other
officials traveling to Siberia.[14]

---

[10] Ogloblin, IV, 168.

[11] Instructions to Eniseisk, 1655, *D.A.I.*, IV, 41.

[12] Ogloblin, III, 27; P. N. Butsinskii, *Zaselenie*, pp. 236–237.

[13] Instructions to Verkhoturie, 1680, *A.I.*, V. 77–79.

[14] Number of horsecarts allotted to the Siberian officials:

Officials of Tobolsk

The chief voevoda of the rank of boiar	25 carts
The chief voevoda of the rank of stolnik	20 carts
The associate voevodas	15 carts each
The diaks	12 carts each
The pismennye golovas	10 carts each

Officials of Tomsk

The chief voevoda	20 carts
The associate voevoda	13 carts
The diaks	11 carts each

Footnote concluded on page 50.

As a rule the voevodas were appointed for a term of two or three years. In Tobolsk from 1587 until 1700 there were forty changes in voevodas.[15] In Berezov between 1592 and 1606 there were six changes.[16] In Iakutsk there were five successive voevodas during the years 1645–1652, but only one, Lodyzhenskii, from 1652 until 1658.[17] In Eniseisk one voevoda held his office for five years, from 1667 until 1672,[18] but five- or six-year terms were rather unusual in Siberian administrative practice. There were too many office seekers, and under the influence of the old idea of "kormlenie" the government tried to distribute the benefits of the office to as many candidates as possible. The belief that a short period would give less opportunity for graft to develop may have been another important consideration. The brevity of the tenure and the hope of obtaining a new appointment, if there were no complaints, may have had a restraining effect upon abuses. In the absence of effective control and supervision over the voevodas the government preferred to change them often, since the only time the voevodas' activities were checked upon was when they were leaving office.[19]

In 1695, however, the Muscovite government issued a decree whereby the voevodas in all towns of Siberia, with the exception of the voevodas of Tobolsk, should have terms of from four to six years, or even longer, if their service proved satisfactory. This was done on account of the expenses involved in the transportation of the voevodas and the burdens imposed on the population along their route of travel. It was also hoped that fewer changes would decrease the amount of smuggling practiced by the voevodas.[20]

Other towns

The voevodas of Berezov, Tara, Surgut	13 carts each
The voevodas of Pelym, Ketsk, Krasnoiarsk, Eniseisk, Narym	12 carts each
The voevodas of Mangazeia	14 carts each
The voevodas of Ilimsk	17 carts each
The voevodas of Iakutsk	30 carts each

While they stayed in Siberia, these officials could ask once every year for horsecarts to bring them additional supplies from European Russia. The number of carts so allotted was one-half the norm specified above. (Compiled from the instructions to Kuznetsk, 1678, *A.I.*, V, 36–37.)

[15] *D.R.V.*, III, 108–288, *passim;* Sobstvennaia ego imperatorskago velichestva kantseliariia, *Dvortsovye razriady, passim.*

[16] V. K. Andrievich, *Istoriia Sibiri*, I, 27.

[17] Chicherin, p. 87.

[18] Ogloblin, I, 27.

[19] Chicherin, p. 86.

[20] Decree, 1695, *P.S.Z.*, III, 203.

About a month prior to the departure of the newly appointed voevodas to Siberia, the Siberian Prikaz issued instructions outlining the duties of the local voevodas for every principal or assigned town, where the change of voevodas was taking place.[21] For the informaton of the voevodas there was kept in every *s'ezzhaia izba* (the town office of the voevodas, called otherwise *prikaznaia izba*) a set of instructions which had been sent to the previous voevodas of the town. After the *Ulozhenie* (the code of laws of the Tsar Aleksei Mikhailovich) had been prepared, a copy of it was forwarded to every town.[22] These documents served together as administrative guides for the voevodas.[23] Whenever all these aids were insufficient, the voevodas, as already stated, were to refer to Moscow for advice and also, if their towns were of secondary rank, to the voevodas of their principal towns. Nevertheless, the voevodas were not completely bound either by earlier or by recent instructions, and in certain matters they were allowed freedom of action.[24]

The opportunity to use their own judgment, presumably "guided by the Lord," left the voevodas a wide field for the abuse of their powers. Late in the seventeenth century attempts were made to curtail the possibilities of arbitrary rule. Some progress was made when, in 1695, Peter the Great ordered the preparation of a permanent set of regulations for the voevodas of each town.[25]

---

[21] Chicherin, p. 90.

[22] Chicherin, p. 92.

[23] "The voevodas administer their town according to instructions ... and according to the Ulozhenie." G. Kotoshikhin, *O Rossii v tsarstvovanie Aleksiia Mikhailovicha*, p. 139.

[24] "If the present articles contain directions which do not apply to the existing conditions, because they are impossible to execute, or their execution would cause a loss to the treasury or a burden to the people, then the voevodas ... shall use their own judgment ... remembering their oath and the fear of God." Instructions to Tobolsk, 1697, *P.S.Z.*, III, 375.

"Perform your duties, taking care of the affairs of the sovereign, according to the present instructions ... and considering the local circumstances. Find the previous instructions and read them carefully. Follow them eagerly in so far as they are good, leading to the profit of the sovereign and to security. If the previous instructions do not lead to any profit, or do not fit into existing conditions, then act according to the present circumstances, whatever is the best to do. Follow the guidance of the Lord so that the sovereign will profit and the men of the sovereign and others will not be unduly burdened." Instructions to Tara, 1633, *P.S.Z.*, III, 568. These directions are found almost word for word in other documents. Instructions to Tobolsk, 1664, *D.A.I.*, IV, 349; instructions to Iakutsk, 1694, *A.I.*, V, 444; instructions to Tobolsk, 1697, *P.S.Z.*, III, 342 ff.

[25] "And in the future a set of articles shall be prepared based on instructions and decrees, to put fear into the voevodas and to keep them from such arbitrary actions as are detrimental both to the treasury and to the population. These articles bearing the signatures of the *dumnye liudi* [members of the *Boiar-*

The voevodas had to follow their instructions carefully when they were taking over their office. This was rather an elaborate procedure. The departing voevodas handed over to their successors the town keys and seal, the lists of the Russian and native population, the inventories of equipment and supplies, and the account books. After this there followed the inspection of the town and its garrison. Then the supplies were weighed and measured, and the money and furs were counted.[26] The new voevodas had to make sure that the previous administration had caused no loss to the treasury either through incompentency or dishonesty. The belongings and even the houses of the former voevodas were searched for concealed furs.[27]

The retiring voevodas had to make up all shortages before they were allowed to depart, and the results of the investigation had to be immediately reported to the Siberian Prikaz. Once, in 1635, when the retiring voevoda of Pelym, Baskakov, did not have the furs shown in the records, and also had paid some of his serving men salaries above the existing norms, the new voevoda, Usov, was instructed to exact the deficit from Baskakov.[28] On another occasion, in 1696, the voevoda of Turinsk, Morev, was short 264.86 rubles in cash and was found responsible for a fire which caused a great deal of damage; he, also, had to make up the losses to the government.[29]

Very often the newly appointed voevodas had to check complaints which were received by the Siberian Prikaz about the voevodas who had finished their term. In 1667 the voevoda of Berezov, Davydov, cruelly suppressed the rebellion of the Ostiaks, who complained to Moscow that he had hanged seventeen innocent "best men"[30] and had confiscated their possessions for himself. Davydov was ordered to remain in Berezov, until the new voevoda, Gagarin, appointed in 1668, finished the investigation of com-

---

skaia Duma] and the seal of the great sovereign shall be sent to towns and placed in the *s'ezzhaia izba* ... the people shall be given charters, demanding obedience to the regulations as stated in the articles. If the voevodas demand anything contrary to these articles, then the people shall not obey them and shall send complaints to Moscow." Decree, 1695, *P.S.Z.*, III, 203–204.

[26] Ogloblin, I, 23–25; instructions to Kuznetsk, 1625, *A.I.*, III, 217–218; instructions to Tara, 1633, *P.S.Z.*, III, 565; Chicherin, pp. 92–93.

[27] Mueller, *Opisanie*, p. 227; Ogloblin, IV, 125.

[28] Ogloblin, I, 23–24.

[29] Decision of the boiars, 1696, *P.S.Z.*, III, 257–258.

[30] The term "best men," when applied to natives, usually means prominent or influential men.

plaints. Davydov had to stay until 1669, when he was finally exonerated.[31]

Contrary to the government regulations, the Siberian voevodas, especially those in the more distant towns, frequently avoided rendering accounts by departing from the town before the arrival of the new voevodas. As a result, the government was kept in ignorance as to the real state of affairs. In 1651 voevoda Lodyzhenskii was sent to Iakutsk with instructions to check the accounts of his predecessor, Akinfov, and, if Akinfov had failed to get the accounts from his predecessor, Frantsbekov, then Lodyzhenskii was to go over the records of the latter as well.[32] In 1658 new voevodas were sent to Iakutsk. They, in turn, received instructions to check Lodyzhenskii's accounts, and, if Lodyzhenskii had not carried out orders, to check the accounts of his predecessors Akinfov and Frantsbekov as well.[33] In other words, for seven years the Muscovite government was not informed about the activities of its agents in Iakutsk. Such conditions led to a decree in 1697 forbidding the voevodas to leave without a statement from their successors that the latter found everything in order. This statement the retiring voevodas were to present to the Siberian Prikaz.[34] Previous regulations had already established the rule that voevodas leaving the towns without rendering proper accounts were liable to a fine at first amounting to two hundred rubles and later to five hundred rubles.[35]

The Staff of the Voevodas

The Muscovite administrative policy avoided conferring wide authority on a single official. Even in the army the chief voevoda shared his command with other voevodas, and the orders of the government were issued to "the boiar-voevoda and to his *tovarishchi* (literally comrades, here meaning associates)."[36] It has been shown above[37] that the decisions of the boiar of a prikaz had also to be approved by the diaks. This idea of having in association with the executive officer one or more councilors who had little power of

---

[31] Ogloblin, III, 25.
[32] Instructions to Iakutsk, 1651, *D.A.I.*, III, 299.
[33] Instructions to Iakutsk, 1658, *D.A.I.*, IV, 101.
[34] Decree, 1697, *P.S.Z.*, III., 402.
[35] Decision of the boiars, 1696, *P.S.Z.*, III, 258; instructions to Nerchinsk, 1696, *A.I.*, V, 466.
[36] *D.R.V.*, III, 218–219.
[37] See *supra*, pp. 7–8.

their own but whose consent was necessary in all important matters was also adopted in the provincial administration of Siberia.[38]

During the early period of the Siberian occupation it was more common to find two voevodas than one in a town. When there were two, the second was known as the *tovarishch* or associate of the first, who was then called the chief voevoda. Appointment of voevodas in pairs continued to the end of the seventeenth century. To some towns the government at one time would send one voevoda, at another time two. However the practice of sending two voevodas to the same town was gradually abandoned. In 1681, only the largest towns, Tobolsk and Tomsk, had two voevodas each.[39]

In addition to the second voevoda, or in his stead, other officials were associated with the chief voevoda of a town. The earliest instructions to Siberia mention the *pismennye golovas* (literally "writing heads," military officers capable of keeping records and of attending to official correspondence) as associates, or even substitutes for the voevodas. At the time of the Ermak expedition, it was the golova Glukhov who led the Russian forces back after the death of the commanding voevoda.[40] Tobolsk was founded by the pismennyi golova, Chulkov, who acted as the first voevoda there.[41] In 1600 the golova, Ianov, was sent to build an ostrog in Iepanchin Iurt (later called Turinsk),[42] and was given charge of it, being replaced later by another golova, Likharev.[43] The pismennye golovas, Pisemskii and Tyrkov, who were sent in 1604 to build Tomsk, remained there, and their successors were also pismennye golovas, Rzhevskii and Bartenev.[44]

During the first quarter of the seventeenth century, the government ceased to designate the pismennye golovas as the associates of

---

[38] Ogloblin, III, 8.

[39] An inspection of the lists of the voevodas taken at random shows: Around 1620–1622 there were 4 towns with a single voevoda and 9 with two voevodas. In 1631 there were 11 towns with a single voevoda and 4 with two voevodas. In 1645 there were 12 towns with a single voevoda and 4 with two voevodas. In 1681 there were 16 towns with a single voevoda and 2 with two voevodas.

Two voevodas were maintained longer in important towns such as Tobolsk, Tomsk, Iakutsk, Mangazeia, and Tara, whereas the two small towns of Narym and Ketsk, which had previously been administered independently, in 1671 were placed under a single voevoda. *D.R.V.*, III, 107, 110, 129–130, 134, 136–138, 149–151, 161–169, 236, 240–242, 262.

[40] Fischer, pp. 161–162; Mueller, *Opisanie*, p. 156.

[41] *D.R.V.*, III, 108; Fischer, p. 169.

[42] Instructions to Ianov, 1600, *R.I.B.*, II, 66; Mueller, *Opisanie*, pp. 283–286.

[43] *D.R.V.*, III, 119; Mueller, *Opisanie*, p. 297.

[44] Ogloblin, IV, 38–39.

the voevodas,[45] although until the end of the century they were still appointed by Moscow to accompany the voevodas.[46] They came to be regarded as special officers attached to the voevodas to be detailed for various important commissions. As such they compiled statistics of the Russian population, of the natives paying the fur tribute, and of land under cultivation; they also investigated the activities of the voevodas and other officials; in case of the absence or death of the voevoda they had charge of towns; sometimes they led military expeditions or performed other tasks.[47]

The role of the pismennye golovas and of the second voevodas as associates of the chief voevodas was taken over gradually by regular clerical officials, either the diaks or the *pod'iacheis s pripis'iu*,[48] whose special duty was to keep records and do other clerical work, although they also took part in the administration of the government. The diaks were officials of the Muscovite prikazes, to which they returned when their term of office was over. They had already been employed in the provincial administration in the time of the namestniks and were retained in similar service when government by the voevodas was introduced.[49] In 1599 the first diak was appointed in Tobolsk.[50] By 1625 there were three associates there, one associate vocvoda and two diaks.[51] In Tobolsk these diaks became known as the *bol'shoi* (senior) diak and the *men'shoi* (junior) diak.[52] In Tomsk the first diak appeared after 1608, and two diaks were appointed in 1629, after Tomsk was made the center of a separate razriad.[53] The diaks served in the big towns as the second and third associates respectively, but in small towns where there was only one voevoda the diak was his only associate.[54] Such a situation existed, for example, in Mangazeia, where in 1639 and again in 1641 the diak, who was then the only associate of the voevoda, had complete charge of the town, on the first occasion, as a result of

---

[45] In Tobolsk after 1599, in Surgut after 1608, in Tara after 1623, etc. *Ibid.*, IV, 32–33.

[46] Instructions to Verkhoturie, 1692, *P.S.Z.*, III, 130.

[47] Ogloblin, I, 31; III, 11; IV, 32–33; *D.R.V.*, III, 145, 151, 225; instructions to Tara, 1631, *P.S.Z.*, III, 557.

[48] Ogloblin, III, 10; IV, 32; for an explanation of the terms, see *supra*, pp. 9, 55.

[49] *Supra*, pp. 27–28.

[50] Ogloblin, IV, 32.

[51] *D.R.V.*, III, 142.

[52] *Ibid.*, III, 240.

[53] *Ibid.*, III, 149; Ogloblin, IV, 33–34.

[54] Ogloblin, III, 9.

the absence of the local voevoda, and on the second, of his death.[55] Like the voevodas, the outgoing diaks were held responsible to their successors.[56]

In some towns the place of a diak was taken by a *pod'iachei s pripis'iu.*[57] Under such circumstances he was the voevoda's associate and had the same functions and rights as a diak.[58] The pod'iacheis s pripis'iu were usually transferred from Moscow or other European towns, where they had held similar positions, or had been ordinary pod'iacheis. In very few instances were pod'iacheis s pripis'iu raised to the rank of diak in Siberia.[59]

Ogloblin makes the statement that "not even the smallest town in Siberia was ever administered by the voevoda alone (without associates)."[60] However, he himself disproves this generalization in one of his articles, where he tells the story of the Siberian merchants who protested against the appointment of a pod'iachei s pripis'iu in Eniseisk. The petitioners explained that in 1644 the Siberian Prikaz had sent a pod'iachei s pripis'iu to this town although until that time there had been only a voevoda without any associate there. The petition was granted by the tsar in 1647 in spite of the efforts of the Siberian Prikaz to prevent such action.[61]

There must have been other towns without either diaks or pod'-iacheis s pripis'iu. Otherwise the government in Moscow would not have issued a decree in 1695 introducing their appointment throughout Siberia.[62] From that time on the government insisted

---

[55] *Ibid.*, III, 9; *D.R.V.*, III, 159.

[56] Ogloblin, 1, 30–31.

[57] "By our order ... you shall have in Verkhoturie the pod'iachei s pripis'iu, Shestakov.... He will be together with you, as an associate.... He is to receive 30 rubles as his salary [per year].... The pod'iachei s pripis'iu, Matiushkin who was sent to Verkhoturie last year received his salary for Siberian service in Moscow ... 20 rubles per year." Instructions to Verkhoturie, 1631, *A.I.*, III, 310–311.

[58] Ogloblin, III, 10.

[59] *Ibid.*, III, 28, 129.

[60] *Ibid.*, IV, 38.

[61] "Command, o sovereign, that the voevoda be maintained in Eniseisk without pod'iacheis, as it was before ... command that the present pod'iachei, Shilkin, be dismissed, in order that your treasury shall not suffer losses, and that we, thy serfs (kholops) and orphans shall not be altogether ruined on account of pod'iacheis and their abuses and extortions." Petition, 1647, Ogloblin, "Proiskhozhdenie provintsial'nykh pod'iachikh," *Zh.M.N.P.*, Vol. CCXCV (Sept., 1894), No. 9, p. 129.

[62] "The diaks and pod'iacheis s pripis'iu must be always appointed to towns ... [because in their absence] the voevodas fail to forward the financial reports ... excusing themselves by the lack of officials capable of preparing them." Decree, 1695, *P.S.Z.*, III, 203.

that documents from every Siberian town bear the signatures of the diaks or the pod'iacheis s pripis'iu, in addition to that of the voevodas.[63]

Usually the voevodas and their associates carried on official business as one body. Together they sent their reports to Moscow,[64] or received communications from petty officials sent on some commission from their town.[65] The correspondence from the assigned to the principal towns was usually addressed also to the whole staff,[66] although sometimes the chief voevoda of the principal town dealt with the assigned towns himself.[67] When he did he usually wrote a personal message to the voevoda of the assigned town, without mentioning the associates of the latter.[68]

The chief voevoda of a town and his associates were usually appointed together and for the same period. The instructions of the Muscovite government issued upon their appointment were addressed to all of them as a body. Individual instructions were issued only on such occasions as when a successor had to be appointed to replace one of the town officials before the end of his term.[69] In 1614 a new associate voevoda of Tara, and in 1631 a new pod'iachei s pripis'iu of Verkhoturie filled vacancies in these towns. Each of these officials received individual instructions similar to those generally sent to the whole group of town officials. The new appointees were advised to count the men and supplies and to investigate the activities of their colleagues. Their findings were to be reported to Moscow. These instructions, however, deserve special mention, because they contain the Muscovite definition of the relations of the chief town voevoda to the other officials. The voevoda and his associates were to administer all local affairs together, *za odno* (as one person, that is, conjointly), *bezvolokitno* (without "dragging," without mutual hindrance), *bezo vsiakia rozni* (without squabbles).[70]

[63] Decree, 1695, *P.S.Z.*, III, 215.
[64] Report from Tobolsk, 1626, *R.I.B.*, VIII, 376; report from Iakutsk, 1640–1641, *D.A.I.*, II, 241; report from Verkhoturie, 1681, *A.I.*, V, 108.
[65] Report to Iakutsk, 1641, *D.A.I.*, II, 249.
[66] Instructions to Ilimsk, 1659, *D.A.I.*, IV, 157; instructions to Tara, 1693, *P.S.Z.*, III, 593; instructions to Tobolsk, 1697, *P.S.Z.*, III, 345.
[67] Ogloblin, IV, 139.
[68] Instructions to Ilimsk and to Tiumen, 1659, *D.A.I.*, IV, 153, 183; instructions to Verkhoturie, 1652, *A.I.*, IV, 169.
[69] Ogloblin, IV, 34.
[70] Instructions to Tara, 1614, Ogloblin, IV, 142–143; instructions to Verkhoturie, 1631, *A.I.*, III, 310–311; instructions to Iakutsk, 1651, *D.A.I.*, III, 314.

This vague, general demand for coöperation was difficult to meet in practice. The lack of a clearly defined relationship led at times to serious quarrels. In 1642 the voevoda Golovin in Iakutsk put his associates, the voevoda Glebov and the diak Filatov in jail. A special messenger from Eniseisk, the pismennyi golova Bakhteiarov, freed the prisoners. The next day Golovin attempted to put the diak back in jail and would have done so had not the serving men prevented him. In order to clear himself in the eyes of Moscow, Golovin reported that his enemies carried on treasonable negotiations with the Iakuts. The other side accused Golovin of collusion with private enterprisers against the serving men.[71] A similar conflict occurred in Tomsk, where in 1650 the associate voevoda, Bunakov, refused to sit in the *s'ezzhaia izba* (office of the voevodas) with the chief voevoda and the diak. With the support of the serving men and the lower clerks, he established himself in the "cossack office" and usurped the functions of the administration. For this action he was later whipped in the market place and sent back to Moscow.[72] In 1668 another incident of the same kind took place in Tobolsk. The chief voevoda, Godunov, after a quarrel with his associates, Belskii and Zhdanov (one a voevoda and the other a diak), removed them from office and placed them under arrest. Accusations from both sides were sent to Moscow, and a decree arrived recalling Belskii and Zhdanov; Godunov, after further punishing Belskii, eventually let him depart, but Zhdanov was detained in Tobolsk, until a special messenger was sent from Moscow for him.[73]

In spite of all these disturbances, the central government was willing neither to abandon the practice of having the town officials dependent on one another, nor to place a single executive officer in charge of a town. When a voevoda acted "without associates," his action was looked upon with suspicion and regarded as unlawful and arbitrary and as a probable indication of graft.[74] The government reasoned that the requirement of a consensus between the voevoda and his associates in all affairs of importance would discourage corruption. Of course, the officials could form a sort of clique, but it takes time to come to an understanding in such matters. Meanwhile the term of office was short, and there was

---

[71] Report of Pushkin, 1645, *D.A.I.*, III, 34–35; instructions to Iakutsk, 1648, *D.A.I.*, III, 138; petition from Iakutsk, 1649, *D.A.I.*, III, 208.
[72] Report from Tomsk, 1650, *D.A.I.*, III, 249.
[73] *D.R.V.*, III, 201–202.   [74] S. Prutchenko, *Sibirskiia okrainy*, I, 16.

always the possibility of an associate's reporting to the Prikaz should he be approached with any irregular proposal. That is why the Muscovite government tolerated the direct reports of the voevoda's associates over his head. Although the communications of the second voevodas were not numerous, there is much evidence of correspondence carried on by the diaks. In 1645 the diak of Eniseisk, for instance, reported the troubles in the administration of Iakutsk; in 1648–1649 the diak of Tomsk sent a report about the local voevodas. The voevodas had good reason to be cautious of the diaks, who always came from the staff of the Muscovite clerks and therefore had "connections" in the Siberian Prikaz.[75]

MINOR OFFICIALS

The voevodas and their associates conducted official business in a special building, called the *s'ezzhaia* or *prikaznaia izba*. In larger towns this administrative office consisted of departments or *stols* (literally tables or desks), which were in charge of clerks—*pod'iacheis*.[76] Unlike the voevodas and their associates, the pod'iacheis were as a rule local men and held their appointments for indefinite periods. Some of them remained in office for as long as forty or even fifty years.[77] They received their appointment through petitions presented to the Siberian Prikaz, or were chosen by the local voevodas, subject to the approval of the Prikaz.[78] They were selected from among the literate serving men, minor unordained church officials, and townsmen; those whose past occupation was that of market scribe, or whose father was also a pod'iachei were preferred.[79] Even former *guliashchie liudi* (itinerant workers or tramps, usually of peasant origin, often runaway serfs) were sometimes appointed as local pod'iacheis.[80]

The number of pod'iacheis varied with the size and importance of the town. In 1640 there were twenty-two in Tobolsk, nine in Tomsk, and from one to seven in other Siberian towns. During this year there were altogether seventy-eight pod'iacheis in Siberian

[75] Ogloblin, III, 8–10.
[76] These minor clerks should not be confused with the pod'iacheis s pripis'iu, who were described above, as the associates of the voevodas.
[77] Ogloblin, "Proiskhozhdenie provintsial'nykh pod'iachikh," *Zh.M.N.P.*, Vol. CCXCV (Sept., 1894), No. 9, pp. 122, 126.
[78] *Ibid.*, No. 9, p. 134.
[79] *Ibid.*, No. 9, pp. 123, 144–145, 147–148, 150; No. 10, pp. 223–224, 229, 232, 236–237.
[80] *Ibid.*, No. 10, p. 234.

service and five vacancies.[81] Their salaries also were subject to variation, with the highest paid pod'iacheis as a rule receiving not more than nine rubles a year.[82] There were exceptions, however, and a petition is preserved where a pod'iachei already receiving ten rubles per year asks for an increase of five rubles.[83] Upon their retirement the pod'iacheis rendered accounts to their superiors, as well as to their successors in office.[84]

Owing to the knowledge of local affairs which they acquired during their long service, the pod'iacheis, in spite of a subordinate position, were officials of some importance. They were especially influential in towns where the voevoda had no associates, and where their signature was required to attest documents. In 1686 the voevoda of Krasnoiarsk was sentenced to a day in jail for sending his report to Moscow without the signature of the pod'iachei.[85]

Another important group of minor officials was the *prikaznye liudi* (literally men under orders, men given a commission). Whenever it was necessary to perform certain administrative tasks, such as taking charge of small ostrogs, taking a census, making an investigation, or sending an important message, the voevoda employed for that purpose some of the men under his command, usually minor military officers, who were then called prikaznye liudi.

Among these officials, the prikaznye liudi who were sent to take charge of ostrogs, *ostrozheks* (small ostrogs), or *zimov'es* (winter quarters or camps), deserve special consideration. They acted as petty voevodas; occasionally, they received direct communications from the Siberian Prikaz, and they had the right to report to the Prikaz over the heads of their immediate superiors, the voevodas of the uezd. In 1626, for instance, the boiar son Dubenskii commissioned to build an ostrog in Krasnoiarsk, complained to the Prikaz that the voevoda of Tobolsk would not let him go to Krasnyi Iar (Krasnoiarsk), and would not allow him any men.[86] The prikaznye liudi in charge of ostrozheks were usually appointed for one year. The appointments were made either by the Siberian Prikaz or by the voevodas themselves who had to notify the Siberian Prikaz.[87]

[81] *Ibid.*, No. 9, p. 132.
[82] *Ibid.*, No. 10, pp. 228, 233, 238–239.
[83] Ogloblin, III, 93.   [86] *Ibid.*, III, 10; IV, 38; Chicherin, p. 386.
[84] *Ibid.*, I, 31–32.   [87] Ogloblin, III, 29–30; IV, 38; *D.R.V.*, III, 149.
[85] *Ibid.*, IV, 120.

In summing up this description of Siberian officials, certain generalizations can be made.

In the beginning of the conquest, the leading role in the administration belonged exclusively to the serving nobility filling the military offices of voevodas and pismennye golovas. Later a bureaucratic element from the Muscovite prikazes was introduced, in the persons of diaks and pod'iacheis s pripis'u, which replaced the second voevodas and pismennye golovas at the head of the administration, although the place of the first voevodas always remained in the hands of nobles. Subordinated to the voevodas and their associates were minor officials: prikaznye liudi (usually military men) and pod'iacheis (clerks).

The town office was held jointly by the voevodas and their associates. In spite of inconveniences caused by this practice, the central government persisted in refusing to confer the administrative authority of the town upon a single chief official. Nevertheless this rule seems to have had some exceptions which were eventually stopped by a decree of 1695.[88]

The circumstances of the appointment of the voevodas and the view, which even the central government itself held, of the voevoda's office as one with possibilities for profit, illustrate the persistence of the traditions of kormlenie. The government sought, however, to limit the "feeding" of the voevodas by means of instructions, regulations, distribution of authority, short terms of office, and compulsory accounting when the voevodas left office.

---

[88] Decree of 1695, *P.S.Z.*, III, 203.

CHAPTER V

MILITARY ADMINISTRATION OF SIBERIA

EVEN A SUPERFICIAL glance at the Siberian administrative structure during the first century of its existence reveals its unmistakably military character. In the words of Prutchenko, Siberia in the seventeenth century was a large "military camp."[1] The chief administrators were essentially military officers with civil duties attached to their office. Most of their subordinates were also military men. Others, even purely clerical assistants such as pod'iacheis, at times were called upon to perform military duties. A review of the unsettled condition of the colony, where military forces were continually employed either for the acquisition of new territories or for the pacification of the natives in the regions already conquered, makes apparent the reasons for the preponderance of military elements in the administration.

The military organization of Siberia, like the military organization of European Russia, was determined by the existing class structure. The upper strata of the aristocracy provided the commanding officers; the petty nobility served as minor officers or made up the picked troops; from the non-noble free classes came the rank and file. The commanding officers in Siberia, the voevodas and pismennye golovas, have been described in the preceding chapter. The present description of the Siberian military forces will begin with the group rating second in the military administrative ladder—the petty nobility of the so-called "boiar sons."[2]

---

[1] S. Prutchenko, *Sibirskiia okrainy*, I, 2.

[2] The term "boiar son" is derived from the word "boiar" (for an explanation of the latter term see *supra*, p. 2, n. 4). In the earliest times the boiar sons were the younger representatives of the boiar families. I. D. Beliaev, "Sluzhilye liudi," *Moskovskii sbornik*, I (1852), 365, quotes the Ipat Chronicle, p. 46; V. Sergeevich, *Russkiia iuridicheskiia drevnosti*, quoted by N. N. Debolskii, in his review, *Zh.M.N.P.*, CCXCV (Sept.–Oct., 1894), 156–157; N. Pavlov-Silvanskii, *Gosudarevy sluzhilye liudi*, p. 93.

Later, during the time of Vasilii Vasilievich Temnyi (the Blind), the title boiar—for the first time in 1433—was retained only for such boiars as were able to maintain an exalted position at the Muscovite court, as the highest officials and members of the Boiar Duma (Boiars' Council). To the rest of the boiars, as a hereditary class, the name "boiar sons" was now applied. I. D. Beliaev, "Zhiteli," *Vremennik*, III (1849), 20; Pavlov-Silvanskii, *loc. cit.*

In 1564 the *oprichnina* was introduced, a social and administrative experiment of Ivan IV, which was followed by the "purges" of the old hereditary nobility. Then during 1565–1566 the title of the upper class of aristocracy was

[62]

THE BOIAR SONS

The first boiar sons in Siberia came as officers of the military units which were brought from European Russia. When Siberia began to furnish its own military men, new boiar sons rose from among the Russian and foreign exiles sent to Siberia,[3] from the *Litva*[4] (to be described below) and from the cossacks.[5] Within the Tobolsk razriad only the chief voevoda of Tobolsk could create new boiar sons, and then only if there were vacancies because of the regulations limiting their number.[6] The heads of the other razriads probably exercised similar rights. At least, it is known that in 1640 the voevoda of Tomsk, as punishment for insubordination and gambling, reduced several local boiar sons to cossacks on foot and replaced them by new boiar sons promoted from the cossacks.[7] Late in the century or, to be more exact, after 1684, some of the boiar sons were granted the newly created rank of the Siberian *dvorianin* (nobleman).[8] As the social status of the Siberian nobility was

changed from boiar sons to *dvoriane*. Beliaev, "Zhiteli," *loc. cit.*; Pavlov-Silvanskii, *op. cit.*, pp. 100–101.

In the time of the early chronicles the name dvoriane had been applied to the lower retainers, sometimes to the slaves of the prince, but in the thirteenth to sixteenth centuries the same name came to be used to denote a group of men somewhat higher in rank, free men who served a prince in exchange for the use of land, and who had a right to change their feudal master for another prince. After 1566 the dvoriane were made up of the old aristocratic element of the boiar sons and the newer element of the recently elevated retainers of the Muscovite prince, representing together the new serving nobility. Meanwhile the name, boiar sons, dropped in repute and after 1566 was used to designate the lower strata of nobility, which occupied the place held in the appanage period by the junior druzhina and later by the free servants of the prince's household. Thus, curiously, the application of the terms, boiar sons and dvoriane was transposed in the sixteenth century: boiar son has come to designate a lower rank and dvoriane, a higher. Beliaev, "Sluzhilye liudi," pp. 367, 369, 371, 373–382; *idem*, "Zhiteli," pp. 21–24. Pavlov-Silvanskii, *op. cit.*, pp. 27–28. Very likely this transposition was brought about by the social reforms of Ivan IV.

From this new group of boiar sons special detachments were formed in the Muscovite military service, or the boiar sons were used as officers of the streltsy and cossacks. It is in this latter capacity that we find them in Siberia.

[3] P. N. Butsinskii, *Zaselenie*, pp. 209, 213.

[4] *Ibid.*, p. 209; N. N. Ogloblin, *Obozrenie stolbtsov* (cited hereafter as Ogloblin), III, 103–104, 111, 129.

[5] Ogloblin, I, 111; III, 101, 105, 146; N. Abramov, "O sibirskikh dvorianakh i detiakh boiarskikh," *Etnograficheskii sbornik* ... , V (1862), 11–13.

[6] Instructions to Tobolsk, 1664, *D.A.I.*, IV, 349; instructions to Tobolsk, 1697, *P.S.Z.*, III, 341.

[7] Ogloblin, I, 123, 135–136.

[8] Singular of dvorniane, see *supra*, n. 2.

considered below that of the nobility in European Russia, the Siberian nobles tried and sometimes succeeded in getting their names into the lists of the Muscovite nobles.[9] Neither the rank of a Siberian-made boiar son, nor that of a Siberian nobleman was hereditary,[10] but the children of the boiar sons or of such officers as *golova* or *ataman* were preferred when filling vacancies.[11] Most often the awarding of these ranks was preceded by the presentation of a petition from the candidate.[12] The ordinary Litvins[13] or cossacks were raised to the rank of boiar son only in consideration of services rendered by themselves as well as by their fathers.[14]

In 1631 there were about 70 boiar sons in all Siberia.[15] But gradually their number increased. In 1682 there were 91 boiar sons in Tomsk alone.[16] In 1737 the Siberian Prikaz compiled a list of Siberian boiar sons and of Siberian nobles, and there were enough of them to make a regiment of dragoons, with 76 nobles and 276 boiar sons remaining for civil service.[17] The boiar sons and later the nobles were appointed as prikaznye liudi in the smaller ostrogs and zimov'es,[18] or as *nachalnye liudi* (commanders, officers) of the various types of serving men.[19] Like the pismennye golovas, they were assigned important commissions, such as the collection of various data for the government, the exploration of new regions, or the conducting of valuable caravans.[20]

The boiar sons and the Siberian nobles formed a sort of colonial aristocracy in Siberia. The development of state farming and certain other circumstances kept this class, unlike the nobles of European Russia, from becoming one of large landowners. However, they enjoyed certain privileges[21] and received better salaries

---

[9] Ogloblin, III, 101. The oath of allegiance taken in 1646 by the serving men of Tomsk mentions four nobles after the names of the voevodas, then enumerates the boiar sons. These nobles, probably from European Russia, were attached to the staff of the voevodas. Ogloblin, I, 88.

[10] Abramov, p. 17.

[11] *Ibid.*, 11–14; instructions to Tobolsk, 1697, *P.S.Z.*, III, 341.

[12] Abramov, p. 11; Ogloblin, III, 101, 284–285.

[13] *Infra*, p. 65.

[14] Ogloblin, I, 111; III, 103–105; IV, 131–132.

[15] "Smetnyi spisok 139 godu," *Vremennik*, Vol. IV (1849), pt. 3, pp. 48–51.

[16] Ogloblin, I, 137.

[17] Abramov, p. 17.

[18] *D.R.V.*, III, 149; Ogloblin, III, 29–30.

[19] Ogloblin, III, 29–31; N. N. Ogloblin, "Iakutskii rozysk o rozni boiarskikh detei i kazakov," *Russkaia starina*, Vol. XCI (1897), No. 8, p. 376.

[20] Ogloblin, "Iakutskii rozysk," p. 376; Ogloblin, I, 60–62, 79, 83, 116; III, 11, 95; Abramov, pp. 14–16.

[21] Ogloblin, II, 83.

than other serving men, and as a result they usually remained loyal to the voevodas in the occasional clashes of the latter with serving men of lower rank.[22]

Litva

An important position below the boiar sons was occupied by the *Litva* or *Litvins*. This group was composed of prisoners of war, immigrants, and foreign mercenaries sent for punishment to Siberia. The Litva was a Siberian foreign legion, consisting of men of many nationalities, Poles, White Russians, Ukrainians, Lithuanians (from whom it derived its name), Swedes, and Germans; there were even Frenchmen in the Litva.[23] The majority of these men had had previous military experience, and their military skill was superior to that of the Russians. They were mounted and armed like the cossacks, alongside of whom they generally fought in military campaigns.[24] In the second half of the seventeenth century, the government introduced in Siberia the organization of troops according to western European standards. Thus in 1660, Colonel William Fanzeits (?) was sent to Siberia to drill "raitars" and "saldats."[25] In 1668 another foreign officer, Egrat (the Danish colonel Egerat?) arrived at Tobolsk with fifty-four foreign "raitars."[26] As soon as troops of this type were introduced, the Litvins were among the first to be enlisted in their ranks.[27]

Not being used to the climate and the conditions of life in Siberia, the Litvins presumably felt the hardships of the Siberian service more keenly than did the Russians. Their common destiny and their cultural level, which was above that of the Russians, tended, despite their motley composition, to unite them whenever their interests had to be defended.[28] Altogether, even though the Litvin group was a small one, they formed an interesting as well as an important part of the Siberian army, and several Litvins rose to the position of boiar sons and officers, and played significant parts in the conquest of Siberia.

[22] N. N. Ogloblin, "Tomskii bunt 1637–1638," *Istoricheskii vestnik*, LXXXV (1901), 236.

[23] Ogloblin, III, 103; Butsinskii, *Zaselenie*, pp. 198–199.

[24] Ogloblin, III, 116.

[25] *Ibid.*, IV, 12.

[26] *Ibid.*, III, 33; N. Ustrialov, *Istoriia tsarstvovaniia Petra Velikago*, I, 181.

[27] Ogloblin, III, 266.

[28] *Ibid.*, III, 115.

STRELTSY

A very considerable portion of the Siberian army was composed of professional soldiers, *streltsy* (shooters),[29] so named because their chief weapons were muskets, although they were armed also with swords, pikes, and battle-axes. Some of them were mounted, but the great majority were infantrymen. The introduction of the streltsy by Ivan IV marked the beginning of the regular army in Russia. In European Russia the streltsy were organized into regiments of about a thousand men each, under the command of golovas, who were usually Muscovite noblemen. A regiment was divided into companies, each commanded by a *sotnik* (commander of a hundred), who was appointed from among the boiar sons. There were also minor officers promoted from the ranks. The privates were either the sons of streltsy, as this service was hereditary, or were conscripted from the free men of lower classes.[30]

Unlike modern soldiers, the streltsy did not live in barracks. Instead, they were given houses by the government in a certain part of a town, specially assigned for the purpose and called the *streletskaia sloboda* (suburb of streltsy). In addition to homes, where they lived together with their families, they received small plots of land, and salaries in money and grain. Also, they were allowed to keep shops and to carry on business on a small scale. They enjoyed a number of privileges, such as exemption from certain court dues, and permission to make alcoholic beverages for their own use, though not for sale.[31]

The service of the streltsy was for life, or rather for the term of their physical fitness. During the first half of the seventeenth century, the streltsy on foot were considered the best infantrymen in Russia. In time of war, they took part in the field, and in the defense of towns. In time of peace, they acted as the town gatekeepers, policemen, watchmen, and firemen. Some of them were attached to the office of the voevodas and to the customhouse in the town where they were stationed. Others were employed to escort

[29] Singular, *strelets*.
[30] N. I. Shpakovskii, "Strel'tsy," *Zh.M.N.P.*, CCCXIX (Sept.–Oct., 1898), 136–138; Kotoshikhin, *O Rossii v tsarstvovanie Aleksiia Mikhailovicha*, pp. 28, 101–102; Ustrialov, I, 174–175; *D.R.V.*, XX, 231–234; H. O. R. Brix, *Geschichte der alten russischen Heeres-Einrichtungen*, p. 57.
[31] Shpakovskii, pp. 136, 141–142, 146–151; Kotoshikhin, p. 101; Ustrialov, I, 175, 294–295.

prominent travelers and valuable shipments. In Siberia, in addition to other duties, the streltsy collected furs from the natives.[32]

During the time of Ivan IV there were about 5,000 streltsy in Moscow and 7,000 in frontier towns.[33] During the period 1625–1636, according to Brix, the number of streltsy, not counting the garrison of Moscow, was increased from 20,539 to 26,353, about ten per cent being streltsy on horse.[34] In 1625, of 2,735 serving men in Siberia 995 were streltsy, 191 on horse, and 804 on foot; in 1636, of 5,004 Siberian serving men 1,558 were streltsy, 75 on horse, and 1,483 on foot.[35]

Documents show that the streltsy served in Siberia throughout the seventeenth century, but as the century advanced, their service, because of frontier conditions, became increasingly like that of the cossacks, and by the middle of the century they were hardly distinguishable from this other body of serving men.[36]

COSSACKS

More important and more numerous than the streltsy in Siberia were the Siberian cossacks.[37] The origin of the word cossack is still in dispute. The Tatars applied the term to the rabble of their army, and it was used also to designate the predatory nomad bands which appeared along the frontiers of the declining Tatar Empire. The name was taken over by the Russians who used it when speaking of free homeless men, tramps, and itinerant laborers, a class later known as *guliashchie liudi* (literally wandering men or tramps).[38]

With the weakening of the Tatar rule, many of these wandering men together with fugitives of all sorts set forth toward the steppes.

---

[32] Shpakovskii, pp. 135, 145–146; Ustrialov, I, 175; Kotoshikhin, p. 102.

[33] Shpakovskii, p. 136.

[34] Brix, *op. cit.*, Beilage No. 4, pp. 580–583; P. N. Miliukov, "Gosudarstvennoe khoziaistvo Rossii v. sviazi s reformoi Petra Velikago," *Zh.M.N.P.*, CCLXXI (Sept.–Oct., 1890), 48.

[35] Compiled from Brix, pp. 575–583; K. B. Gazenvinkel, *Knigi razriadnyia*, quoted by D. Korsakov, review in the *Istoricheskii vestnik*, LII (1893), 509–511.

[36] P. A. Slovtsov, *Istoricheskoe obozrenie*, I, 6, n. 2; instructions to Tiumen, 1652, recommend changing the name of the 150 local streltsy on horse to that of cossacks on horse. *D.A.I.*, 378–379.

[37] Ogloblin, III, 104.

[38] "Should any of the itinerant cossacks hire themselves out to live at the monastery working as salters, cooks, water carriers, wood choppers and carriers, or performing other tasks, have them report to our namestniks, volostels, and tiuns." Charter to the ... monastery, 1543, *A.A.E.*, I, 179; see also charter to ... peasants, 1564, *A.A.E.*, I, 303–304; customs charter to ... monastery, 1591, *A.A.E.*, I, 426.

In the first half of the sixteenth century they started a number of settlements along the upper Don, and later along the Volga and Iaik (Ural) rivers. Here they led an adventurous life, selling fish and game to passing merchants, plundering them when they had an opportunity, fighting similar Tatar cossacks, raiding towns beyond the frontier, and causing grief to the Tatar and Russian governments alike.[39]

The cossack communities developed a democratic, if crude, system of self-government. The most important among these communities were the Don Republic, nominally under the suzerainty of the Muscovite tsars, and the Zaporog Republic in the Ukraine, which was established a little later within the sphere of influence of the Polish crown. The Don cossacks apparently are mentioned first in 1549, when the Nogai chief Iusuf wrote to Moscow that there were two or three cossack towns on the Don, and that these cossacks robbed the Tatar merchants.[40] The most notable military achievement of the Don cossacks was the capture of Azov in 1637, which they offered to the Muscovite tsar.

These rough, warlike frontiersmen were good fighters and on several occasions the Muscovite government availed itself of their aid. The cossacks took an active part in conquering Kazan and Astrakhan.[41] During the war in Livonia (1558–1560), there was a detachment of cossacks under the command of Ermak within the Russian army; according to Platonov, it was the same Ermak who later led an expedition to Siberia.[42]

The Muscovite government tried to utilize and stabilize the restless elements migrating toward the steppes by inducing them to enter into special frontier service. In return for comparative freedom and exemption from taxes, the cossacks settled along the Russian southern frontier, guarded the river fords and the trails on land, and watched for possible Tatar raids. Many cossacks

[39] G. V. Vernadskii, *Nachertanie russkoi istorii*, Pt. 1, p. 136; S. M. Solov'ev, *Istoriia Rossii s drevneishikh vremen*, I (V), 1684–1687; V. O. Kliuchevskii, *Kurs russkoi istorii*, III, 131–132.

In 1538, in answer to the complaints of the Nogai Tatars, Moscow responded: "There are many cossacks in the steppe, men from Kazan, Azov, Crimea, and others. . . . The cossacks of our frontier mingle with them, and all of them are bandits giving trouble to you as well as to us." Vernadskii, *op. cit.*, p. 136.

[40] Vernadskii, *op. cit.*, pp. 136–137; Solov'ev, II (VI), 313–315.

[41] Solov'ev, II (VI), 66–75, 93.

[42] S. F. Platonov, "Ocherk nizovskoi kolonizatsii severa," Russkoe geograficheskoe obshchestvo, komitet severa, *Ocherki po istorii kolonizatsii severa*, p. 63.

formed a part of the town garrisons where their duties were not distinguishable from those of the streltsy.[43] With the opening up of Siberia the cossacks became the most active group among the Siberian serving men and carried on their shoulders the conquest and the establishment of Russian authority there.[44] In 1625 there were 333 cossacks on horse and 658 cossacks on foot in the Siberian service.[45] In 1631 there were already about 2,000 cossacks in Siberia, and their numbers were steadily increasing.[46]

The cossacks in Siberia were of two kinds: the town cossacks who received a salary and were in active service on horse or on foot, and the village cossacks, agricultural colonists, *belomestnye* (freeholders), who served not for salary but for the use of land exempt from taxes. The latter group appeared with the development of agricultural colonization. They were settled among the peasants to protect them from the natives. In 1625–1626 the authorities of the town of Verkhoturie settled 87 peasants along the river Nev'ia. In 1626 these peasants asked for protection against the Kalmucks. A small ostrog was built at the settlement and manned at first by the serving men from Verkhoturie, who were sent there in turns, one group at a time. Soon it was found more convenient to replace them with a permanent garrison, and in 1635 17 belomestnye cossacks were settled there, armed with 27 muskets and 5 small cannon.[47] About the same time, the settlement along the Nitsa River had a population of 144 peasants and 30 belomestnye cossacks.[48] There must have been a great number of belomestnye cossacks in Siberia, because the voevoda of Eniseisk alone, in 1669, settled 134 belomestnye cossacks on land to guard the ostrozheks on the rivers Belaia, Kem', and Usolka, as well as to reinforce the Makovskii and Irkutskii ostrogs.[49]

AUXILIARY TROOPS

In addition to the Russian serving men, natives also were employed for military purposes. In 1594 the voevoda of Surgut, in response to his report, received a reply from Moscow with instructions to undertake an expedition against the hostile tribe of Pegaia Orda

---

[43] Brix, p. 55.
[44] Ogloblin, III, 104.
[45] Compiled from Brix, p. 575.
[46] Compiled from the "Smetnyi spisok 139 godu," pp. 48–51.
[47] Butsinskii, *Zaselenie*, p. 40.
[48] *Ibid.*, p. 48.
[49] Ogloblin, I, 127.

(Grey Horde). The voevoda was to be aided by troops from Tobolsk composed of Russian serving men and Tatar auxiliaries. In addition to these the chief Igichei was supposed to bring his Ostiaks from Berezov. If Igichei failed to appear, the local Ostiaks were to be enrolled to strengthen the army of Surgut.[50] Among the men sent to build the strategic town of Tara there were 300 Irtysh Tatars on horse and 150 Irtysh Tatars on foot, armed with firearms, 50 Tiumen natives on horse, 50 natives from Koshuki and Tabory, and others. Mueller has noted with surprise that in this army the natives greatly outnumbered the Russians.[51]

The natives served either as special troops, or, if baptized, they were enrolled among the Russian streltsy[52] or among the cossacks, with whom they came to be on an equal footing.[53] In the Tobolsk garrison in 1631 there were 17 baptized Tatars and 9 other baptized natives, evidently of the better class, who served together with the Litvins on horse, 4 newly baptized natives who served with the cossacks, and two detachments of *iurtovskie sluzhilye liudi* (special native troops), of 260 and 265 men respectively. Thus, the natives composed about half the total garrison.[54]

During the conquest of eastern Siberia, native troops were used probably on an even greater scale because of the shortage of Russian serving men. The record of the expedition sent in 1659 against the Chukchis shows that the troop sent from the Kolym zimov'e numbered 150 native Iukagirs and only 19 Russian serving men and volunteers.[55] In 1684 the Tungus of Uda were used against other Tungus tribes.[56]

The volunteers in these enterprises were *promyshlenniks* (Russian private traders and hunters, similar to the Canadian *coureurs*

[50] *Ibid.*, III, 209–210.

[51] Instructions for the building of Tara, 1594, Mueller, *Opisanie*, pp. 207–218; Ogloblin, III, 221.

[52] "To the newly baptized . . . issued three rubles apiece and good clothing on account of their baptism . . . enroll them into our service as streltsy and pay them our salary in money and grain, the same as to the other [Russian] streltsy." Instructions to Verkhoturie, 1603, *A.I.*, II, 56.

[53] Ogloblin, III, 110–111.

[54] "Smetnyi spisok 139," p. 48; S. V. Bakhrushin, "Sibirskie sluzhilye tatary v XVII veke," *Istoricheskie zapiski*, I, 55–80, *passim*, but especially pp. 67, 76–77.

[55] Report from Kolym, 1659, I. M. Trotskii, comp., "Kolonial'naia politika moskovskogo gosudarstva v Iakutii XVII v." *Trudy istoriko-arkheograficheskogo instituta akademii nauk S.S.S.R.* (to be cited hereafter as "Kolonial'naia politika"), Vol. XIV, No. 5, p. 64.

[56] Petition of Tungus, 1684, *D.A.I.*, XI, 203–204.

de bois).[57] They often aided the regular serving men in expeditions against the natives.[58] In 1648 the voevoda of Ilimsk sent 200 pro- myshlenniks to the rescue of the Verkholensk ostrog beseiged by the Buriats.[59] In 1683 in the expedition sent from Iakutsk 30 pro- myshlenniks were added to the 33 cossacks.[60] The documents dealing with actions against the natives often refer to promyshlenniks with such comments as "killed a man," "wounded in the belly," "wounded in the face," which are indicative of the active partici- pation of promyshlenniks in military service.[61]

It is worth mentioning that the promyshlenniks, even while pursuing their own interests, often served the cause of the govern- ment. Crisscrossing Siberia in boats and sleighs, on their wander- ings, they played an enormous part in breaking ground for the eventual conquest, especially in eastern Siberia. While keeping ahead of the government expeditions in order to obtain the best furs before the government officials could visit the natives, they opened the way for the systematic military occupation which was to follow. Often, however, they joined the serving men in subju- gating the new tribes. The early exploits of the Stroganovs and the later exploits of Khabarov provide illustrations of the activities of such "promyshlennik-conquistadors."[62]

When the natives seriously menaced the Russian settlements, all able-bodied men had to be ready to take up arms. To provide the population with means of defense, the government had to supply guns and ammunition: in 1635 Moscow sent a shipment of muskets to be distributed among the townsmen and peasants in Siberia;[63] in 1653 the Kuznetsk authorities delivered nineteen muskets with sufficient lead and powder to a village inhabited by 45 peasants.[64] In 1647 large masses of Kalmucks moved along the rivers Ishim and

---

[57] For a description of promyshlenniks, see R. H. Fisher, "The Russian Fur Trade 1550–1700," Univ. Calif. Publ. Hist., Vol. 31, pp. 30 ff.
[58] "These promyshlenniks often went into expeditions against the hostile tribes together with the serving men and, together with the serving men they subjugated these hostile natives and brought them under thy great sovereign's exalted hand." Report from Iakutsk, 1682, *D.A.I.*, VII, 365.
[59] J. E. Fischer, *Sibirskaia istoriia*, 535–536.
[60] Report from Iakutsk, 1684, *D.A.I.*, X, 347.
[61] G. V. Vernadskii, "Gosudarevy sluzhilye i promyshlennye liudi v vostochnoi Sibiri XVII veka," *Zh.M.N.P.*, new series, LVI (March–April, 1915), 336.
[62] Vernadskii, "Gosudarevy sluzhilye i promyshlennye liudi ... ," p. 342; Slovtsov, I, 7, 47.
[63] Ogloblin, III, 47.
[64] *Ibid.*, I, 34.

Tobol, threatening Tobolsk. Hearing the news, the local voevodas prepared a plan of defense whereby the townsmen, peasants, and even unordained churchmen were assigned different duties in case of attack.[65]

ORIGIN OF THE SIBERIAN ARMY

Importation of the serving men from European Russia.—At first, the Siberian army was composed of troops from European Russia. Some of them were sent as permanent military colonists, others for a limited period.[66] Serving men for Siberia were obtained in two ways. One way was by transferring part of the garrisons from Russian towns, as was done in 1635 when 500 streltsy were sent to Tiumen from Kholmogory.[67] Another way was by enlisting volunteers. Such an enlistment took place in 1631 when 500 men were gathered in the towns of Pomorie[68] for enrollment in the Siberian service.[69] Sometimes a combination of both methods was resorted to. Thus, the detachment of serving men sent in 1635 from Velikii Ustiug was made up partly of the local garrison and partly of newly enlisted men.[70]

Most of the serving men sent to Siberia came from the Pomorie, the rest from other parts of Russia, such as the cossack settlements

---

[65] "The Bykasov tower is to be in charge of the boiar son Chernitsyn and the ataman Antonov. Under their command there are to be 180 cossacks on foot ... the tower cannon is to be handled by the *pushkar* (artillery man) assisted by two peasants.

"The corner tower and the space (i.e., wall) as far as the 'cossack gate' is to be in charge of the boiar son Bovykin and the murza-ataman Vykhodtsev. Under their command there are to be 30 streltsy, 50 cossacks on foot, and 81 townsmen. ... The tower cannon is to be handled by the pushkar ... with three peasants to turn the cannon and four cossacks to attend to the tower embrasures.

"The space from the 'cossack gate' to the Perm gate is to be in charge of the boiar son Kibarov and the ataman Syrkov. Under their command 81 peasants, 30 townsmen ...

"The space from the Perm gate to the Bazaar gate is to be in charge of the boiar son Arshinskii and the ataman Vykhodtsev. Under their command are to be 20 men from the archbishop's retinue, 10 sons of churchmen, 78 non-enlisted cossacks [boys]...." *Osadnyi spisok* (siege list), quoted by Slovtsov, I, pp. 65–66.

[66] "Announce the favor of the sovereign to the ataman Temir Ivanov and to the cossacks whom he has enlisted; the cossacks from Terek, from the villages [of the southern frontier], and from the Don. Tell them to bear the hardships of service and [faithfully] to serve the sovereign, who will reward them for their endurance with a large salary, and, by the new year, will relieve them, sending other men to take their place." Instructions to Surgut, 1595, *Chteniia*, Vol. CCXXIX (1909), Bk. 2, pt. 4, p. 7.

[67] Butsinskii, *Zaselenie*, pp. 99, 193; Ogloblin, III, 32–33.

[68] Pomorie was the region of maritime towns along the Arctic Sea in European Russia.

[69] Butsinskii, *Zaselenie*, p. 190.   [70] *Loc. cit.*

along the Don and Terek rivers and in the Pole (steppe frontier).[71] The methods of transferring troops to Siberia show the difficulty of the problem of military colonization and the inefficiency of the government in coping with it. The migration to Siberia involved a great deal of trouble for the colonists themselves, and was a veritable calamity for the population of the regions through which the troops had to pass. The transferred serving men received a small subsidy from the government (*desiatnik* or commander of ten men, 2.25 rubles, married streltsy, 2.00 rubles each, and single streltsy, 1.50 rubles each),[72] but that was hardly sufficient.[73]

The misfortunes of the streltsy, however, were nothing as compared with the sufferings of the population. As soon as rumors of approaching troops on the march to Siberia reached a town or a village, the inhabitants would lock their houses, hide their wives and daughters, drive their cattle to the woods, and fearfully await the coming horde, which would bring back memories of Tatar invasions. In order not to detain the passing streltsy, the carts, wagons, and other conveyances which the townsmen and peasants had to provide on such occasions would be ready for a week or two ahead. Upon arriving in a village, the serving men were met with food, drink, and money, for the inhabitants were ready to do anything to get rid of their unwelcome guests as soon as possible. But the serving men were usually in no hurry and would stay a week or longer in one place.[74] Several documents describe how passing serving men terrorized the local population.[75]

For the local authorities they had little respect, beating the

---

[71] *Ibid.*, p. 231; instructions to Surgut, 1595, *Chteniia*, Vol. CCXXIX (1909), Bk. 2, pt. 4, p. 7; instructions to Pelym, 1594, *R.I.B.*, II, 110.

[72] Butsinskii, *Zaselenie*, p. 191.

[73] "On the way from Kholmogory we and our wives and children lost everything and became poor. We had to leave behind our homes and belongings, because as soon as the order arrived we were forced to move, not even having time to sell our property, and now we cannot buy horses and neither can we perform our service." Petition of the streltsy, 1636, Butsinskii, *Zaselenie*, p. 99.

[74] *Ibid.*, pp. 191–192.

[75] "A rumor reached the sovereign that the boiar son V. Saraev together with the ataman Eustrat and cossacks [under their command] were guilty of several offenses during the journey. Passing the land of the boiar D. I. Godunov, they robbed and flogged peasants and raped women. In the village of Zabolot'e they killed a peasant, butchered cows and pigs, and stole clothing. Other boiar sons, atamans, and cossacks who were sent from Moscow flogged and robbed several people and refused to pay for transportation. . . . Prince Peter [the voevoda of Pelym] . . . must carefully investigate. . . . The offenders are to be painfully flogged." Instructions to Pelym, 1594, *R.I.B.*, II, 115–117.

The serving men while passing Ustiug in 1599 "demanded from the inhabi-

minor officials, insulting and threatening the voevodas. If they behaved in this way in towns with voevodas and garrisons, one can imagine what went on in the villages, and how such poorly disciplined and violent soldiers treated the natives in Siberia. The torturing of men, ravishing of women, stealing of cattle and grain, and the purposeless destruction of property marked the path of the serving men.[76] The Muscovite government in response to numerous complaints tried to investigate these disorders, and ordered the Siberian voevodas to punish the offenders. Sometimes men were flogged and officers demoted,[77] but more often such orders remained a dead letter, because the enforcement of discipline was difficult, misconduct was general, and the voevodas on their way to Siberia, did not behave much better themselves.[78]

Enlistment in Siberia.—The transfer of serving men, in addition to the expense to the government, resulted in devastation of land, spoliation of peasants, and decrease of population in the regions which were on the road to Siberia. Fortunately, by the 'thirties and 'forties of the seventeenth century, the population of Siberia had increased so much, both through private and state colonization, that the government could draw upon the immigrants for its serving men.[79] Most of the men enlisted in Siberia were drawn from the exiles and sons and relatives of the serving men, from *guliashchie liudi, promyshlenniki,* and baptized natives.[80]

The right to enlist new men as streltsy or as cossacks on foot was granted to the voevodas of all towns, but boiar sons, Litva, and cossacks on horse could be enlisted only in the chief town of a

---

tants wine and beer, and upon refusal started to slash the people with swords and to shoot at them with muskets. They killed three men and wounded two fatally." Investigation in Ustiug, 1599, Ogloblin, IV, 136.

"This year [1635] the golova of streltsy Danilov [there follows enumeration of other officers] and 500 streltsy passed through Sol Vychegodskaia.... Orders were received to provide them with wagons.... We prepared 950 wagons according to instructions and waited for them for two weeks.... When they arrived they started to beat and flog [enumeration of local officials] and extorted from us 200 rubles." Complaint from Sol Vychegodskaia, 1635, Butsinskii, *Zaselenie,* p. 193.

"They [the passing serving men] seized the caps from women's heads and tore their earrings through the flesh." Result of the investigation in the uezd of Solikamsk, 1636, Ogloblin, III, 326.

[76] Butsinskii, *Zaselenie,* pp. 193–194.
[77] Ogloblin, III, 326–337.
[78] Butsinskii, *Zaselenie,* pp. 194–195, 239–241; Ogloblin, III, 171.
[79] V. K. Andrievich, *Istoriia Sibiri,* I, 147.
[80] Instructions to Iakutsk, 1651, *D.A.I.,* III, 311, and others.

razriad. With its regard for the principle of caste, the central government insisted that boiar sons should be enlisted from the children of boiar sons, and similarly that Litva and cossacks on horse be chosen from unenlisted members of their own group. The rise of a Litvin or a cossack on horse to the rank of boiar son could take place only with the consent of the sovereign. Similarly, the voevodas could not enroll boiar sons into other groups of serving men such as Litva or cossacks.[81]

Concerning the enlistment of streltsy and cossacks, government regulations emphasized the demand that they be "free men."[82] The voevodas were prohibited from accepting as serving men the agricultural colonists cultivating land for the state, whether they were peasants or exiles.[83] All newly enlisted men had to meet certain qualifications with respect to their character and military fitness.[84] The recruiting officers were prohibited from conscripting any bonded or runaway peasants, debtors, or fugitives from justice.[85]

Because of the scarcity of serving men in Siberia, these regulations were not strictly observed, especially in the more remote regions, where every man able to carry arms was valuable.[86] To discourage irregular enlistment and promotion, as well as to check fitness for service, the government ordered occasional inspections of the lists of serving men. Those who held their rank irregularly or above their social status were accordingly demoted. In 1660, for instance, such an inspection took place in Tobolsk.[87] The inspectors, because of the need for agricultural colonists, looked especially for former peasants who had cultivated land for the state, and returned them to the land. In 1680, former guliashchie liudi, who otherwise were not under obligation to the state, were retained in service, but several belomestnye cossacks, enlisted from among the

---

[81] Instructions to Tobolsk, 1697, *P.S.Z.*, III, 341.

[82] Instructions to Verkhoturie, 1604, *A.I.*, II, 58; instructions to Tomsk, 1630, Ogloblin, III, 151.

[83] Ogloblin, I, 110; III, 64.

[84] "When you receive this message, [choose in place of 115 streltsy who died or were killed] free volunteers, good, strong men, who know how to shoot and are familiar with military service." Instructions to Verkhoturie, 1604, *A.I.*, II, 58.

"To fill up the vacancies, choose men fit for such service . . . , men who could stand [the hardships of] service in the expeditions; do not take them too young, too old, crippled, sick, or drunkards." Instructions to Tobolsk, 1697, *P.S.Z.*, III, 341.

[85] Instructions to Pelym, 1594, *R.I.B.*, II, 120; Ogloblin, I, 110.

[86] Ogloblin, III, 64.

[87] *Ibid.*, I, 110–111.

peasants in 1669, were reduced to peasants again.[88] During 1680–1681 inspections took place in Verkhoturie, Tomsk, Kuznetsk, Iakutsk, and probably in other towns as well.[89]

In organizing a new detachment, the general practice was first to find a *sotnik* (commander of a hundred), who was to enlist ten *desiatniks* (commanders of ten), who in turn each had to find ten privates.[90] The newly enlisted men, when entering the service, had to give a pledge indicating the place and kind of service they accepted, and containing a promise of good behavior and the acceptance of responsibility for other men of the group.[91] When enlisted men were added to an already organized unit, the men of this unit were compelled to pledge that their newly acquired comrades would serve faithfully and would not run away after receiving their salaries. This pledge signified also that the new men were acceptable to the serving men, without whose consent the enlistment would not be effective.[92] The serving men of European garrisons who were transferred to Siberia were required upon their arrival to swear that their unit was composed of the same men who had received orders to go and that among them there were no substitutes, either relatives or hired men.[93]

This procedure illustrates an interesting policy of the Siberian army, the institution of mutual responsibility. The group was made to have an interest in the conduct of the individual members, since the desertion or misbehavior of any individual would bring a penalty upon the entire group. For the government this was a means of maintaining discipline, and within the mass of the serving men it led to the development of an *esprit de corps*, of a group consciousness, and of the idea of the *mir* which manifested itself, as we shall see later, on several occasions.

---

[88] *Ibid.*, I, 109.

[89] *Ibid.*, I, 113–114.

[90] Butsinskii, *Zaselenie*, pp. 190–191.

[91] "I [name], and [enumerations of names of the other nine men] guarantee among ourselves in the whole group of ten, one for another ... to be in the tsar's service in the new town of Tabory [Pelym]. We pledge to serve in the tsar's service, not to rebel, not to get drunk, or live in a disorderly manner, not to gamble, not to steal, not to rob, not to desert.... And if any of our number should run away I, *desiatskii* [same as desiatnik—commander of ten], and my comrades will provide as security our remuneration in salary, in money and grain, and we shall take his place and suffer penalty according to the tsar's order." Mueller, *Opisanie*, p. 188; compare Butsinskii, *Zaselenie*, p. 191; pledges of streltsy, 1593–1594, *R.I.B.*, II, 99–101.

[92] Ogloblin, II, 131.

[93] Butsinskii, *Zaselenie*, p. 191; Ogloblin, I, 205.

THE BURDENS AND HARDSHIPS OF THE SIBERIAN SERVICE

The chief duties of the serving men were military: protection of the Russian settlements, conquest of new territories, suppression of uprisings, and repulsion of raids. In addition, they were called upon to perform a number of other tasks which, under the conditions existing in Siberia at that time, required armed men. The search for new territories rich in furs, the collection of the *iasak* (fur tribute) from the natives, the transportation of supplies and furs, the collection of customs at the customs barriers required military protection. At the same time, the shortage of men in the garrisons turned the serving men into Jacks-of-all-trades, carpenters, smiths, boat builders, farmers, fishermen, and miners.[94] Ogloblin discusses a document describing the duties of the one hundred men who composed the garrison of Eniseisk in 1629; every one of them was assigned some special task besides purely military duties.[95] Very often the serving men complained to the government of the excessive demands imposed upon them. In 1604 the streltsy of Verkhoturie asked to be excused from the cultivation of hops for the government brewery.[96] The streltsy of Eniseisk petitioned in 1629 to be relieved from transportation service.[97] As the number of Siberian serving men was never large,[98] there were many requests to augment their ranks in the towns in order that their numerous duties might be performed properly.[99] The greatest need for men

---

[94] "They [the serving men] have to perform all kinds of duties: they serve on foot and on horseback, keep watch over the town and the ostrog, and they are sent on all sorts of commissions. They have to build the ostrog and towers and to dig a moat around the ostrog; they accompany messengers, supervise peasants and, themselves, harvest and thrash the grain." Instructions to Pelym, 1596, Mueller, *Opisanie*, pp. 192–193.

[95] Ogloblin, III, 239.　　　[96] Instructions to Verkhoturie, 1604, *A.I.*, II, 59.

[97] Ogloblin, III, 117.

[98] The following table shows the number of the serving men in Siberia:

1622,　6,500(?) Slovtsov, I, 83, an estimate, probably exaggerated.
1625,　2,696　Gazenvinkel, *Knigi razriadnyia*, quoted by Korsakov, see *supra*, p. 67, n. 35.
1625,　2,735　Brix, p. 575, compiled.
1631,　3,705　"Smetnyi spisok 139 godu," pp. 48–51.
1636,　5,004　Gazenvinkel, *op. cit.*, quoted by Korsakov, see *supra*, p. 67, n. 35.
1662, 10,000(?) Slovtsov, I, 84, an estimate, probably exaggerated.
1681,　8,916　Including also Churchmen and some other nonmilitary men. Ogloblin, IV, 162.
1709, 17,375(?) Slovtsov, I, 181, an estimate, hardly accurate.

[99] Ogloblin, III, 121; reports from Iakutsk, 1651 and 1653, *D.A.I.*, III, 330–332; 396–403.

was, of course, in the remote regions. In 1684 the voevoda of Iakutsk was completely helpless when a flood undermined the ostrog and endangered the buildings where the hostages and furs were kept. All the available older men had been sent after furs, and the garrison duties were carried out by boys, sons of local cossacks who were too young to be sent on expeditions and for whom there were no guns in the local arsenal.[100]

The service in Siberia, dangerous and burdensome as it was, was made more severe by various privations, the lack of the elementary necessities of life—even of food. Those who served in the distant and isolated ostrogs and ostrozheks as *godovalshchiks* (men sent out to serve at a given post for one year) probably suffered most.[101] Even the larger ostrogs, like Iakutsk and Okhotsk lacked simple articles of copper and iron, such as cooking pots, nails, and other supplies.[102] When these commodities arrived, the prices were too high for the low salaries paid common cossacks and streltsy.[103]

Most serious of all was the problem of food. In 1626 the men of Eniseisk complained that their "food is such, that in Russia even animals would not accept it."[104] In 1629 a petition from Krasnoiarsk stated that the serving men during an expedition suffered from hunger and exposure, died of starvation, and "endangered their souls by eating foul food."[105] Some documents record cases of cannibalism.[106] That the Siberian serving men suffered excessive hardships was admitted by the central government itself, when it expressed its gratification for the loyalty of the garrison of Eniseisk which refused to join the rebellion of six hundred newly enlisted men sent to Dauria[107] in the Amur region.

---

[100] Reports from Iakutsk, *D.A.I.*, X, 343; XI, 156–157.

[101] See a picturesque account of dangerous explorations, shipwrecks, travel across moving ice in the Arctic Ocean, and starvation, in a report from Kolym, 1651, *D.A.I.*, III, 280–283. Similar are a report from Indigirka, 1651, *D.A.I.*, III, 277, and a report from Uiandinskoe zimov'e, 1651, *D.A.I.*, III, 276.

[102] Report from Okhotsk, 1684, *D.A.I.*, XI, 157; report from Iakutsk, 1684, *D.A.I.*, XI, 201.

[103] Ogloblin, III, 119.   [104] *Loc. cit.*

[105] Ogloblin, III, 120.

[106] Documents about expedition of Poiarkov, 1646, *D.A.I.*, III, 58–59.

[107] "The serving men of Eniseisk, like their fathers and grandfathers, served in near and remote lands for eight, ten, or more years, without treachery and desertion, fought battles with the natives, where many of them were killed and wounded, as they did not spare themselves. Sent on distant service, where they had themselves to drag sledges, they brought many hostile lands under the exalted hand . . . of the great sovereigns and forced the natives to deliver iasak. They suffered privations, poverty, cold, and hunger, and, from the natives, vio-

Although perhaps the central government appreciated their hard and hazardous service, nevertheless the serving men were often subjected to abuses by the local officials. The voevodas persistently tried to impose more duties upon them, to restrain their freedom, and to decrease their salaries, obliging them to cultivate land instead.[108] In addition, the voevodas did not pay salaries on time,[109] took from the serving men their best furs, and otherwise exploited them. In 1639 the Muscovite government ordered that one-third of the salaries of the married men who had been sent on remote expeditions be held back for their families. The voevodas immediately took advantage of this order. They proceeded to pay only two-thirds of the salary to all men sent away, whether married or not, and to appropriate the rest for themselves. These conditions lasted from 1639 until 1647 when the tsar finally ordered an investigation to discover why the serving men did not receive their full salary.[110]

The serving men also suffered in other ways at the hands of the voevodas. For infractions of discipline the punishments meted out by the voevodas and other superior officers were not only harsh but frequently unreasonable. Of course, the serving men were hardly a group which could be handled by gentle methods. It is sufficient in this connection to recall the brutal treatment of the peaceful population by the troops marching to Siberia. Besides, the ideas of the times were such that the government itself recommended "flogging without mercy" as a corrective for insubordination and other offenses. In 1629, by order of the government, the serving men who were sent to apprehend deserters and failed to do so were flogged in the market place, whereas the deserters when eventually caught were flogged and tortured, and their leaders were hanged.[111] Some of the Siberian administrators went far beyond government instructions in elaborating refinements of cruelty. The voevoda of Iakutsk, Golovin, for instance, acquired an outstandingly unwhole-

lence, insults, and robberies. In the distant service, in the absence of grain, they had to eat grass and roots, and still in such need they served faithfully, obediently . . . and would not be lured into any treachery." Tsar's message, 1685, *D.A.I.*, XII, 14–15.

[108] Ogloblin, "Tomskii bunt 1637–1638," *Istoricheskii vestnik*, LXXXV (1901), 230.

[109] In 1691 the government owed to the serving men in Siberia 143,000 rubles of back pay. Ogloblin, IV, 113.

[110] Butsinskii, *Zaselenie*, pp. 250–251.

[111] Report from Tobolsk, 1629, *R.I.B.*, VIII, 601–606.

some reputation for his ingenuity in devising different methods of torture.[112] His henchman Poiarkov, following the example of his chief, robbed, tortured, and flogged men under his command and ordered them to eat the flesh of killed natives.[113] Golovin's successor was known for his extreme cruelty in using rods of particular pliability and thickness, not only on those who needed disciplining but also on men who merely aroused his displeasure.[114] A similar record was left by the prikashchik of the ostrog of Okhotsk, Iaryshkin, who insulted, abused, and flogged men for no reason whatsoever and even destroyed the homes and barns of his serving men.[115] Unfortunately for the serving men, such mistreatment was by no means exceptional.[116]

DISCONTENT AND DISTURBANCES AMONG THE SERVING MEN

It is not surprising that the severity of the Siberian service produced discontent among the serving men which found vent in occasional outbursts of rebelliousness. Responsible for one another, permanently established within the same town or uezd, and often related to each other by family ties, the Siberian serving men tended to form a homogeneous social group.[117] In Europe, the streltsy and cossacks represented army elements of a different historical origin and, as a general rule, were clearly distinguishable from one another. In Siberia, however, where they were drawn from the same strata of society and from the same type of men, the distinction faded, a circumstance explaining why writers sometimes refer to both groups as cossacks.[118] Common grievances strengthened their solidarity and made them aware of common interests. The adventurous life, and the continuous struggle with

---

[112] "He has tortured us [the serving men] ... and our wives ... , he ordered 150 and more knout blows at a time, he burned us over the bonfire, pulled limbs out of joint, poured water with ice over the head, he pulled at the veins and the navel with hot pliers, ... twisted the head." [There follows a particularly gruesome torture.] "... broke the ribs, scattered hot ashes on the back, drove needles under the finger nails ... and besides he ordered that men be placed on a hot frying pan." Petition of mir, 1645, "Kolonial'naia politika," p. 28, and more details on p. 32.

[113] Documents on the expedition of Poiarkov, 1645, *D.A.I.*, III, 58; petition of mir, 1645, "Kolonial'naia politika," p. 46.

[114] "His associates would ask him to stop beating innocent poeple ... but he would only strike harder." Petition from Iakutsk, 1649, *D.A.I.*, III, 211.

[115] Documents on the uprising of the Tungus, 1677–1681, *D.A.I.*, VII, 282–283.

[116] Ogloblin, I, 181; instructions to Krasnoiarsk, 1680, *D.A.I.*, VIII, 275 ff.

[117] Ogloblin, I, 193.   [118] Andrievich, *op. cit.*, I, 147; Slovtsov, I, 7.

the natives made them tough, self-reliant, and ready to defend these interests. To the hardships of service and the oppression of the administration they responded not only with numerous petitions to Moscow, but also with riots and desertions.

In 1625, in Pelym, some disorders broke out which were accompanied by an attempt to knife the voevoda and his associate.[119] In the same year, the serving men of Eniseisk threatened and insulted the local voevoda ("pulled his beard") and made preparations to desert; the situation was saved by the timely arrival of a detachment from Tobolsk.[120] In 1628 the cossacks who had been sent from Tomsk to Kuznetsk refused to obey until their salary was paid; they were flogged, but persisted in their refusal.[121] In 1629 the cossacks of Krasnoiarsk killed their *ataman* (the cossack officer corresponding to the golova of the streltsy) Kol'tsov, because he failed to bring grain and they also intended to attack the garrison of Eniseisk, with which they had accounts to settle.[122] The same year a group of serving men at Kuznetsk made an attempt to run away to the "Don or Volga."[123] In 1638–1639 there were serious riots in Tomsk following the announcement of the voevodas that the grain salary due since September, 1637, would be stopped for all serving men who cultivated large portions of land, while the rest of the serving men would receive less grain salary than before.[124] Another big riot occurred in Tomsk in 1649–1650, when the serving men took advantage of a quarrel between the local voevodas in the course of which the associate voevoda, Bunakov, usurped full authority, issuing orders from the "cossack office." It is worth noting that later investigations traced the causes of the disturbance to the agitation of serving men who had just returned to Tomsk from Moscow, where they had witnessed a popular uprising.[125] At the same time, troubles occurred in Narym and Surgut, where the serving men were saying "improper things" about events in Moscow.[126] When in 1651 an expedition was sent against Devlet Kirei, the grandson of Kuchum, 150 cossacks, exasperated at the lack of

[119] Ogloblin, III, 225–226.
[120] *Ibid.*, III, 233–235; Andrievich, *op. cit.*, I, 154; Fischer, p. 341.
[121] Report from Tobolsk, 1628, *R.I.B.*, VIII, 539–540.
[122] Andrievich, *op. cit.*, I, 151, 154.
[123] Report from Tobolsk, 1629, *R.I.B.*, VIII, 601–602.
[124] Ogloblin, "Tomskii bunt . . . ," p. 230; Ogloblin, I, 193.
[125] Ogloblin, I, 192–193; B. Chicherin, *Oblastnyia uchrezhdeniia . . .* , p. 78.
[126] Ogloblin, I, 193; III, 176.

supplies, the nonpayment of salaries, and the hardships of the expedition, revolted against their commander and deserted him.[127]

Rumors and stories about the ideal climate and the wealth of the Amur region brought new determination to the restless masses of serving men. In 1653, led by Kislyi and Cherkashenin, a party of 300 men escaped the vigilance of the voevodas and departed to seek the new Promised Land. This group included, among others, 27 men from the ostrog of Verkholensk as well as several men from Ilimsk.[128] In 1654 another large body of serving men deserted under the leadership of Egorov and Baran. Luck, however, did not favor this group. The men were intercepted by government forces and the leaders severely punished.[129] Nevertheless, the wave of desertions was not stopped, and by 1655 the voevoda of Ilimsk reported that "there are altogether about 1,500 runaways on the Amur." But it must be noted that military deserters formed only a minority of these, most of the runaways being *guliashchie liudi,* exiles, peasants, and *promyshlenniks.*[130]

In 1655 the movement to the Amur assumed serious proportions. It started with the revolt of the serving men in the ostrog of Verkholensk. The ranks of the rebels were quickly swollen with serving men who flocked from other places, especially from the ostrog of Ilimsk. Ilimsk might easily have been taken by the insurgents, but they decided to leave for the Amur and "in the future not to be commanded by the tsar's voevodas." About 300 men, mostly cossacks, commanded by the ataman Sorokin, carried out their intentions.[131]

Of all the rebellious cossacks who went to the Amur, the most successful were the ones led by an exiled Pole, Chernigovskii. In 1665 they founded the Albazin ostrog on the ruins of a Daurian town which had been ruled formerly by a native chief, Albaza. Subsequently they built several other ostrogs along the river Zeia and its tributary Selinba, and organized in Albazin a sort of free cossack republic. This republic existed until 1672 when the government gained control over the Albazin region.[132]

---

[127] Andrievich, *op. cit.,* I, 157. For another example of the desertion of men sent on an expedition, see Ogloblin, III, 78.

[128] Ogloblin, "Bunt i pobeg na Amur vorovskogo polka M. Sorokina," *Russkaia starina,* LXXXV (1896), 206.

[129] *Ibid.,* p. 207.   [130] *Ibid.,* p. 212.

[131] *Ibid.,* pp. 204–222; Ogloblin, I, 195.

[132] S. V. Bakhrushin, *Ocherki po istorii kolonizatsii Sibiri v XVI i XVII v.v.,* p. 167.

The uprising of Stenka Razin in European Russia (1667–1670) seems to have sent reverberations to Siberia. In 1668 the serving men in Tobolsk rioted against the new grain regulations.[133] During 1667–1668 there was a great deal of discontent in Iakutsk caused by antagonism between the social groups within the garrison. Here, the cossacks, the nonprivileged group, clashed with the boiar sons, who represented the petty aristocracy of the town. The boiar sons had better salaries, privileges in service, and positions of command over the ordinary serving men. They were the chief instrument of the voevodas in oppressing the common serving men. For these reasons they were universally hated and envied. The trouble in Iakutsk started with a petition by the cossacks who unanimously asked that boiar sons should not be sent with them on expeditions. A long list of grievances was presented to the local voevodas. The boiar sons used military grain supplies "to make beer and wine for sale"; for the least fault "they beat our brethren, and break their legs by putting them in stocks"; they refused to send cossacks to collect furs from the natives, and instead sent the private traders with whom they could share illicit profits gained by robbing the government of furs. The boiar sons never captured any hostages themselves but, for a bribe, would allow the important hostages seized by the cossacks to escape. Owing to the mismanagement of the boiar sons, a detachment of 50 cossacks lost 46 men. The boiar sons tortured innocent, loyal natives with fire and hanged them, and when the natives rose in revenge, the cossacks had to pay with their lives for the cruelty of their superiors. Yet, whenever the cossacks performed any deed of importance, the boiar sons claimed all the credit.[134] The history of this quarrel, in which the boiar sons responded with counteraccusations against the cossacks, provides instructive material for a study of the interrelationships among different classes of serving men.

Disturbances among the Siberian serving men continued to the end of the century. In 1677 there was a conspiracy against the voevoda in Iakutsk.[135] In 1680 the serving men of Albazin murdered the voevoda Obukhov, who had been robbing them and mistreating

---

[133] Ogloblin, I, 193.

[134] Ogloblin, I, 188, 363–364; *idem*, "Iakutskii rozysk o rozni boiarskikh detei i kazakov," *Russkaia starina*, Vol. XCI (1897), No. 8, pp. 375–392, esp. pp. 375–381.

[135] Ogloblin, I, 194.

their wives and daughters.[136] In 1685 a detachment of 600 men sent to Dauria revolted on the way and robbed the voevoda of Nerchinsk, Voeikov.[137] In 1690 there was a riot of serving men against the voevoda Zinov'ev in Iakutsk, the serving men planning to run away to distant zimov'es.[138] In 1695–1696 the serving men of the Udinsk, Selenginsk, and Kabansk ostrogs rose against their officers and tried to seize Irkutsk.[139] About the same time, in 1696–1697, there was a riot against the voevoda in Irkutsk,[140] while in Krasnoiarsk, during 1696–1700, the serving men refused to recognize the authority of three successive voevodas.[141]

The disturbances among serving men were not confined to protests against their superiors. On several occasions different garrisons fought bloody battles with one another, usually over some fur region which each side claimed as its own. It is sufficient to mention the conflicts which took place in 1629–1630 between the men of Krasnoiarsk and Eniseisk,[142] in 1634 between the men of Mangazeia and Eniseisk,[143] in 1638 between the men of Tomsk and Eniseisk,[144] and in 1643 between the men of Krasnoiarsk and Tomsk[145] and between the men of Irkutsk and Selenginsk.[146]

In order to get a full understanding of the restless and riotous spirit of the Siberian serving men, it is very important to keep in mind the persistence among them of the traditions of the first conquerors of Siberia, the cossacks of Ermak, and of the ideal of the free cossack life, such as existed on the Don River, where there was a free cossack republic in which all men were equal, the officials were popularly elected, and the community was without taxes and burdensome obligations to the government and without the hated voevodas and diaks.

On many occasions the serving men displayed the "cossack spirit." In their petitions to the tsar they often indicated that unless their requests were granted they might seek a better life

[136] Instructions to Krasnoiarsk, 1680, *D.A.I.*, VIII, 275.
[137] Tsar's message, 1685, *D.A.I.*, XII, 14–15; Ogloblin, 1, 188.
[138] Ogloblin, III, 331.
[139] *Ibid.*, I, 195.
[140] *Ibid.*, III, 170.
[141] *Ibid.*, III, 189, 329–330.
[142] *Ibid.*, III, 121; Andrievich, *op. cit.*, I, 154.
[143] P. N. Butsinskii, *Mangazeia i mangazeiskii uezd, 1601–1645 g.g.*, pp. 18, 24; instructions to Iakutsk, 1638, *R.I.B.*, II, 967.
[144] Message from Eniseisk to Iakutsk, 1639, *D.A.I.*, II, 231.
[145] Fischer, p. 481.   [146] Ogloblin, I, 188.

through desertion.[147] They insisted on the right to elect their own officers. In 1632 the cossacks of Tobolsk protested against the appointment by the government of the boiar son Arshinskii as their golova. Their petition stated that many of them had long been in the service, some of them for forty or fifty years, and since the time of Ermak they had been commanded by their own atamans, not by the golovas appointed by the government. They asked permission to retain the ataman whom they had elected. The cossack petition was granted,[148] and on several other occasions the government took into consideration the wishes of the serving men regarding appointments of their officers.[149] In small ostrogs the serving men, on some occasions, demanded participation in the planning of the "sovereign's affairs."[150]

Whenever the serving men made a stand against the administration, they called *krugi* (literally circles, general assemblies), after the fashion of the Don and Zaporog cossacks. Here decisions were made, leaders were elected, and the men swore allegiance to a common cause.[151] More than once, attempts were made to establish free cossack communities in Siberia. In 1649–1650 one of the accusations against the recalcitrant associate voevoda, Bunakov, was that he and the serving men planned to "start a Don [meaning a free republic] on the upper Ob'."[152] The parties of serving men who ran away to the Amur intended to establish free settlements there which would not be "commanded by the tsar's voevodas."[153] The short-lived Albazin republic is probably the best illustration of what they were trying to accomplish.[154]

The unsettled conditions in Siberia and the continuous advance into new regions in the search for furs put a military emphasis upon the Siberian administration. The voevodas and their associates,

---

[147] "So we, your serfs, would not go away and desert your sovereign's service." Petition from Nerchinsk, 1676, *D.A.I.*, VII, 374, and others.

[148] Butsinskii, *Zaselenie*, pp. 108–109.

[149] In 1629 in Tobolsk (Ogloblin, III, 129), in 1668 in Tara (Ogloblin, II, 130), in 1688 in Kuznetsk (Ogloblin, I, 115).

[150] Report from Okhotsk, 1652, *D.A.I.*, III, 338–340.

[151] In 1626–1627 in Eniseisk (Ogloblin, III, 233), in 1637–1638 in Tomsk (Ogloblin, "Tomskii bunt ... ," p. 230), in 1696–1697 in Krasnoiarsk (Ogloblin, III, 329). The voevodas were instructed to prevent attempts to organize *krugi* (instructions to Iakutsk, 1651, *D.A.I.*, III, 312).

[152] Ogloblin, I, 194.

[153] Ogloblin, "Bunt ... Sorokina," pp. 206, 210–211.

[154] S. V. Bakhrushin, *Ocherki ... kolonizatsii Sibiri*, p. 167.

who received their orders direct from Moscow, stood at the head of the military forces in Siberia and commanded the mass of serving men, corresponding to the different types of military men in the Muscovite armed forces. These men, unlike their voevodas, were permanent military colonists who bore the burden of the conquest. The most important single group among them were the cossacks.

The serving men were in part transferred from European Russia, in part enlisted from among the Siberian colonists. With the increase of population in Siberia the government ceased to send troops from European Russia, because of the expense involved and the disorderly conduct of these troops on their way to Siberia.

The conditions of service in Siberia were very severe, and the serving men suffered from various privations as well as from abuses by local officials. As a result there was continuous discontent among the men, who frequently took advantage of the frontier conditions to rebel against the authorities.

The management of the cruel, unruly, and freedom-loving frontiersmen must have presented a difficult problem to the central government in carrying out its designs and policies in Siberia.

CHAPTER VI

ADMINISTRATION OF THE NATIVES

THE METHODS OF CONQUEST

Ostrogs.—The conquest of the khanate of Sibir during the latter part of the sixteenth century, first undertaken by the Volga pirate, Ermak, and completed by the tsar's voevodas, laid the foundation for the Russian Empire in Asia. After defeating the khan Kuchum, the Russians continued their eastward advance until the whole of Siberia became the possession of the Muscovite sovereign.

The Siberian natives, politically disunited, backward, and unfamiliar with firearms, were invariably defeated whenever they dared offer open resistance to the military organization and superior military equipment of the Russians. The latter, however, were handicapped by inferiority in numbers and by the fact that they had to scatter their forces over such a vast territory. These unfavorable circumstances the Russians overcame by building a well-planned system of forts and blockhouses, generally referred to as *ostrogs.*[1]

To control the chief means of communication and transportation, the Russians chose the sites for ostrogs along important waterways. By virtue of their location, ostrogs prevented any organized hostile action on the part of the natives in whose territory they were erected. In time of peace the ostrogs were administrative centers; in time of war they became bases for military operations.

The main feature of an ostrog was a stockade made of large timber; the tops of the stocks were sharpened, and along the stockade at certain intervals there were embrasures for marskmen. On the corners of the stockade and above the gates towers equipped with artillery were erected. The largest ostrogs were built in western Siberia. The towns there were fenced off by one or two lines of the stockade which protected the town population; within the stockade stood a wooden citadel, which contained the government buildings and storehouses. The walls of the citadel were surmounted by towers, twenty to thirty feet high, parapets and *gorodni* (places for marksmen). Sometimes a moat was dug along

---

[1] R. J. Kerner, *The Urge to the Sea: The Course of Russian History (The Role of Rivers, Portages, Ostrogs, Monasteries, and Furs to the Eighteenth Century)*, p. 84.

the walls of the citadel and stockade. Special care was taken to safeguard the landing place on the river with two or three rows of *nadolby* (palisades), so that during a seige communication with other towns would not be interrupted.[2]

Ordinary ostrogs, like those in eastern Siberia, had no citadel and were protected merely by the stockade and towers.[3] Some of them were small and were called *ostrozheks* (small ostrogs). In the outlying districts, instead of ostrogs the government kept *zimov'es* (literally, winter lodgings, winter camps) consisting of a single hut with a garrison of perhaps half a dozen men.[4] In addition to the ostrogs, the Russians, in order to impede movements of large masses of natives, built across the trails leading to the hostile tribes *zaseki* (obstacles formed by cut trees) and nadolby, similar to the palisades used for the defense of towns.[5]

The ostrogs proved indispensable for consolidating the conquest and maintaining Russian authority in Siberia. Naturally the ostrog-building program became a matter of very keen interest to the Muscovite government. Until the colonial administration reached the point where detailed guidance by the government ceased to be of practical value, the local officials received elaborate instructions for locating and constructing the new ostrogs.

One such instruction contains directions concerning the foundation of Pelym. To build this ostrog an expedition was to be sent from Lozvinsk into the territory dominated by a hostile chief Ableghirim. The expedition had to start early in the spring, as soon as the river Lozva was free from ice. After reaching Tabory (territory of Pelym), the Russians were to occupy the native town there. If for military reasons the site of this town was unsatisfactory, it had to be destroyed and a new one built. For safety an ostrog had to be erected first. Later the storehouses for military equipment and food supplies, and other buildings were to be con-

---

[2] Instructions to Pelym, 1595 and 1597, *R.I.B.*, II, 121, 138; instructions to Verkhoturie, 1624, *R.I.B.*, II, 428; Description of Mangazeia, 1625–1626, *R.I.B.*, II, 431–433; P. N. Butsinskii, *Mangazeia* . . . , p. 16; *idem, Zaselenie* . . . , pp. 86–87, 149–150; M. A. Friede, "Russkie dereviannye ukrepleniia po drevnim literaturnym istochnikam," *Izvestiia rossiiskoi akademii istorii material'noi kul'tury*, III (1924), 113–143, *passim.*

[3] Report from Verkolensk, 1641, *D.A.I.*, II, 255; documents concerning building of towns, ostrogs . . . in Siberia, 1676–1682, *D.A.I.*, VII, 346, 358, 362–363, 369.

[4] I. M. Trotskii, comp., "Kolonial'naia politika moskovskogo gosudarstva v Iakutii" (cited hereafter as "Kolonial'naia politika"), p. ix, fn.

[5] Ogloblin, *Obozrenie stolbtsov* . . . (cited hereafter as Ogloblin), I, 39.

THE GATE TOWER OF THE FORMER OSTROG OF ILIMSK

structed within the ostrog. The work was to be done by serving men and natives. The latter had to be segregated from the Russians, constantly watched, and prohibited from entering the ostrog, lest they should learn about the number and equipment of the serving men. The ostrog had to be ready before the onset of winter.[6]

The building of ostrogs was not without difficulties. In order to speed construction, builders had to use a light wood which did not last very long, and the results of the hurried construction of the early ostrogs were not satisfactory. A voevoda of Berezov reported that when he arrived there he found that the wood used for the ostrog had already rotted and that two of the town walls were dilapidated.[7] Voevoda Shakhovskoi found the walls, towers, stockade, and moat in Pelym in dire need of repair, although they were built only two years before his appointment there.[8] Narym and Ketsk were originally built in places so low that they suffered from floods and they had to be moved to better locations.[9] Tiumen was fortified in 1586, rebuilt in 1595 and again in 1622.[10]

Some ostrogs had to be moved from their original sites for military reasons. In 1636 the serving men of the ostrozhek Vagai (built on the Vagai River) reported to Tobolsk that the ostrozhek did not serve its purpose because it could not keep watch properly over the main trail from the steppe. As a result the Kalmuks, while making raids on the Russian villages and Tatar iurts in the uezd of Tobolsk, were able to pass the ostrozhek unnoticed. The ostrozhek had to be moved to another place along the same river, where the trail was narrowly confined between the impassable swamps and forest, and where there was no way to go around the ostrozhek.[11]

Application of "Divide et empera."—Once an ostrog was established, the immediate problem of providing for the safety of the Russian expeditionary force was solved, and the local voevodas could proceed with subduing the natives within the vicinity of the ostrog and imposing upon them delivery of the *iasak* (fur tribute).

---

[6] Instructions about the building of Pelym, 1592–1594, G. F. Mueller, *Opisanie*, pp. 183–185; also in *R.I.B.*, II, 103–111.

[7] Instructions to Berezov, 1601, Mueller, *Opisanie*, p. 205.

[8] Instructions to Pelym, 1597, *R.I.B.*, II, 138.

[9] Mueller, *Opisanie*, pp. 251–260; correspondence between Tobolsk and Ketsk, 1611, *R.I.B.*, II, 206–213.

[10] G. F. Mueller, "Sibirskaia istoriia," *Ezh. soch.*, 1764, p. 5; Butsinskii, *Zaselenie*, p. 86.

[11] Butsinskii, *Zaselenie*, pp. 117–118.

For such purposes military prowess alone was not sufficient; the voevodas had to be diplomats as well as warriors. I. M. Trotskii, in his preface to the recently published collection of Siberian documents, remarks with surprise that

... it is curious to note that the hostility among the natives themselves, apparently, increased with the advent of the conquerors: the iasak-paying natives helped to impose iasak on their neighbors, while the hostile natives chose as their victims those who accepted the domination.[12]

As a matter of fact, it seems to have been a deliberate policy of the Russians to isolate the tribes by building ostrogs and fomenting intertribal hostility in the Russian interest. There are abundant proofs that such a policy bore fruit.

In the territory of Berezov, the Ostiaks, under their chief Igichei, lent a willing hand against their old enemies, the Voguls of Konda.[13] The Ostiaks of Kazym were employed by the voevodas of Berezov to collect furs from the Samoeds of this uezd.[14] Abak, chief of the Telenguts, sought the protection of the Russians against Altyn-Khan, and for his part of the bargain, promised to be a faithful ally of the Russians.[15]

In eastern Siberia there was continuous hostility between the Tungus and the Iukagirs, both sides appealing to the Russians for help.[16] The Iukagirs were also having trouble with the Chukchis, and the Russian expeditionary force against the latter in 1659 consisted largely of Iukagirs,[17] who in 1678–1679 again asked Russian protection against the Chukchis.[18] The Tungus chief, Mozheul, offered his services in leading the Russians against his enemies, the Buriats, who had not as yet paid the iasak.[19] Not only did the Russians profit from the quarrels among the different tribes, but often they found ready allies in one part of the same tribe against

---

[12] "Kolonial'naia politika," p. x.

[13] Mueller, *Opisanie*, pp. 200–204; J. E. Fischer, *Sibirskaia istoriia*, p. 249.

[14] Butsinskii, *Zaselenie*, p. 11; documents of ... Berezov, 1668, *D.A.I.*, V, 375–378.

[15] Fischer, p. 211.

[16] "A Iukagir, Toguriamko, fled to the ostrozhek with three boys, saying that the Lamuts [branch of the Tungus, see V. Ogorodnikov, *Ocherki istorii Sibiri* ..., Part I, p. 266] had massacred the Iukagirs, Ganzha and his kinsmen." "Kolonial'naia politika," p. ix.

"In 1678 the Iukagirs ... captured our wives and children and took away from us our reindeer and other possessions." Petition of the Lamuts, 1678–1679, "Kolonial'naia politika," p. 213.

[17] Report from the zimov'e of Kolym, 1659, "Kolonial'naia politika," p. 64.

[18] Petition of Iukagirs, 1678–1679, *ibid.*, p. 238.

[19] Report of an iasak collector to Iakutsk, 1641, *D.A.I.*, II, 255.

another part. Thus in 1640 the Tungus shaman Niriulko, asked the serving men to make war on the Tungus chief, Zveroul, who had killed two of Niriulko's relatives.[20] During the expedition of Khodyrev from Eniseisk to the Lena River one clan of the Iakuts assisted the Russians against another clan of the same tribe.[21] The documents of Iakutsk are full of various accusations which the Iakuts made against each other in expectation of redress from the Russians.[22]

Russian Treatment of the Native Upper Class

As soon as the natives in the newly acquired territory became more or less reconciled to Russian domination, the Russian administration, in order to establish regular and uninterrupted delivery of the iasak, tried to introduce peace and order among them.[23]

The government sought especially to win the favor of the wealthy and influential natives. This policy was pursued from the very beginning of the Siberian occupation. Captured members of the native nobility were treated with consideration and sometimes released in the hope that they would bring their relatives and supporters to the Russian side.[24] Mametkul, a relative of Kuchum, was taken prisoner by Ermak's cossacks and sent to Moscow, where he was well received and later given a military rank in the Russian service. As a voevoda he participated in the Swedish war of 1590 and in the Crimean expedition of 1598.[25] Other members of Kuchum's family were treated in Moscow with the courtesy due their rank. The chiefs captured by the golova, Chulkov, were granted estates in Russia.[26]

Native chiefs who went over to the Russian side were given certain privileges. Thus the chief Lugui, who in 1595 recognized

---

[20] Case of the chief Zveroul, 1640–1641, "Kolonial'naia politika," pp. 2–3.

[21] Communication of the voevoda of Eniseisk to Iakutsk, 1639, *D.A.I.*, II, 231.

[22] "Kolonial'naia politika," p. x.

[23] "The raids of Igichei's men into the Great Konda, the massacres of the Voguls, the kidnapping of their wives and children, and any other molestation of the Voguls [by Igichei's men] must stop . . . the offenders shall receive severe punishment." Instructions to Berezov, 1600, Mueller, *Opisanie*, pp. 200–204.
"Protect the chief Mikhail . . . and his men from the Ostiaks of Pelym. . . . Punish [offenders] according to the circumstances, to stop their lawlessness." Instructions to Berezov, 1604, Mueller, *Opisanie*, pp. 200–204.

[24] Instructions to iasak collectors, 1660, *D.A.I.*, IV, 219; Fischer, p. 243; petition of Murza [chief] Baiseit, 1599, *S.G.G.D.*, II, 129.

[25] Mueller, *Opisanie*, p. 138.

[26] *Ibid.*, p. 174.

the authority of the Muscovite sovereign, was exempt from the iasak for service rendered to the Russians.[27] The chiefs Alachei and Onzha were granted volosts from which they collected iasak for themselves.[28] The volost of Obdorsk in the uezd of Berezov and the volost of Bardak in the uezd of Surgut remained for some time practically independent principalities under the native chiefs, who were given the title of princes.[29]

The descendants of even the hostile chiefs were allowed to retain their rank and to exercise their authority over their former subjects. In the uezd of Turinsk there once existed the Vogul-Tatar principality of the chief Iapancha, who distinguished himself in the struggle with Ermak. In 1628–1629 the son of Iapancha was the "best man"[30] in the volost created from this principality. The chief of the Pegaia Orda, Vonia, seemed so dangerous that the Russians were forced to build an ostrog at Narym in order to check his activities. Yet two volosts of the uezd of Narym were later ruled by his descendants and relatives.[31] The favoritism of the administration toward the native *luchshie liudi* (best men) was at times so great as to cause dissatisfaction among the serving men.[32]

The alliance of the Russian government with the upper class of natives was a great administrative convenience. Most of the volosts organized within the uezds of the Siberian towns were nothing but former native petty principalities, or other tribal units. Thus, the former component parts of the old khanate of Kuchum within the uezd of Tobolsk, the native "hundreds" within the uezd of Verkhoturie, the principality of Pelym within the uezd of Pelym, the principality of Iapancha within the uezd of Turinsk, the former tiny principalities of Lugui and Samar within the uezd of Berezov, the Ostiak principalities within the uezd of Surgut, the "uluses" of nomads within the uezds of Kuznetsk, Krasnoiarsk, Tomsk, and other towns were all converted into volosts and became Russian administrative units for the collection of iasak. The native

---

[27] Mueller, *Opisanie*, pp. 159–160; S. V. Bakhrushin, "Iasak v Sibiri v XVII veke," *Sibirskie ogni*, May–June, 1927, p. 101.

[28] Mueller, *Opisanie*, p. 199; charter to Igichei, 1594, *S.G.G.D.*, II, 127.

[29] Bakhrushin, "Iasak," p. 101; Ogloblin, IV, 126.

[30] The term used to designate prominent or wealthy men.

[31] Bakhrushin, "Iasak," p. 101.

[32] "Because they [the natives] sit near the voevoda, while he orders that we be beaten with a knout, the natives call us *khudye liudi* (inferiors, men of lowest rank, of no importance)." Petition of the mir of Iakutsk, 1645, "Kolonial'naia politika," p. 25.

chiefs and many "best men" were transformed into Russian officials who sent their former subjects to gather furs, were responsible for the delivery of the iasak, and even collected dues from passing Russian merchants. As government officials they often attended the voevoda of their uezd, and, together with their own agents, *esauls,* were rewarded for their service by gifts and by exemption from the iasak.[33]

The good will and support of the native chiefs was a weighty factor in the country, where the natives greatly outnumbered their conquerors.[34] To win them over to the Russian side, special methods were used. Whenever a new voevoda was appointed, one of the first things he had to do was to invite the native chiefs and the "best men" from the surrounding territory to the ostrog, and to meet them in an impressive fashion, appealing to the natives' psychology. A solemn "reception" was held, with the voevoda and the serving men garbed in gala "colored dress." The chiefs passed between the ranks of serving men standing in military formation, while cannon and muskets were discharged in salute. Then the voevoda delivered a speech, emphasizing the power and benevolence of the government, enumerating the injustices from which the natives suffered, and promising, in the future, new favors and the elimination of evil practices. The procedure ended with a feast, where the natives were given an opportunity to gorge themselves with food and drink.[35] Strong drinks were especially popular, and a petition has been preserved in which the natives complained that they were served beer instead of strong liquor.[36] Similar feasts were held on the occasions when the chiefs arrived in town with the iasak from their volosts and were rewarded with various gifts in the form of cloth, metal tools, and brightly colored beads.[37]

Some of the native chiefs, however, did not respond to the induce-

---

[33] Bakhrushin, "Iasak," pp. 99–102; Ogloblin, I, 93–94; II, 112; IV, 126; instructions to Kuznetsk, 1651, *A.I.,* IV, 148; charter to the Voguls of the Chusovaia River, 1660, *A.I.,* IV, 287–288; Bakhrushin, "Sibirskie sluzhilye tatary," pp. 71–72.

[34] For instance, in 1676 there were 16,687 natives under the jurisdiction of Iakutsk, while the voevoda had under his command only 670 serving men. Documents on serving men in Iakutsk, 1675–1676, *D.A.I.,* VI, 407–408.

[35] Directions for the reception are found in nearly all the instructions given at the time of appointment to the Siberian voevodas.

[36] Ogloblin, III, 158.

[37] Bakhrushin, "Iasak," pp. 118–119; instructions to a iasak collector, 1660, *D.A.I.,* IV, 216, 219; instructions to a iasak collector, 1676–1682, *D.A.I.,* VII, 137, 140–141.

ments offered by the Russians and remained stubborn in their
resistance to the invaders. Toward them the government used ruthless and unscrupulous methods, quite in keeping with the times.
There was no room for sentimentality, and treachery as a political
weapon was lauded. The history of the ostrog of Tobolsk may
illustrate this point.

After the family of the khan Kuchum left Sibir, the local Tatars
recognized the authority of the prince Sediak, a descendant of the
former khans. The Russians built the ostrog of Tobolsk in the heart
of his possessions. The founder and commandant of the ostrog,
Chulkov, decided to do away with the powerful chief. He invited
Sediak and other notables to a feast, and, while the dinner was in
progress, the Russians massacred his escort and seized Sediak and
other chiefs. Soon afterwards the people of Sibir, disheartened by
the loss of their leaders, either left for other places or recognized
the Russians as their rulers.[38]

On another occasion, the government instructions to the founders
of the town of Pelym plainly advised the voevodas to lure the local
chief Ableghirim to the ostrog by false promises, so that they could
later kill that enemy of Russia.[39]

Such harsh treatment of the hostile natives was not ordinarily

---

[38] Mueller, *Opisanie,* pp. 171–174. According to the chronicle, the Russian
commander Chubukov invited Sediak and other Tatar nobles to the feast. During the meal he urged them to prove their good will by drinking the health of
the Great Sovereign Feodor Ioannovich. The Moslem Tatars were not used to
drinking wine. However, in order not to offend the host each took a cup of
vodka. The potent liquor nearly choked them. The Russians were quick to inter-
pret the inability of the Tatars to swallow their toast as a Divine omen indicating their evil intentions toward the Tsar. The guests were instantly seized by
the guards. Arkheograficheskaia Kommissiia, *Sibirskiia letopisi,* pp. 228–231.

[39] "Build the ostrog first, then try to ensnare Ableghirim, the chief of Pelym,
with his oldest son Tagai, his nephews and grandsons, and execute all of them;
seize also five or six of his best men, choosing those who gave us the most
trouble, and execute them also. Send to Tobolsk [as a hostage] the younger son
[of Ableghirim], Tautii, with his wife and children. Announce the favor of the
sovereign to their subjects, the iasak men, and tell them to bring iasak and to
come to the town without fear. . . . Tell them that they are free from any obligations to the chief of Pelym. . . .

"If Ableghirim . . . will not come and attempts to flee, then the voevodas must
send boats with the serving men in pursuit. They [the serving men] must seek
Ableghirim, his wives and children, and fight and kill his men, as well as burn
his *gorodok* [fortified village]. . . . Send messages to the chief of Pelym, his
children and best men [warning them] not to bring upon themselves the further
anger of the sovereign, but to come without fear to the voevodas. If the chief of
Pelym and some of his children should happen to come to the voevodas, they

a part of the government policy, although the government could not restrain its local officials from erring in this direction. The government was interested in preserving the lives of the natives because the loss of a native's life meant the loss of the furs which he could deliver, and extreme cruelty toward one native was likely to drive away several others.

If the natives rejected an opportunity to come "under the exalted hand of the great sovereign" and refused to deliver the iasak, armed forces were sent against them. Before opening hostilities, however, the men in charge had to try persuasion. Through interpreters, the serving men were to promise peace and security if the natives would consent to deliver hostages, to take the oath to the tsar, and to bring furs. Only after all peaceful methods had failed, might the serving men use force to subdue the natives—punishing them "slightly" and pillaging them "moderately."[40]

Similar policies were used against disobedient natives who had already been subdued. In 1676 the Tungus chief, Baltuga, and his men killed a cossack and two Russian peasants. An expedition was sent from Iakutsk against his tribe; the heads of the expedition were advised to promise mercy and forgiveness if the natives would admit their guilt and continue to deliver iasak. If, however, they refused obedience, then, "with the Lord's aid" they should be thoroughly chastised and brought in irons to Iakutsk.[41]

Government Policies toward the Natives in General

Oaths of loyalty and hostages.—Whenever expeditions sent against the natives succeeded in their purpose, either by persuasion or by force, the natives had to take a solemn oath of loyalty to the Russian tsar and pledge faithful fulfillment of their duties. Appeal was made to the local superstitions, and the supernatural agencies operating in a given tribe were invoked to bring a terrible fate and

---

should be assured of their safety, in order to attract the rest of the family. When, however, the chief of Pelym and all his children are in the hands of the voevodas, then execute the chief himself, his older son, and five or six other men. The younger son with his wife and children should be taken to Tobolsk." Mueller, *Opisanie*, pp. 180–186; instructions to Pelym, 1592–1594, *R.I.B.*, II, 108–109.

[40] Instructions to a cossack officer on the Olekma River, 1639, *D.A.I.*, II, 162; instructions to Iakutsk, 1651, *D.A.I.*, III, 310; instructions to Iakutsk, 1658, *D.A.I.*, IV, 112; instructions to Iakutsk, 1670, *A.I.*, IV, 448; instructions to Iakutsk, 1694, *A.I.*, V, 432.

[41] Case of Baltuga, 1676–1679, *D.A.I.*, VII, 5.

destruction upon those who broke the oath.[42] After some experience with the natives, the Russians learned to investigate carefully whether or not the oath was a "straight" one, because the natives, counting on Russian ignorance of the local beliefs, might stage a "fake" oath which they did not consider efficacious.[43]

Another method of assuring the obedience of the natives, much more certain than by demanding the oath of loyalty, was the practice of taking hostages. The intimidated natives of the newly conquered territories were forced to hand over to the Russians their chiefs and other influential "best men."[44] In the subdued territories some of the chiefs who brought furs were detained at the ostrog by the Russians. The more important the hostage and the more numerous the tribe he represented, the greater was the guarantee that the natives would fulfill their obligations. Usually the Russians kept one or two hostages from every volost. At intervals ranging from one month to a year the hostages were exchanged for new ones.[45] When the natives came again with furs, hostages were shown to them to dispel any doubts as to their fate.[46]

The voevodas were instructed to keep hostages well guarded, under lock, sometimes in irons, in order to prevent their flight or rescue by their kinsmen. Apart from these precautions, the prisoners were supposed to be well treated and fed at the government's expense.[47] It is hardly necessary to add that the local officials often took very poor care of their charges. The hostages received bread

---

[42] The Ostiaks swore in front of a bear skin on which were placed a knife, axe, and other sharp instruments. The ceremony consisted of eating a piece of bread from the end of the knife. The person breaking the oath was supposed to choke himself with food, to become the prey of a bear, or to perish from the axe or knife.

The Iakuts had the custom of cutting a dog in two and the person taking the oath had to walk between the two halves, inviting upon himself, in case of treason, a fate similar to that of the dog. Bakhrushin, "Iasak," p. 111; Ogloblin, III, 98; decree, 1606, *S.G.G.D.*, II, 306.

[43] S. V. Bakhrushin, "Istoricheskie sud'by Iakutii," p. 16.

[44] V. I. Ogorodnikov, "Russkaia gosudarstvennaia vlast' i sibirskie inorodtsy v XVI–XVIII v.v.," *Sbornik . . . irkutskogo universiteta*. Otdel I, Nauki gumanitarnye, I (1921), 73.

[45] "Luckily for the sovereign, the Lord gave us a wealthy shaman of a numerous tribe as a hostage." Report of an iasak collector, 1656, *D.A.I.*, IV, 57. See also instructions to Ilimsk, 1659, *D.A.I.*, IV, 159; instructions to Iakutsk, 1670, *A.I.*, IV, 443.

[46] Instructions to Iakutsk, 1670, *A.I.*, IV, 448.

[47] Instructions to Ilimsk, 1659, *D.A.I.*, IV, 164; instructions to a iasak collector, 1660, *D.A.I.*, IV, 222; instructions to iasak collectors, 1676–1682, *D.A.I.*, VII, 138, 142, 149; instructions to Iakutsk, 1670 and 1694, *A.I.*, IV, 448, V, 432.

only when they were displayed to their kinsmen. Dog food and carrion flesh were likely to be included in their diet, and there are records to show that sometimes they were starved to death.[48]

The practice of taking hostages, although widespread, was not universal; to keep hostages involved expense, and to guard them required serving men who were needed for other duties. When sure of its authority, the administration in some places dispensed with hostages. The institution was officially abolished in 1769.[49] Moreover, sometimes the seizure of hostages did not accomplish anything, as their relatives deserted them and fled from the Russians.[50]

Paternalistic attitude of the government.—Once the government felt confident that the loyalty of the natives was reasonably assured, it prescribed that local officials use kindness and consideration in their treatment of them.[51] The general tendency was to regard the natives as special wards of the state who needed supervision and protection. It was considered necessary to keep arms from reaching the natives, who might be tempted into some mischief, and to prevent, as far as possible, their demoralization by vices imported by the Russians, because it would affect their economic welfare and their ability to deliver the iasak. Therefore, in spite of protests from the natives,[52] the merchants were forbidden to sell them axes, knives, or any arms or objects which could be converted into arms, as well as wine, tobacco, or any gambling devices.[53]

While taking such precautions, the government tried to keep the natives satisfied with Russian rule. It listened attentively to their complaints and gave prompt and often favorable replies. For instance, in response to their petition, the men of Konda were granted

---

[48] Ogloblin, I, 250; Butsinskii, *Mangazeia*, pp. 22–23; petition of mir, 1645, "Kolonial'naia politika," p. 45.

[49] Ogloblin, III, 222; "Kolonial'naia politika," p. xiii.

[50] Petition of mir, 1645, "Kolonial'naia politika," p. 25; report of a iasak collector, 1655, *D.A.I.*, IV, 12.

[51] "You [the officials] should treat well those natives who would come under the exalted hand of the sovereign tsar and who would deliver the iasak. See that they do not suffer from any offenses or insults; do not take anything away from them by force and protect them against other people." Instructions to Tara, 1631, *P.S.Z.*, III, 561; instructions to Kuznetsk, 1625, *A.I.*, III, 222; and others.

[52] "We cannot cut wood or make traps for animals without axes, we cannot make footwear without knives." Complaints of Tatars and Voguls, 1599, *R.I.B.*, II, 147.

[53] Charter to promyshlenniks, 1600, *A.I.*, II, 27–28; Ogloblin, III, 210; instructions to Tara, 1633, *P.S.Z.*, III, 574; instructions to Timen, 1699, *P.S.Z.*, III, 545; instructions to Iakutsk, 1694, *A.I.*, V, 439; and others.

a smaller assessment of iasak;[54] The natives from Tabory were allowed to cultivate less land for the government than originally required;[55] the misconduct of the Ostiak princes toward the Voguls was investigated;[56] the natives of Tiumen were freed from the transportation service imposed upon them;[57] the Tatars of Tara were relieved from several burdensome duties imposed upon them by the local administrators;[58] certain natives of the uezd of Tobolsk were relieved from the payment of the iasak because "they did not hunt sables."[59]

A number of instructions intended to protect native interests from the Russian colonists were issued. When the merchants of Verkhoturie received a grant of land, the local authorities were advised to see that the distribution of land would not affect the local Voguls unfavorably.[60] In 1678 the government prohibited the founding of new ostrogs in places which had been used by the natives for hunting.[61] In the Lena basin the Russian serving men and promyshlenniks were forbidden even to visit certain regions preserved entirely for native hunting.[62] The voevodas were told repeatedly to protect the natives from any injustice or violence at the hands of either serving men or promyshlenniks, and offenders were to be severely punished.[63] In the voevodas' court the natives received preferential treatment in their litigation with the promyshlenniks.[64]

The government had shown considerable leniency toward the natives even in the matter of fur collection, which was its chief

[54] Mueller, *Opisanie*, pp. 194–195; instructions to Pelym, 1596, *R.I.B.*, II, 123–135.

[55] Instructions to Pelym, 1596, *R.I.B.*, II, 122.

[56] Instructions to Berezov, 1600, Mueller, *Opisanie*, pp. 202–203.

[57] Instructions to Verkhoturie, 1598, *A.I.*, II, 10.

[58] Ogloblin, III, 221–222.

[59] *Ibid.*, IV, 131.

[60] Instructions to Verkhoturie, 1599, *A.I.*, II, 26.

[61] Documents dealing with the foundation of the towns, ostrogs, 1678, *D.A.I.*, VII, 347.

[62] Documents dealing with the iasak, 1678–1681, *D.A.I.*, VIII, 4.

[63] Instructions to Pelym, 1596, *R.I.B.*, II, 123; instructions to Mangazeia, 1601 and 1603, *R.I.B.*, II, 820–821, 839; instructions to Iakutsk, 1649, *D.A.I.*, III, 214; instructions to Tobolsk, 1664, *D.A.I.*, IV, 347; instructions to Iakutsk, 1694, *A.I.*, V, 439–440; instructions to Iakutsk, 1680, *D.A.I.*, Vol. VII, 295–296; Ogorodnikov, "Russkaia gosudarstvennaia vlast'. . .," p. 89.

[64] "If the Samoeds complain about merchants or anybody else, try their cases without delay . . . but if the merchants complain about the Samoeds, do not hold a court without orders from the sovereign." Instructions to Mangazeia, 1601, *R.I.B.*, II, 820–821.

concern. In 1599 the natives of Siberia were informed with all due pomp and ceremony that the tsar, Boris Godunov, on account of his ascension to the throne, had released them from the delivery of iasak for one year.[65] In general the voevodas were instructed not to require the delivery of iasak from poor, old, sick, or crippled natives.[66] If, for some good reason, the iasak men could not deliver furs on time, the voevodas were to extend the date of delivery.[67] Collection of the iasak had to be made with "kindness and not by cruelty and flogging ... corporal punishment was not to be used ... so as not to insult the natives and drive them away."[68]

Noninterference in the affairs of the natives.—Although the government was interested in bringing the natives into submission, it did not bother them by interfering in their affairs. So long as the safety of the serving men or the amount of the iasak and its regular delivery were not affected, the government did not feel any need to change the old customs or the tribal organization. In accordance with its policy of making an alliance with the "best men," the government found it advantageous to allow them to handle in their own fashion the tribesmen whom they had under their control. In particular, the administration of justice for the natives, unless it involved Russians, was left in the hands of the native chiefs. The government repeatedly reminded the local officials "not to try any cases involving natives."[69]

Many of the natives, however, preferred to seek justice from

[65] Instructions to Verkhoturie, 1599, *R.I.B.*, II, 63–65; Ogloblin, III, 221; decree of Boris Godunov, 1599, *S.G.G.D.*, II, 156–157.

[66] "We grant a favor and order you not to collect iasak from the old men, crippled men, and small children." Tsar's message, 1610, *R.I.B.*, II, 176; see also, instructions to Verkhoturie, 1598, *A.I.*, II, 11–12; documents quoted by Butsinskii, *Zaselenie*, p. 327; instructions to Tobolsk, 1664, *D.A.I.*, IV, 362–363; report about the assessment of iasak, 1627, *R.I.B.*, VIII, 490–494; report from Tobolsk, 1630, *R.I.B.*, VIII, 668–669; Ogloblin, III, 159–160, 222.

[67] "If the iasak men come to Tobolsk and present petitions to the great sovereign asking for postponement of the delivery of iasak because of famine, unsuccessful hunting, scarcity of animals caused by the floods, or sickness ... the boiar and the voevodas [of Tobolsk] should give them time in which to complete delivery.... When the final date comes, then all the arrears in delivery must be collected.... The voevodas must insist on that very firmly, so there will be no failure, but they must use kindness, they should not flog the iasak men, so the latter will not become embittered." Instructions to Tobolsk, 1664, *D.A.I.*, IV, 362–363.

[68] Documents quoted by Butsinskii, *Zaselenie*, p. 327; instructions to a iasak collector, 1660, *D.A.I.*, IV, 215.

[69] Instructions to the prikashchik of the Aiansk sloboda, 1685–1687, *A.I.*, V, 228; Butsinskii, *Zaselenie*, p. 305; Ogorodnikov, "Russkaia gosudarstvennaia vlast'... ," p. 87.

their new masters, rather than from their own chiefs. They came to the voevodas with cases involving murders, the purchase price of their wives, sorcery, robbery, and grievances of all sorts.[70] The voevodas were willing to try these cases because in doing so they saw a chance of weakening the influence of native chiefs who still remained unreliable, and because they found the role of judges extremely profitable.[71] Occasionally the voevodas authorized the serving men who were sent to collect the furs to act as their deputies.[72]

To avoid confusion, the government, between 1678 and 1685, settled the question of authority in the following manner. The "mixed cases," involving both Russians and natives, cases of murder, and suits involving amounts of more than five rubles were to be judged by the voevodas alone. Cases involving five rubles or less could be settled by minor officials, usually iasak collectors, deputized by the voevodas, but only conjointly with the local chiefs.[73]

Whenever Russian officials handled native cases, attention was given to bringing in verdicts in accordance with native customs. A curious situation resulted. Murder, according to the *Ulozhenie* (Russian code of laws of 1649) was punished by death, whereas according to the customs of the Ostiaks and Voguls the murderer had to pay damages to the relatives of the dead man. Thus, a native murderer had to compensate the relatives but remained alive, whereas a Russian for a similar crime was condemned to die. It seemed as if the life of a iasak man was more precious than that of a Russian serving man. According to the government regulation, the execution of a native could take place only with the consent of Moscow.[74] Another privilege given the natives was the

---

[70] Complaints from the natives, 1638–1688, "Kolonial'naia politika," pp. 201–218.

[71] "From the Iakuts [the voevoda Lodyzhenskii] receives every year 200 head of cattle and more [for administration of justice]. Statement of the merchant Malakhov, 1658, "Kolonial'naia politika," pp. x, 61.

[72] The complaint of mir on the voevoda Golovin, 1645, "Kolonial'naia politika," pp. x, 21.

[73] Instructions to the iasak collectors, 1678–1682, *D.A.I.*, VII, 147–154; instructions to the prikashchik of the Aiat village, 1685–1687, *A.I.*, V, 228; instructions to the iasak collector in Iakutsk, 1685, *A.I.*, V, 194; Ogorodnikov, "Russkaia gosudarstvennaia vlast'. . . ," p. 88; instructions to Iakutsk, 1688, "Kolonial'naia politika," p. 132.

[74] Butsinskii, *Zaselenie*, pp. 306–307; Ogorodnikov, "Russkaia gosudarstvennaia vlast'. . . ," p. 88; instructions to Iakutsk, 1686, "Kolonial'naia politika," p. 246.

waiving of the customary court fees in their cases, whereas the Russians were required to pay theirs.[75]

Christianization of the natives.—In accordance with its policy of preserving native tribal organization and native customs, the Muscovite government did not interfere with the religious beliefs of the natives. However, the conversion of the natives to Christianity had certain advantages. The baptized men, alienated by the change of religion from their kinsmen and former associates,[76] were enlisted into Russian service and thus strengthened the garrisons. The baptized women solved the problem of the shortage of women in Siberia because they might marry serving men, as well as baptized natives.[77] Therefore the government had reason to encourage somewhat the spread of Christianity and it did so by making gifts to those who embraced the new faith.[78] As the Russians had no race prejudice and regarded religion as the only barrier separating them from the natives, the newly baptized were treated on equal terms with the Russians.

Nevertheless, in spite of the proselyting zeal of the churchmen, the government was not at all eager to baptize large numbers of natives. The advantages gained by their conversion were more than overbalanced by the financial losses, as the baptized natives, in effect, received Russian citizenship and ceased to pay iasak. Consequently, both the clergy and the local officials were repeatedly and explicitly forbidden to use any coercion in converting the natives. Christianity, if introduced at all, should prevail by "love and not by cruelty."[79] For each baptism it became necessary to ask special permission from the administration.[80]

The local religious ideas and superstitions were treated with some consideration. When "Paltysh," an image of a deity belonging

---

[75] Instructions to Iakutsk, 1694, *A.I.*, V, 442.

[76] "Since we abandoned the old faith we can live with our brethren no longer, because they would not let us in their land." Report of the voevoda of Tomsk, quoting the baptized natives, 1609, *R.I.B.*, II, 184.

[77] Ogloblin, III, 110–111, 211; Butsinskii, *Zaselenie*, p. 310.

[78] "To the newly baptized . . . issue three rubles apiece and good cloth on account of their baptism . . . order them into our service as *streltsy* in place of those who left, and pay them our salary and grain the same as the other streltsy." Instructions to Verkhoturie, 1603, *A.I.*, II, 56.

[79] Ogorodnikov, "Russkaia gosudarstvennaia vlast'. . . ," p. 84.

[80] "The newly baptized Ulianka brought to the priests another girl to be baptized instead of the one for whom permission was granted. For that Ulianka was flogged." Case of the newly baptized girl, 1648, "Kolonial'naia politika," p. 164.

to the Konda Ostiaks, somehow found its way into the treasury of the town of Berezov, it was returned to the chief Onzha upon his request and served as a symbol of his authority in the tribe.[81] When the Muscovite government learned that the newly baptized Ostiaks and the Russian serving men desecrated the graves of the pagan Ostiaks, it demanded an investigation by the local officials and punishment of the offenders.[82] Even some of the Russians in Siberia fell under the influence of the local shamans. Both the voevodas and the ordinary serving men made use of native medicine men when they wanted to read the future or to impose a curse on their enemies.[83] Human sacrifices, however, were strictly forbidden, and when in 1618 the Ostiaks of Pelym sacrificed a child at the foot of "the sacred larch" the local voevodas prosecuted the participants.[84]

Attitude toward slavery.—The same considerations which determined the attitude of the central government toward the Christianization of the natives also affected its policy with regard to the enslaving of natives by the Russians. Here, however, the government had to give way, eventually, to the actualities of Siberian conditions. Desiring to preserve as many as possible of the iasak-paying natives, the Muscovite government tried to suppress the acquisition of natives as *kholops* (serfs or slaves) in Siberia, or their transportation to Russia. In 1599 vigorous instructions were sent to Siberia, commanding that all captured Tatars, Ostiaks, and Voguls be set free. Those who already had been exported to Russia were to be returned to their homes. Traffic in natives was explicitly forbidden and subject to "strict punishment and the death penalty." With regard to the baptized natives, however, the instructions recommended that they be left in Russian settlements, that the men be enlisted in the streltsy or cossacks, and that the women be married to Russian serving men.[85]

The broad interpretation of the exceptions made for the baptized natives opened a way for evading the prohibition of slavery. The Russians in Siberia found they could keep baptized slaves, and by

---

[81] Instructions to Berezov, 1606, Mueller, *Opisanie*, 317–318; also in *S.G.G.D.*, II, 315–316.

[82] Instructions to Berezov, 1610, *R.I.B.*, II, 213–216.

[83] Account of the protopop Avvakum, quoted in "Kolonial'naia politika," p. xii; report of the voevoda of Iakutsk, 1679, *D.A.I.*, VIII, 244; criminal cases decided by the voevoda of Iakutsk, 1684, *D.A.I.*, XI, 30.

[84] Butsinskii, *Zaselenie*, p. 308.

[85] Instructions to Surgut and Tobolsk, 1599, Ogloblin, III, 221; IV, 132.

1625 it was necessary for the government again to issue instructions forbidding baptism by force and the enslavement of captives taken during military expeditions or seized from the iasak men.[86] In 1631–1641, the government energetically confiscated the *iasyrs* (as the native captives were called) from the serving men, especially from the voevodas and their relatives.[87] The evil, however, had taken too strong a root in Siberia; slaves were easy to get because among the natives slavery was an established and widely spread institution,[88] and the serving men were very eager to obtain cheap labor and concubines. As a result, in spite of government prohibitions, the trade in iasyrs continued. The document of 1638 mentions a "Bukharin" selling iasyrs in Tobolsk, evidently with the consent of the local authorities.[89] The book of customs receipts in Tara, under the date 1654, records the sale of a native woman by two cossacks who received fifteen rubles for her and out of this sum paid a ten per cent government sales tax.[90]

In the middle of the seventeenth century the spread of serfdom in European Russia and the legal recognition of it by the Ulozhenie resulted in a change of the government views upon the enslavement of natives in Siberia.[91] A document of 1681 shows that in the ostrozhek of Anadyr the boiar son (in charge of the ostrozhek?), the local cossacks, local promyshlenniks, and even a monk openly had one or more natives, usually women, in their possession.[92] Similarly, in 1693, two local priests and a deacon owned iasyrs in Berezov.[93] By the end of the century, ownership of native slaves was completely recognized. In 1698–1699 the voevoda of Iakutsk was formally sued because he confiscated iasyrs from the local merchants.[94] By 1702 regular title deeds on native slaves came into existence, issued upon payment of three per cent of the purchase price, whereby the purchasers could choose either to possess permanently, or mortgage, or sell their iasyrs.[95] Thus, the Muscovite government, which at first vigorously opposed the enslavement of

[86] Ogloblin, III, 228.
[87] *Ibid.*, I, 24–25, 259; II, 61.
[88] "Kolonial'naia politika," p. xxi.
[89] Ogloblin, I, 169.
[90] *Ibid.*, II, 26, 103.
[91] Ogorodnikov, "Russkaia gosudarstvennaia vlast' . . . ," p. 95.
[92] List of the iasyrs in the ostrozhek of Anadyr, 1681, "Kolonial'naia politika," p. 193.
[93] Ogloblin, I, 108.   [95] Ogloblin, I, 178–179.
[94] *Ibid.*, I, 172.

natives, gradually accepted the existence of native slavery, although the local administrators were still forbidden to possess or to export natives.[96]

In the administration of its colony, Moscow showed a marked concern for the welfare of the natives as well as tolerance for their peculiarities. This policy was dictated by the practical consideration of filling the state treasury with precious furs. Unfortunately, a lack of efficient central control, together with the abuses of the local officials, prevented this farsighted policy from being put into practice effectively.

Obligations and Grievances of the Natives

The delivery of the iasak was the most important obligation the natives had toward the government.[97] In addition to this the natives were called upon to perform other duties in connection with the various problems which confronted the colonial administration. The extensive use of natives in the military service has already been discussed.[98] An attempt was also made to use them as farmers.

The shortage of food supplies was one of the greatest difficulties which the Russians had to face in Siberia. At the beginning of the conquest, the grain had to be brought at considerable expense from European Russia. Therefore, one of the first tasks of the Siberian administration was to develop the local cultivation of land, and in an attempt to do this the voevodas of several uezds (Pelym, Verkhoturie, Turinsk, Tiumen, and later Eniseisk) tried to organize state farms operated by native labor.[99] For the most part such enterprises were unsuccessful; the natives made poor farmers and repeatedly complained that they were not accustomed to agriculture.[100] Fortunately, the gradual arrival of Russian colonists made further encouragement of farming among the natives unnecessary.

The natives were also used for other purposes. Shortage of guides

[96] Ogorodnikov, "Russkaia gosudarstvennaia vlast'...," p. 95; instructions to Tiumen, 1699, *P.S.Z.*, III, 547; instructions to Iakutsk, 1694, *A.I.*, V, 433.
[97] Iasak will be discussed in detail in the following chapter.
[98] See *supra*, pp. 69–70.
[99] Mueller, *Opisanie*, p. 185; Butsinskii, *Zaselenie*, pp. 100–102; Ogorodnikov, "Russkaia gosudarstvennaia vlast'...," p. 80; Shcheglov, *Khronologicheskii perechen'*..., pp. 60, 62; P. A. Slovtsov, *Istoricheskoe obozrenie*, I, 20; Ogloblin, III, 240.
[100] Complaints of the natives, 1599, *R.I.B.*, II, 146; Butsinskii, *Zaselenie*, pp. 311–312.

and interpreters among the serving men necessitated the employment of natives in these roles,[101] and the shortage of labor led to
the use of them in the building and repairing of town fortifications
and roads.[102] For transportation, the Russians had to use natives
as rowers of boats and drivers of carts.[103] This caused a great deal
of dissatisfaction among the natives, who were forced to provide
horses, oxen, dogs, and even reindeer to carry men, supplies, and
furs.[104] They disliked the transportation service so much that in
exchange for release from it some of them offered to pay triple the
required amount of iasak.[105] Frequently, the natives, besides their
iasak obligation, had to catch fish, gather berries, bring wood for
fuel or for building purposes, furnish hunting hawks, and, in
general, "to serve the sovereign's service at the orders of the voevodas."[106] Some of the voevodas interpreted this as justification for
using natives for all kinds of personal service as well.[107]

Imposition of the iasak delivery and of other forms of service
constituted a heavy burden for the natives, who, because of their
cultural backwardness and their inability to cope with the severe
climate, already led a wretched and precarious existence. They
needed all the "clemency and kindness" which were mentioned so
often in the government instructions. The same instructions, however, demanded that the voevodas "seek profit for the sovereign
with zeal." It is hardly surprising that the local officials, eager to
win a reputation for financial efficiency (which might lead to
another lucrative appointment) and more than anxious to fill their
own pockets, were likely to forget all about "clemency" and to
concentrate on "profit"—especially to themselves.

Acting on their own iniative some of the voevodas raised the
established quota of furs required from the natives. Thus in 1624
the voevodas of Pelym and Narym demanded ten and eleven

[101] Ogloblin, III, 221; Ogorodnikov, "Russkaia gosudarstvennaia vlast' . . . ,"
p. 81.
[102] Instructions for building of Pelym, Tara, Turinsk, *R.I.B.*, II, 122; Mueller, *Opisanie*, pp. 183, 207–216, 290–291; Ogloblin, IV, 141.
[103] Instructions to Berezov, 1610, *R.I.B.*, III, 173.
[104] Instructions to Verkhoturie, 1598, *A.I.*, II, 10; petition of the natives,
1599, *R.I.B.*, II, 146; report from Tiumen, 1629, *R.I.B.*, VIII, 588; Ogorodnikov, "Russkaia gosudarstvennaia vlast' . . . ," pp. 82–84.
[105] Butsinskii, *K istorii Sibiri*, p. 14.
[106] Instructions to Berezov, 1608, *R.I.B.*, II, 173–174; documents about the
uprising of Tungus, 1677–1681, *D.A.I.*, VII, 280; Butsinskii, *K istorii Sibiri*,
p. 22; Ogloblin, IV, 131.
[107] Butsinskii, *Zaselenie*, p. 322.

sables per native instead of the regular five,[108] while an increase of the quota by one or two sables was a common practice among the Siberian administrators.[109] Some of these extra sables went to the government, but a great many of them found their way into the personal coffers of the voevodas. If there were an investigation, the voevodas would declare that the extra sables had been presented to them as gifts or that the furs delivered were of such low value that the additional furs were needed to protect the treasury from deficit.[110]

The more cautious officials, in order to be beyond suspicion of graft, pretended to buy the furs from the natives. Such commercial transactions in reality differed very little from downright robbery, inasmuch as the natives received a price far below the actual value of the furs.[111] The excessive demands for furs, under one pretext or another, brought about complaints from the natives that they had to sell their last miserable possessions, and had either to sell or to pawn their wives and children, in order to satisfy the greedy officials.[112]

To make matters worse, the Siberian officials, especially when they made the rounds to collect the iasak, were likely to take away from the natives not only their furs but even their means of existence. Thus the golovas Rzhevskii and Bartenev seized from the natives the furs remaining after delivery of the iasak, as well as their dogs and food supplies of fish and fat.[113] The voevoda Barneshlcv robbed the Iakuts of their horses and cattle.[114] The officer in charge of the ostrog of Okhotsk took the natives' reindeer from them.[115] The records show that the serving men sometimes even destroyed the property of the natives without any apparent profit to themselves, as when they burned the native settlement on the Kolyma River. The natives there lost their winter clothing, food, and fishing equipment.[116]

---

[108] Butsinskii, *Zaselenie*, p. 321.

[109] Ogorodnikov, "Russkaia gosudarstvennaia vlast' ... ," p. 90.

[110] Butsinskii, *Zaselenie*, p. 321; Documents dealing with the uprising of the Tungus, 1677–1681, *D.A.I.*, VII, 281–282, 284–289, 299, 301.

[111] Butsinskii, *Zaselenie*, p. 321.

[112] *Ibid.*, 322–324; petition of the Iakuts, 1664, "Kolonial'naia politika," p. 212.

[113] Report from Tomsk, 1609, *R.I.B.*, II, 182.

[114] Report from Iakutsk, 1679, *D.A.I.*, VIII, 244.

[115] Documents on the uprising of the Tungus, 1677–1681, *D.A.I.*, VII, 278.

[116] Petition from the natives of Kolyma, 1653, "Kolonial'naia politika," p. 56.

The natives suffered from the Russian rule in many other ways. The government imported a number of colonists from Russia and a great many other Russian colonists came on their own initiative. In order to give room to these settlers, the natives often had to abandon their hunting grounds and fishing places, although some were able to recover at least a part of their land through appeals to Moscow.[117] On several occasions, because of the lack of Russian women in Siberia, both colonists and serving men abducted native women, especially when their fathers and husbands were away hunting.[118] In general, the conduct of the Russian settlers, as well as of numerous promyshlenniks, was frequently such that, as we have seen, the government had to issue special instructions to the local officers demanding protection for the natives.

Instead of following the government instructions, the local administrators themselves often mistreated the natives. The voevoda of Narym kidnapped a son of the local chief and kept him until a ransom of one hundred rubles was paid.[119] An official of Okhotsk gathered together all the children of the local tribe of Tungus and required the natives to bring a sable in return for each child.[120] The officials of Tomsk, traveling in 1606 along the Ob' River, "tortured the natives and extorted exorbitant gifts."[121] The voevoda of Tobolsk reported that in Pelym the local voevoda had flogged many Ostiaks to death.[122] Golovin, the notorious voevoda of Iakutsk, "hanged 23 of the best men" and "flogged many Iakuts to death, used torture, and starved others to death in a dungeon."[123] The boiar son Pushkin, in charge of the ostrog of Olekminsk, in order "to satisfy his greed, flogged the natives with rods and kept them in irons."[124] The stolnik Bibikov in Okhotsk, repeating the methods of his predecessor, Krizhanovskii, hanged a number of Tungus,

---

[117] Ogorodnikov, "Russkaia gosudarstvennaia vlast' . . . ," p. 91; Butsinskii, *Zaselenie*, pp. 37–38; S. Okun', "K istorii Buriatii," *Krasnyi arkhiv*, LXXVII (1936), 188.

[118] Statement . . . of Malakhov about the voevoda of Iakutsk, Lodyzhenskii, 1658, "Kolonial'naia politika," p. 57; documents on the uprising of the Tungus, 1677–1681, *D.A.I.*, VII, 286, 301, 303; report from Iakutsk, 1679, *D.A.I.*, VIII, 244; instructions to Iakutsk, 1680, *D.A.I.*, VIII, 266; Butsinskii, *Zaselenie*, p. 321; and others.

[119] Butsinskii, *Zaselenie*, p. 321.

[120] Documents about the uprising of the Tungus, 1677–1681, *D.A.I.*, VII, 278.

[121] Report from Tomsk, 1609, *R.I.B.*, II, 182.

[122] Butsinskii, *Zaselenie*, p. 321.

[123] Petition of mir, 1645, "Kolonial'naia politika," pp. 24, 39.

[124] Instructions to Iakutsk, 1680, *D.A.I.*, VIII, 263.

flogged others with a knout or mutilated them by cutting off their ears and noses.[125] The golova Poiarkov, who was sent on an expedition to subdue a hostile chief, Kamuk, not only drove away the cattle belonging to the natives and appropriated all their possessions, but also burned the native town with its three hundred inhabitants, including the chief and his family.[126]

The natives, in response to the burden of the iasak delivery, the demands of the various services, and the incessant plundering and cruelty of the invaders, resorted to petitions to Moscow, refusals to furnish the furs, migrations, assassinations, and open, armed uprisings.

The petitions to Moscow, whenever they reached their place of destination, usually brought favorable replies from the central government, but Moscow was far away and a long time would elapse before the answer to the petitions was known. The illiterate natives had difficulty in finding scribes who would consent to compose such petitions. The voevodas naturally tried to suppress any written protests whenever they heard about them and did their best to prevent them from reaching higher authorities. In Moscow the machinery of the government functioned slowly, and the wheels of justice had to be oiled by bribes. Consequently, favorable replies to their petitions would reach the natives only long after the abuses they complained of had been perpetrated. Meanwhile the voevodas would have had time to prepare for an investigation and to "fix" the witnesses in their own favor or to intimidate the natives so that they were afraid to complain to the investigators. Correction of the evils was left in the hands of the local administrators who, more or less, shielded each other in these matters.[127] All these factors minimized the effectiveness of petitions.

Another form of protest by the natives was their refusal to pay the iasak. In 1599 the chief of the Surgut Ostiaks, Vonia, consented to see only one of the five iasak collectors who had been sent to him by the voevoda of Surgut, and he told the collector that his tribe did not intend to deliver the iasak.[128] In 1603 the Ostiaks of the Middle Ob' refused to pay iasak,[129] as did the Tatars of Kuznetsk in

[125] Documents on the uprising of the Tungus, 1677–1681, *D.A.I.*, VII, 297–299.
[126] Petition of the mir, 1645, *D.A.I.*, III, 36.
[127] Butsinskii, *Zaselenie*, pp. 321–323.
[128] Ogloblin, III, 209.
[129] *Ibid.*, III, 214.

1630.[130] In 1670–1680 several nomad Tungus, living in the basin of the river Argun', ceased to bring furs, offering instead horses and cattle of little value. They objected also to visits from iasak collectors and threatened to kill them.[131] In 1684, instead of hunting for furs, the Tungus from the river Indigirka came to the ostrog Zashiversk, where they went on a kind of "sit-down strike" and apparently planned to attack the ostrog.[132] These and many other refusals to deliver iasak did not, however, help the natives; they only resulted in armed expeditions against them, which, either by intimidation or by reprisals, brought the natives once more into obedience.[133]

Not infrequently did the natives become tired of delivering iasak and bearing the abuses of the administration, and they did not wait for punitive expeditions against them. Instead, to avoid punitive expeditions, the tribes and isolated groups moved to regions where they hoped they would be safe from the Russians. At the beginning of the conquest such flight was comparatively easy. In 1599 many Tatars and Voguls of Pelym "ran away and lived in forests, in places unknown."[134] In the 'forties of the seventeenth century the boiar son V. Shakhov found on the river Viliui about three thousand Tungus and Iakuts, who had evidently migrated there from the regions occupied by the Russians, because, when at an earlier date the cossacks from Mangazeia visited the Viliui, they did not see any Iakuts there.[135] About 1660 the Tungus from the region of the river Indigirka moved from their place of habitation and escaped payment of the iasak until 1671.[136] In 1665 a big exodus of the natives from the uezd of Krasnoiarsk[137] took place, and in the same year the Buriats of Baikal migrated to the river Selenga.[138] Around 1670 the Tungus of Barguzin fled to the Amur.[139] In 1680 the Iukagirs left the river Penzhina and departed "for other distant rivers."[140] In 1681 the iasak collector sent to the

---

[130] Report from Kuznetsk, 1630, *R.I.B.*, VIII, 597–598.
[131] Report from Nerchinsk, 1681, *D.A.I.*, VIII, 326.
[132] Instructions to Zashiversk, 1684, *A.I.*, V, 191–192.
[133] Ogorodnikov, "Russkaia gosudarstvennaia vlast'...," p. 98.
[134] Petition of the Tatars and Voguls, 1599, *R.I.B.*, II, 147.
[135] "Kolonial'naia politika," p. xv.
[136] Report from Zashiversk, 1671, *A.I.*, IV, 473–474.
[137] Documents on invasion of the Kirghiz, 1665, *D.A.I.*, V, 39.
[138] Instructions to Eniseisk, 1667, *D.A.I.*, V, 175.
[139] Report from Nerchinsk, 1675, *A.I.*, IV, 561.
[140] Documents concerning wars with the Kalmucks ... and other natives, *D.A.I.*, VIII, 176.

river Olenka reported that some of the local Iakuts had migrated to the river Anabora, some to a place called Zhigany, and others to unknown places.[141] In 1683 a detachment of serving men was sent to the river Bystraia to catch runaway Iakuts, who had formerly lived in the vicinity of Iakutsk.[142]

The flight of the natives from Russian rule, especially of tribes living along the southern frontier, was a source of worry to the central government. Once the natives crossed the border and united with the hostile Kirghiz, Kalmucks, or Mongols they were irretrievably lost as suppliers of iasak for the treasury. Accordingly, the local officials were instructed to pursue the fugitives. When, for instance, in 1616, some Tatars fled from Tiumen, a posse was organized by the voevodas and when the runaways were overtaken, a battle took place in which several Tatars were killed. Some saved themselves by flight, but nine families were brought back.[143]

On certain occasions when the natives knew that they could not escape from their oppressors and had no means of protecting themselves, they resorted to desperate action. There are mass suicides recorded in the Siberian documents. In 1627, for instance, the Ostiaks of Surgut "jumped from their boats and drowned themselves" rather than suffer under Russian rule.[144] Quite frequently the natives were inclined to meet violence with violence, but their resistance was ineffective. They lacked cohesive political and social organization, and were too disunited by mutual petty jealousy and hatred to agree on any common action against the Russians. It was in western Siberia, within the boundaries of the former khanate of Sibir, where intertribal ties were the strongest, that most of the serious attempts, involving several tribes, were made to shake off the Russian yoke.

The first large conspiracy against the Russians was formed in 1604, when the Tatars of Tomsk, Kirghiz, and Ostiaks from the middle Ob' and Ket' joined forces. The uprising was suppressed and as a result the ostrog of Ketsk was built.[145] Soon afterward the Ostiaks of the Berezov uezd revolted and for two months unsuc-

---

[141] Report of the iasak collector, 1681, "Kolonial'naia politika," pp. 120–121.
[142] Message from Nerchinsk to Eniseisk, 1683, *D.A.I.*, X, 231.
[143] Instructions to Tiumen, 1617, *R.I.B.*, II, 342–343; Butsinskii, *Zaselenie*, p. 8.
[144] Ogloblin, III, 175.
[145] Report from Ketsk, 1605, *R.I.B.*, II, 161–164; Mueller, *Opisanie*, p. 249.

cessfully besieged the ostrog of Berezov.[146] The revolt was crushed and several leaders were hanged, but the next year a baptized woman chief, Anna of Koda, was at the head of an even larger and more dangerous enterprise. This time the conspiracy included practically all the tribes of western Siberia: the Ostiaks, Samoeds, Voguls, Tungus, and Kirghiz. They planned to seize all important towns and ostrogs, to kill all the Russians and to overthrow Russian rule completely. This conspiracy was discovered by accident when a messenger from one tribe to another fell into Russian hands and the voevodas were enabled to prepare for the emergency.[147]

Another grave situation arose in 1612. The Siberian natives heard that "there was no tsar in Moscow" and they knew that "there were few Russian men in the Siberian towns." Accordingly, the Voguls, Tatars, and Ostiaks formed an alliance and intended first to capture Pelym, then to follow with the invasion of Perm, and eventually to reëstablish an independent Siberian state, "as it had been in the time of Kuchum." It is known that the native army started to move toward Pelym,[148] but about further developments the data are lacking. At any rate, the revolt was doomed to failure and was probably subdued with the usual severity. After 1612, attempts on the part of the natives to put up a joint resistance did not cease, but never again were they as dangerous as were those just described. Apparently not until the second half of the century was there any significant effort at united action. In 1662–1663 the natives of western Siberia, including the Tatars, Voguls, Bashkirs, and Ostiaks tried again to organize, but the movement was crushed at the beginning by the ruthless voevoda of Berezov, Davydov.[149]

Most of the disturbances in Siberia were local and were undertaken by individual tribes or groups within a single tribe. Murders of the iasak collectors and of the promyshlenniks as well as rob-

---

[146] Instructions to Berezov, 1608 and 1610, *R.I.B.*, II, 170–172, 199–200; Ogorodnikov, "Russkaia gosudarstvennaia vlast' . . . ," p. 101.

[147] Communications to Pelym from other towns, 1608–1609, A. M. Gnevushev, comp., *Akty vremeni pravleniia tsaria Vasiliia Shuiskago*, pp. 70–73, 374–376; reports from Ketsk, 1609, *ibid.*, pp. 75–77; Slovtsov, *Istoricheskoe obozrenie*, I, 15; Ogorodnikov, "Russkaia gosudarstvennaia vlast' . . . ," pp. 101–102.

[148] Communication from Tobolsk to Tiumen, 1612, *R.I.B.*, II, 283–288; instructions to Verkhoturie, 1613, *A.I.*, III, 1; Butsinskii, *Zaselenie*, pp. 303–304; Slovtsov, I, 15; Ogorodnikov, "Russkaia gosudarstvennaia vlast' . . . ," pp. 103–104.

[149] Bakhrushin, *Ocherki . . . kolonizatsii Sibiri*, p. 155; Ogloblin, IV, 13; documents about the uprising of 1662–1663 and about an attempt to loot Berezov, 1662–1663, *D.A.I.*, IV, 282–312.

beries of fur and grain shipments occurred almost every year.[150] Occasionally, fairly large parties of Russians were attacked. In 1601 the Russian expedition sent to build the ostrog in Mangazeia was scattered by the Samoeds and 30 cossacks were killed.[151] In 1616 the Ostiaks of Surgut killed 30 cossacks.[152] In 1628 a boiar son and 18 cossacks were killed by the revolting natives of Tara.[153] In 1634 the slaughter of 53 promyshlenniks in Mangazeia was investigated by the government.[154] In 1644–1645 "the iasak paying Tungus, Iakuts, and others killed 30 promyshlenniks on the Viliui, 11 on the Iana, 12 on the Vitim rivers . . . and there were promyshlenniks killed on other rivers."[155] In 1665 on the river Okhota the Tungus murdered a iasak colector and 50 men.[156] In 1678 a cossack officer and several cossacks perished on the river Uraka.[157] In 1680 the son of the voevoda of Iakutsk and 39 men were killed while convoying a transport of furs.[158] In 1683 the Iukagirs killed a *desiatnik* (commander of ten) and 15 cossacks on the Kovyma River.[159] This enumeration of illustrations is by no means exhaustive.

In addition to these attacks upon isolated groups of Russian serving men and promyshlenniks, from time to time local revolts broke out threatening the garrisons of the ostrogs. In 1595[160] and again in 1607[161] the Ostiaks threatened Berezov. In 1627–1628 there was a rebellion of the Tungus on Enisei.[162] In 1630 there was serious trouble among the Tatars of Kuznetsk.[163] In 1634 there were uprisings of Tatars in Tiumen and Tara.[164] In 1635 the Buriats

[150] Ogloblin, I, 196–197; III, 79, 179, 197; IV, 16; Ogorodnikov, "Russkaia gosudarstvennaia vlast' . . . ," p. 99; instructions to Mangazeia, 1627, *R.I.B.*, II, 851; report of the serving man from Indigirsk, 1651, *D.A.I.*, III, 283; documents on rebellion of the Tungus, 1666, *D.A.I.*, V, 68–73; report from Tobolsk, 1670, *D.A.I.*, VI, 85; documents about the uprising of the Tungus, 1677–1681, *D.A.I.*, VII, 277–278; report from Iakutsk, 1680, *D.A.I.*, VII, 291; and many others.

[151] Butsinskii, *Mangazeia*, p. 13; instructions to Mangazeia, 1601, *R.I.B.*, II, 815, 824.

[152] Slovtsov, I, 35; Fischer, p. 253.

[153] Fischer, p. 323.

[154] Ogloblin, I, 196.

[155] Instructions to Iakutsk, 1644–1645, *D.A.I.*, II, 279.

[156] Documents on rebellion of the Tungus, 1666, *D.A.I.*, V, 68.

[157] Documents on the uprising of the Tungus, 1677–1681, *D.A.I.*, VII, 277–278.

[158] Report from Iakutsk, 1680, *D.A.I.*, VII, 291.

[159] Ogloblin, IV, 16.

[160] Bakhrushin, *Ocherki*, p. 157.

[161] See *supra*, p. 111, n. 146.

[162] Ogloblin, III, 234.

[163] Report from Kuznetsk, 1630, *R.I.B.*, II, 587–598.

[164] Slovtsov, I, 41; Ogloblin, III, 39.

stormed the ostrog of Bratsk and massacred its entire garrison.[165] In 1641 there was an uprising of the iasak-paying natives in the uezd of Krasnoiarsk,[166] and in 1642 another uprising of the Iakuts under the leadership of Mamyk in the uezd of Iakutsk.[167] In 1648 the Buriats besieged the ostrog of Verkholensk, which was saved only by the arrival of reinforcements from Ilimsk.[168] In 1649–1650 the Tungus chief Zelemei Kovyrin attacked the serving men and captured their military supplies.[169] In 1658 the Buriats around the ostrog Balagansk revolted, slaughtered the Russian emissaries who were sent to them, and migrated to Mongolia.[170] In 1666 Kovyrin again started a large uprising of the Tungus which spread along the northern coast of the Sea of Okhotsk and in the basin of the river Indigirka. The Tungus besieged the ostrog of Okhotsk and the ostrozhek of Zashiversk.[171] During the years 1673–1678 there was a series of uprisings in the uezd of Krasnoiarsk.[172] In 1675–1676 an uprising of Iakuts took place under the leadership of Baltuga.[173] The disturbances among the Tungus lead by the old enemy of the Russians, Kovyrin, broke out again in 1677 and continued until 1684; the ostrog of Okhotsk was in special danger in 1678, when it was surrounded by a force of one thousand Tungus. The ostrozhek of Zashiversk was threatened in 1684.[174] In 1679 there were serious riots of the Samoeds, who made attempts to capture the towns of Obdorsk and Mangazeia and the zimov'e of Khatang.[175]

---

[165] Bakhrushin, *Ocherki*, p. 161; V. K. Andrievich, *Kratkii ocherk istorii Zabaikal'ia ot dreveishikh vremen do 1762*, p. 15.

[166] Ogloblin, IV, 103.

[167] "Kolonial'naia politika," p. xvi.

[168] Fischer, pp. 535–536; Andrievich, *Kratkii ocherk istorii Zabaikal'ia*, pp. 19–20.

[169] "Kolonial'naia politika," p. xviii; instructions to the iasak collector, 1660, *D.A.I.*, IV, 213–214.

[170] Fischer, p. 543.

[171] Documents on the rebellion of the Tungus, 1666, *D.A.I.*, V, 69; report from Zashiversk, 1668, *D.A.I.*, V, 337–339; report from Iakutsk, 1668, *D.A.I.*, V, 379–381.

[172] Ogloblin, III, 39; instructions to Krasnoiarsk, 1678, *D.A.I.*, VIII, 148–149.

[173] Documents about Baltuga, 1676–1679, *D.A.I.*, VII, 4–45; "Kolonial'naia politika," pp. xvi–xviii.

[174] Documents about the uprising of the Tungus, 1677–1681, *D.A.I.*, VII, 277–304, esp. pp. 277–281, 290, 300–301; instructions to Iakutsk, 1679, *D.A.I.*, VIII, 157–158; Ogorodnikov, "Russkaia gosudarstvennaia vlast'...," pp. 160–109; "Kolonial'naia politika," p. xviii; instructions to Zashiversk, 1684, *A.I.*, V, 191–192.

[175] Documents dealing with the warfare against Kalmucks, ... Samoeds, ... 1678–1682, *D.A.I.*, VIII, 161, 163, 166–168.

The uprisings of the natives continued well into the eighteenth century, especially in the northeastern part of Siberia. All these enterprises eventually failed, but occasionally the rebellious natives were partially successful and able to seize Russian prisoners. The captives then became victims of elaborate torture which reflected the bitterness of the natives toward their masters.[176]

The policy of the Muscovite government toward the Siberian natives was determined by its interest in Siberian furs. The control of the fur colony was to be firmly established and the security of the government agents was to be insured. In order to achieve this purpose the government sent military forces to Siberia and ordered the building of ostrogs in strategic places. The ostrogs were so situated as to prevent concerted action on the part of the natives; for the same reason—that is, to keep the natives disunited—the government encouraged the hostility of one tribe toward another.

In dealing with the natives, the government tried to make alliance with their upper class; even hostile chiefs were well treated and allowed to keep their hold over their subjects, thus becoming a part of the administration. On certain occasions the native chiefs were entertained by feasts and were given presents. Stubborn enemies of the Russians, however, were severely dealt with.

As a sign of their submission, the natives had to take an oath of allegiance and had to deliver hostages. Once they were subdued, the government was not interested in their Russification; on the contrary, the natives were allowed to preserve their institutions and customs. Nor did the government desire the extermination of the natives, indeed it exhibited a degree of anxiety over their welfare. Forced Christianization and enslavement of the natives were banned and many regulations were issued for the protection of natives from the Russians in Siberia. These measures were due to utilitarian considerations; in the hands of the government the natives were destined to become state serfs, whose chief duty was to hunt fur animals and to deliver the fur tribute to the government.

Unfortunately for the natives, the humane intentions of the

---

[176] "The iasak natives murder and torture us, cut open the breast and expose the heart, cut off arms, dig out the eyes, even burn us on a fire and butcher us like pigs." Documents about uprisings of Baltuga, 1676–1679, *D.A.I.*, VII, 32, 34, 37; petition of mir, 1645, "Kolonial'naia politika," pp. 21 ff.

Muscovite government were usually thwarted by the local officials and their unruly serving men. The natives suffered a great deal from the duties imposed upon them and from the extortion and cruelty of the Russian administrators.

In response to oppression, the natives tried to protest to Moscow, to refuse the delivery of the iasak, to move to other lands, and, finally, to oppose the Russians with arms. Continual murders of the iasak collectors and attacks upon shipments of furs and food seriously hampered the collection of furs, and required constant military viligance, while some of the largest uprisings even threatened the towns and centers of the administration.

CHAPTER VII

FINANCIAL ADMINISTRATION OF SIBERIA

THROUGHOUT THE SEVENTEENTH century the army and finance were the greatest problems of the Muscovite government. The solution of these problems, however, required different emphasis in Europe and in Russia. In Europe the continuous wars and internal unrest placed military affairs first, and the chief function of the financial administration was to provide means for the maintenance of a strong army. In Siberia, where the Russians went in search of economic gain, the situation was reversed. Stress was laid on the exploitation of colonial resources; the army was used largely to aid the state financial agents.

Siberia in the sixteenth and seventeenth centuries was regarded by the Russians as a fabulous El Dorado, where, instead of an abundance of gold, one could find a fortune in furs. It attracted the particular attention of the Muscovite rulers who, following the examples of earlier princes of Suzdal and Vladimir, deservedly earned the reputation of being good businessmen, and who, after crushing the wealthy republic of Novgorod, had no serious competition from private interests. When the expedition of Ermak demonstrated the feasibility of exporting furs on a large scale from Siberia, the government of the Muscovite tsar took advantage of this opportunity and set up administrative machinery to exploit the Siberian wealth of furs, without neglecting other sources of profit in that region. The purpose of this chapter is to examine this administration and to evaluate the significance of the conquest of Siberia as a financial investment of the "great sovereign."

PERSONNEL OF THE SIBERIAN FINANCIAL ADMINISTRATION

The most important officials in the Siberian financial administration were the voevodas and their associates, who, in addition to their other duties, were the chief business managers of the colonial enterprise of the Muscovite government and watched over "the profits of the sovereign." The serving men under their command were also not purely military men, but revenue officers as well, delegated particularly to the collection of furs from the natives for the state treasury.

Besides these regular agents of the state, the government employed for its financial service in Siberia an additional force which it recruited from private individuals—businessmen of the middle class. These representatives of the community, enlisted in government service, played a very prominent part in the history of the Siberian administration.

It has been explained above that in the middle of the sixteenth century, in order to stop the abuses of the namestniks and their satellites, certain communities were given, through their representatives, participation in the management of the local judicial, financial, and police affairs. The introduction of popular government was not carried out in the spirit of recognition of the right of the population to manage its own affairs. It meant merely that responsibility for the performance of administrative functions was being transferred to the community itself. Representatives of the population served not the community but the state, and were chosen from the wealthiest inhabitants because it fell upon them to make up any deficiency in local government revenues. These chosen men took an oath upon assuming office and hence were called *tselovalniks* (sworn men, literally, those who kissed the cross and the Bible). No one was anxious to fill such an office, which, although honorable, was burdensome and involved too many responsibilities. Hence, men qualified for the office would take turns in holding it. With the introduction of government by the voevodas, the judicial and police functions were taken over by them, but the tselovalniks were retained in the financial administration.[1]

In Siberia the practice of using "sworn men" started from the beginning of the conquest. A document of 1596 states that the voevoda of Pelym sent a serving man together with a sworn man to collect furs from the region of Bol'shaia Konda.[2] At first, however, when the management of all revenues and expenditures was a comparatively simple matter, it was controlled almost entirely by the voevodas. The growing complexity of the financial administration and the ever growing abuses of the voevodas and their serving men brought about a transfer of many functions to the sworn men.[3]

---

[1] B. Chicherin, *Oblastnyia uchrezhdeniia*, pp. 39–48; V. O. Kliuchevskii, *Kurs russkoi istorii*, II, 460–470.

[2] Instructions to Pelym, 1596, G. F. Mueller, *Opisanie*, p. 194.

[3] N. N. Ogloblin, *Obozrenie stolbtsov* (cited hereafter as Ogloblin), I, 225; instructions to the customs head in Turinsk, 1646, *D.A.I.*, III, 43–44; instructions to Verkhoturie, 1646, *A.I.*, IV, 32–35.

Moreover, as time went on, the Russian population of Siberia increased, and the administration had little difficulty in finding men qualified for the office of sworn men.

There were several advantages in having sworn men in the Siberian financial administration. The use of sworn deputies chosen from the population helped to solve the problem of the shortage of serving men. The sworn men, because of their business experience, handled the financial affairs more competently than did the serving men. They received no salary and did not cost the state anything because their service was regarded as a duty to the state. The sworn men provided the central government with a certain measure of control over the serving men and even the voevodas. Finally, if there was a deficiency the government lost nothing because either the sworn men or their electors had to make up the deficit.[4]

In view of this last consideration, the government demanded that the sworn men in Siberia, like those in Europe, be chosen from the wealthier businessmen, merchants, and promyshlenniks. This rule was rather difficult to enforce. Drawing no salaries and prohibited from trading, the sworn men were likely to suffer financially while in office. As a result, the so-called "best men," fearing the disadvantages connected with the office of a sworn man, often manipulated elections in such a way as to have other and comparatively poor men elected in their place.[5]

The sworn men varied in degrees of importance. There were ordinary sworn men who were sent by the voevodas to accompany the serving men in their collection of furs, or were assigned different petty duties about the towns. Of greater importance were the sworn men who had charge of particular financial functions in connection with the local town treasuries. Thus, by the end of the century there appeared a somewhat superior group of *vybornye kazennye tselovalniks* (treasury sworn men). Although under the supervision of the voevodas, they conducted all operations which dealt with receiving, keeping, and expending treasury funds, whether in the form of money, goods, food supplies, or furs. The voevoda still rendered an account of the condition of the treasury to the government, but he had to do so with the close collaboration of the treasury sworn men. Various books containing records of

---

[4] Ogloblin, III, 320–321.
[5] P. N. Butsinskii, *Mangazeia*, p. 47; Chicherin, pp. 404–419.

income and expenditures of money, grain, and other commodities were still kept in the office of the voevoda, but they were now based on data furnished by the treasury sworn men, who gradually acquired the duty of composing nearly all the financial records of the voevoda's office.[6]

Usually the activities of the sworn men were guided by the *golovas* (heads) of separate departments of the financial administration, who handled the collection of customs, the distilling of alcoholic beverages and their disposal, the management of public houses, or any similar business of the government. Within this group the most prominent were the customs heads. Whereas the rest of the sworn men in a Siberian uezd were local men,[7] the customs heads were ordinarily sent to Siberia from the Russian towns, Vologda, Ustiug, Sviazhsk, Tot'ma, Sol Vychegodsk, and even from Moscow.[8] They were elected by the citizens of their respective towns and appointed by the Siberian Prikaz, which supplied them with the *nakazy*, instructions concerning their office. After a term of one or two years they returned to their home town and other men were chosen and sent to Siberia to take their place. Only when the Siberian towns developed a substantial class of their own businessmen did the government begin to appoint Siberian merchants and traders as heads in customhouses and in the *zastavy* (customs barriers), but never in their own town. For instance, a man from Tobolsk would be appointed to Tomsk. This procedure, of course, tended to make them independent of the local voevodas and local influences, although to a lesser degree than the heads who came from the European towns and who, outside their Siberian service, often had close connections with Moscow.[9]

The customs heads rose to a position of special importance in 1646, when the government sent instructions to Siberian towns, whereby, with the exception of Tobolsk, the local voevodas and diaks were ordered to refrain from handling the collection of customs and passage dues from the merchants and promyshlenniks.

---

[6] Ogloblin, I, 225; *Rospisnoi spisok* (memorial) of the treasury sworn men in Ilimsk contains under the year 1699 an act of acceptance by a new treasury sworn man, Ustianets, of the treasury in money, grain, goods, gunpowder, and furs from the former treasury sworn man of the voevoda's office, Nikiforov. Ogloblin, I, 226.

[7] Ogloblin, I, 225.

[8] *Ibid.*, II, 4, 7, III, 48–49, 196 n., 320; instructions to Iakutsk, 1670, *A.I.*, IV, 447; the same instructions to Ilimsk, 1659, *D.A.I.*, IV, 163.

[9] Ogloblin, II, 4, IV, 42.

In explanation of its action, the government pointed out that the voevodas of several towns, including Eniseisk, Narym, and Ketsk, meddled in the customs business and used it as an opportunity to collect their own private customs, amounting to three to four per cent of the value of declared goods. In case of refusal they detained the merchants or used "force and violence." In order to put an end to further encroachments upon the state prerogative by the voevodas, the charge of customs collection henceforth was placed entirely in the hands of the customs heads and their subordinate sworn men.[10]

In 1652 the government again ordered that supervision over the passage of the merchants and promyshlenniks should be exercised jointly by the voevodas and customs heads, because, according to to the new reports from Siberia, probably written or inspired by the resentful voevodas, the customs heads were accepting bribes and allowing valuable furs to be smuggled into European Russia.[11] In spite of the regulation of 1652, the customs heads retained a very considerable authority and freedom of action. Their office, the *tamozhennaia izba* (customhouse), was still entirely separated from the *prikaznaia* or *s'ezzhaia izba* (office of the voevoda), and their staff of sworn men and *tamozhennye pod'iacheis* (customs clerks) worked free from interference on the part of the pod'iacheis of the voevoda.[12]

The relation between the customs heads and the voevodas was defined in such a way that each of them served as a check on the other. On the one hand, while collecting customs revenues from merchants and promyshlenniks, the customs heads and their staff watched for the disguised *pokrucheniks*[13] of the voevodas,[14] the voevodas being strictly forbidden to trade.[15] Discovery of such pokrucheniks resulted in severe punishment of the latter and confiscation of their goods which in reality belonged to the voevodas.[16] The customs heads also resisted any attempt of the voevodas to interfere with the functioning of the customhouse, and if necessary, they

---

[10] Instructions to Turinsk, 1646, *D.A.I.*, III, 43–45; instructions to Verkhoturie, 1646, *A.I.*, IV, 33–34; M. N. Pokrovskii, *Russkaia istoriia*, II, 249.

[11] Ogloblin, IV, 21–22.

[12] *Ibid.*, II, 3–4.

[13] *Pokrucheniks* here means the agents of the voevodas who carried on undercover business transactions of the voevodas.

[14] Instruction to a customs official in Iakutsk, 1645, *D.A.I.*, III, 41.

[15] Instructions to Iakutsk, 1651, *D.A.I.*, III, 309.

[16] Instruction to a customs official in Iakutsk, 1645, *D.A.I.*, III, 41.

remonstrated with the voevodas and not infrequently reported them to the Siberian Prikaz.[17]

On the other hand, the voevodas, every month or so, received money, furs, and other goods collected in the customhouse, inspected the customs documents and exacted the shortage.[18] In its instructions to the voevodas, the government stated that some of the heads and sworn men continued their private trade, let their relatives pass through the customhouse without payment of proper dues, and embezzled the customs collections.[19] Consequently, to oversee the honesty and efficiency of the customs officials became a duty of the voevodas. The voevodas could punish ordinary sworn men with flogging, but so far as customs heads were concerned the voevodas' hands were tied, and they could only complain to Moscow.[20] When the customhouse was outside of town, the local voevoda sent his inspectors to supervise its operation. Thus in 1692 the voevoda of Tobolsk sent inspector Feofilov to the Sobskaia customs barrier, because in the past, "owing to the dishonesty and inefficiency" of the local customs officials, "there has been a great

---

[17] Instruction to a customs head in Verkhoturie, 1692, *P.S.Z.*, III, 138.

[18] In addition to the supervision by the voevodas, the customs heads, at the end of their term, were also carefully investigated by their successors, who otherwise were responsible for the deficit incurred by their predecessors. Ogloblin, II, 11; III, 321; Butsinskii, *op. cit.*, p. 44.

[19] Instructions to Tobolsk, 1697, *P.S.Z.*, III, 357.

[20] "To collect the customs revenues and attend to the treasury the sworn men on the Lena should be chosen for one year, in turn, from the best merchants and promyshlenniks.... The voevoda and the diak must often inspect them, in order to make them attend to their duties properly and to prevent stealing from the treasury....

"The voevoda and the diak must order the sworn men to bring to the office of the voevoda every month or so the money collected as well as their books, and the money must be checked according to the books. If any money be lacking and the sworn men be made to cover a deficiency, a proper record [description follows] should be made. In case of the disclosure of serious abuses or stealing, the sworn men should be punished: for a serious offense by the knout and for less important ones with rods. Such men should be dismissed, and the merchants and promyshlenniks must be ordered to choose new and good men in place of the offenders.

"The heads are purposely being sent to the Lena from Russia and from the Pomorie. If a customs head on the Lena should disobey the sovereign's order and neglect the sovereign's taxes, or should he profit himself or oppress the merchants, then the voevoda ... and the diak ... must write about it to the great sovereign, but without the sovereign's order they should not remove the head from his office. The voevoda and the diak are under no circumstances allowed to interfere with the customs affairs, so that the sovereign's customs tax will not show a deficit." Instructions to Iakutsk, 1670, *A.I.*, IV, 447; see also instructions to Ilimsk, 1659, *D.A.I.*, IV, 163; instructions to Iakutsk, 1651, *D.A.I.*, III, 308–309; instructions to Iakutsk, 1694, *A.I.*, V, 435–436; instructions to Tobolsk, 1664, *D.A.I.*, IV, 351.

deficit in customs duties." Feofilov received instructions to watch closely the searching of passing travelers, but not to interfere in the procedure.[21]

The extent of the subordination of the customs heads to the voevodas is not clear. From time to time the customs heads submitted written accounts of their activities to the voevoda, who sent them to the Siberian Prikaz.[22] The customs heads, however, frequently corresponded directly with the Siberian Prikaz, and sent their reports there over the heads of the voevodas.[23] Whenever the voevodas needed some expert advice, especially when they had to buy, sell, or build anything, they employed the service of the customs heads.[24] On the other hand, if the customs head was in difficulty and needed armed force to enforce the customs regulations, the voevodas were supposed to send the boiar sons and the streltsy to assist the customs officials.[25] On rare occasions the customs head was given extraordinary administrative functions taken away from the local voevoda. In 1665, for instance, the customs head in Eniseisk, Zviagin, was placed in charge of thirty of the wealthiest local business men, who were accordingly removed from the jurisdiction of the local voevoda, Golokhvastov, on account of the "prosecutions, abuses, and ill treatment," which they had suffered from the latter.[26]

Of all the customs officials, the customs heads in Verkhoturie probably exercised the greatest authority, because through this border town went all government traffic and most of the legitimate private traffic to and from Siberia. In 1695 the government attempted to direct all the traffic through Verkhoturie, closing other routes to Siberia.[27] Not only did the local customhouse handle an

---

[21] Instruction to Feofilov, 1692, *A.I.*, V, 363–366.

[22] Ogloblin, II, 26.

[23] *Ibid.*, III, 14–18; IV, 42–43.

[24] *Ibid.*, II, 4.

[25] "If merchants, traders or any others who are passing through the customs barrier with goods should object to the customs heads and sworn men, and should refuse to have their goods registered and appraised, then the customs heads and sworn men are to report to Vavila [the name of the officer]. The latter must send the serving men to the aid of the customs heads and sworn men so as to enable them to register and appraise the goods, sables, and other furs and to collect a ten per cent tax and other duties." Instruction to Vavila Vyndomskii (sent to the Sobskaia barrier by the voevoda of Tobolsk to inspect the activities of the customs officials), 1676, *A.I.*, 6–7; instructions to a customs head in Verkhoturie, 1692, *P.S.Z.*, III, 137.

[26] Instructions to the customs head in Eniseisk, 1665, *A.I.*, IV, 346–348.

[27] Boiars' decision, 1695, *P.S.Z.*, III, 206–207; S. V. Bakhrushin, *Ocherki*, pp. 104–109.

enormous volume of passing furs, but it also became a strategic point for the detection of various abuses practiced by the Siberian voevodas and their staff.

Iasak

Assessment.—Throughout the seventeenth century the most important function of the financial administration of Siberia was the acquisition of furs for the government. These were obtained by different methods. The simplest, oldest, and most primitive was that of levying a fur tribute following a raid on the native tribe. This was the method used by Oleg, Igor, and Olga in the beginning of Russian history,[28] and by the Novgorodians who raided northeastern Russia and northwestern Siberia.[29] This was the way the spoils of the earlier trans-Ural expeditions of Moscow and of the expedition of Ermak were acquired. So long as there was a frontier with weak tribes beyond, living in territories rich in furs, the raids continued, accompanied by the sacking of the natives. In this fashion in 1644 Poiarkov collected from the Giliaks 12 forties of sables and 16 fur coats,[30] in 1656 Khabarov obtained from the Giliaks and Duchers 120 forties of sables,[31] and Atlasov gathered in Kamchatka 80 forties of sables in addition to the 11 forties which he supposedly bought.[32] The method of fur collection by plunder was, however, too crude, irregular, and wasteful. Therefore the government followed these freebooting expeditions with the building of ostrogs, the subjugation of natives, the establishment of administrative machinery, and the introduction of regularly paid tribute, or the so-called *iasak.*

The word iasak is of Turkish origin and originally meant a law, a statute, or a regulation. Gradually it acquired the meaning of tribute established by the law, which was paid by the conquered to their conquerors. The Russians first encountered iasak in the thirteenth century among the natives of the Volga basin, who paid it to the Tatars, and the term was adopted by the Russians. In Siberia, iasak existed long before the advent of the Russians, having been taken over by the peoples of Siberia from the Tatars who penetrated the shores of the Irtysh and Ob'. In short, both the

---

[28] Lavrentii Chronicle, *P.S.R.L.*, I, 10, 18, 25.

[29] Lavrentii Chronicle, *P.S.R.L.*, I, 107; Novgorodian Chronicle, *P.S.R.L.*, III, 19; R. H. Fisher, "The Russian Fur Trade," pp. 5 ff.

[30] Fischer, *Sibirskaia istoriia*, p. 578.

[31] *Ibid.*, p. 623.

[32] P. A. Slovtsov, *Istoricheskoe obozrenie*, I, 136.

Russians and the Siberian natives were familiar with the idea of iasak, so that its imposition did not present any novelty to either.[33]

The principles of the assessment of iasak, its amount, and the technique of its collection varied according to the time, the place, and the habits of the natives. Nevertheless it is possible to discern three main principles of assessment. The first was to demand the furs as a sort of feudal due imposed upon a few princelings who, as a special favor, retained semi-independence and became vassals of the Muscovite sovereign. These princelings brought their furs as *pominki* or supposedly voluntary gifts to honor their sovereign. The term iasak was not used for this assessment, because it implied complete subjugation and carried with it the connotation of degradation.[34] This principle was in use during the early period of the conquest.

The second principle was that of "collective assessment"; furs were demanded from a group of natives as a whole, without regard to its individual members. This method, very useful in dealing with nomadic natives who often refused to give their names or the number in their tribes, was also used, especially in the beginning of the seventeenth century, in the assessment of the sedentary tribes.[35] The amount of iasak paid by these natives was fixed only approximately on the basis of the family or *rod* (clan), and varied with the change of voevodas and the zeal of the iasak collectors, as well as with the natives' ability and willingness to pay.[36] The practice of collective assessment of the nomadic natives was very similar to the *tiaglo* (collective tax and other obligations), which had long been in use in European Russia. There a tiaglo was assigned to a town

[33] S. V. Bakhrushin, "Iasak," *Sibirskie ogni*, No. 3, 1927, pp. 95–97; Fisher, pp. 50–51.

[34] Bakhrushin, "Iasak," pp. 96, 100–101; Mueller, *Opisanie*, pp. 59, 169–170.

[35] Instructions to Pelym, 1596, *R.I.B.*, II, 125; report from Okhotsk, 1652, *D.A.I.*, III, 335–336; report from Iakutsk, 1662, *D.A.I.*, IV, 267; Mueller, *Opisanie*, pp. 99, 338–341; Butsinskii, *op. cit.*, p. 21; V. I. Ogorodnikov, "Russkaia gosudarstvennaia vlast'...," p. 74; Ogloblin, I, 92–93.

[36] The Tatars of the Kourdatskaia volost complained about the periodic increase of iasak in their volost. At first, as a group, they paid 480 sables per year; in 1594 the voevoda of Tara, A. Eletskoi, increased the iasak to 720 sables per year; in 1595 the voevoda, F. Eletskoi, further increased it to 760 sables per year, while in 1597 the voevoda, Kuzmin, demanded 900 sables and some black foxes besides. Ogloblin, III, 221.

In 1596 the government ordered that the iasak assessment upon the Tatars of Bol'shaia Konda be lowered from 1,500 sables to 900 sables. Instructions to Pelym, 1596, *R.I.B.*, II, 123–125.

Also, instructions to Mangazeia, 1627, *R.I.B.*, II, 850; Butsinskii, *op. cit.*, pp. 19–22; Ogorodnikov, *op. cit.*, p. 75.

and the townsmen distributed their shares of it among themselves, the government being concerned only with the total amount.[37]

The third principle was that of "individual assessment," which by the end of the century replaced to a large extent the two other principles. A census of all natives in a given locality was taken;[38] it was checked from time to time, and a quota of sables assigned to every man from eighteen to fifty years old.[39] *Podrostki* (adolescents) and *zakhrebetniks* (dependents) were at first exempt, but later they also were called upon to pay, not at the regular rate, however, but whatever amount they could.[40] The regulations exempted the "old, crippled, blind, and dead," but local officials tried to collect iasak from all these groups, including even the dead.[41]

In many native volosts a combination of the last two principles of assessment was in use. Through the census, the administration ascertained the number of natives, fixed the average quota of furs per individual, and on this basis determined the total amount of the iasak to be delivered from each volost. The natives were then permitted to distribute individual shares among themselves. The charter of the Tsar Vasilii Shuiskii, for instance, demanded from the natives of Pelym a number of furs calculated on the basis of

---

[37] Chicherin, p. 193.

[38] The first attempt to take a census of the iasak-paying natives in Siberia was made by the boiar Suleshov (the chief voevoda of Tobolsk, 1623–1625). Document about the service of Suleshov in Siberia, *R.I.B.*, VIII, 350; instructions to Tara, 1631 and 1633, *P.S.Z.*, III, 556, 572; instructions to Tobolsk, 1664, *D.A.I.*, IV, 362; Butsinskii, *Zaselenie*, p. 312.

[39] Ogorodnikov, *op. cit.*, p. 74.

[40] Fisher, p. 57.

[41] "If any of the natives do not deliver iasak, send them to the Iakutsk ostrog to the voevoda. . . . [Find out] if any native, whether *kholop* [serf or slave], or lame, or blind, or incapacitated by old age, or so sick that he cannot leave the *iurt* [native settlement], or one who has no cattle of his own, is in arrears in his delivery of foxes. Make the people upon whom they are now dependent deliver sables and foxes for the current year and for the past years," Instructions to the iasak collector in Iakutsk, 1680, *D.A.I.*, VII, 148.

"Find out about the Iakut chiefs and the best men of the *ulus* (native encampment) who died [during the recent epidemics of smallpox]. . . . Find out about the property, cattle, horses [enumeration follows] of these dead Iakuts, and who has it now. Let these people [who inherited the property] pay iasak and pominki formerly delivered by the men who have died . . . so that in the future there will be no decrease of iasak. Do not tell the Iakuts . . . that you take the inventories [of the property of the deceased] for the collection cf iasak and pominki, but tell them that the voevoda and the diak have ordered such records made to prevent the property of the deceased from being stolen by the Iakuts who do not pay iasak." Instructions to the iasak collector in Iakutsk, 1652, *D.A.I.*, III, 377–378.

Ogloblin mentions the existence in the archives of Iakutsk of the "Book of the iasak assessment of the dead Iakuts," which was in use in 1678. Ogloblin, I, 107.

so many sables per man, but it left to the natives the adjustment of individual contributions according to their position in the tribe, their ability to pay, and other conditions. The Voguls of Pelym agreed among themselves that the chiefs and wealthy men should pay 7 sables each, men of medium means from 5 to 6 sables, and poor people from 1 to 4 sables. Similarly, under 1628–1629, there is this comment in the records of the iasak collection of Berezov: "The natives do not deliver the sovereign's iasak . . . at equal rates, which they are supposed to pay according to the books, . . . they distribute the total amount [required from the volost] among themselves according to their standing and prosperity." Later on, when the government, in preference to this system, adopted the principle of individual assessment and individual responsibility, the distribution of the iasak, as it was established by the natives among themselves, was used as a basis for dividing the native population into groups paying on a different scale.[42]

The quota assigned to an individual varied with circumstances. Thus, in 1601, the Ostiaks of Turinsk delivered 10 sables per married man and 5 sables per single man.[43] The same rule was applied in many other places.[44] In Surgut, in 1610, the iasak was changed from 11 to 9 sables per man.[45] In 1625 the Surgut Ostiaks still paid 9 sables per man.[46] Around 1629, according to Butsinskii, in some places the natives paid iasak as high as 10 to 12 sables; in the uezd of Mangazeia it varied from 2 to 10 sables, the most common payment being 3 sables per man, and outside of Mangazeia the usual minimum was 5 sables.[47] Fisher has found records of payments as high as 18 and 22 sables per man, but more often the rate was from 5 to 7 sables.[48] The irregularity of the iasak assessment may be further illustrated by the fact that within the same uezd, and even the same volost, there existed different quotas for different men.[49] These variations probably were determined largely by the wealth of furs in a given locality.

---

[42] Bakhrushin, "Iasak," pp. 104–105.
[43] Instructions to Turinsk, 1601, Mueller, *Opisanie*, pp. 290–291.
[44] Ogorodnikov, *op. cit.*, p. 75.
[45] Instructions to Surgut, 1600, Mueller, *Opisanie*, p. 261; instructions to Surgut, 1610, A. M. Gnevushev, comp., *Akty vremeni pravleniia tsaria Vasiliia Shuiskago*, p. 370; Ogloblin, III, 215.
[46] Ogloblin, I, 317–318.
[47] Butsinskii, *Mangazeia*, pp. 19–22.
[48] Fisher, p. 56.
[49] Ogloblin, I, 91; Butsinskii, *Mangazeia*, pp. 19–22.

The Muscovite government of the seventeenth century usually classified its revenues into *okladnye* and *neokladnye*. Okladnye revenues were fixed, definite enough to be relied upon in financial estimates, whereas the neokladnye were indefinite, more or less haphazard and fluctuating. The natural tendency of the government was to convert as much of the neokladnye revenues as possible into okladnye. It was with this purpose in mind that the government tried, as soon as circumstances permitted, to introduce assessment of the iasak on an individual basis. But the establishment of individual responsibility for a definite quota was not satisfactory so long as the natives brought merely a fixed number of skins. It was necessary to establish the iasak on a basis of quality rather than quantity,[50] because the prices of pelts fluctuated from year to year, and because the natives sold valuable furs to the merchants and brought furs of inferior quality as iasak.

About 1626 the iasak quota was determined by the value of the furs instead of the number of pelts. In 1627 in Tara the natives had to bring furs to the value of from 1 to 3 rubles per man.[51] In 1628–1629 in the uezds of Berezov and Surgut the natives brought furs at rates varying from 1½ to 4 rubles.[52] On the river Lena the Tatars offered to bring furs to the value of 3.30 rubles per married man and 1.15 rubles per single man, instead of carrying on the transportaton service.[53] The introduction of iasak in terms of its value in money met with protest from the natives, who complained that the voevodas, in their efforts to demonstrate their anxiety about the "sovereign's profits" or to satisfy their own cupidity, valued the furs at too low a price.[54] As a result, some natives attempted to pay iasak in money instead of furs, but the voevodas were told to refuse such payments and to demand furs, because the assessment was made according to Siberian prices, which were lower than prices in Moscow, and payments in money would decrease government profits.[55]

Collection.—The technique of iasak collection depended chiefly on whether the natives were near or far from an ostrog, and, if they were distant, on the degree of their familiarity with the Rus-

---

[50] Bakhrushin, "Iasak," pp. 103–104; Fisher, p. 56.
[51] List of Tara natives, 1627, *R.I.B.*, VIII, 430–436, 490–493.
[52] Bakhrushin, "Iasak," p. 104.
[53] Document of 1629, *R.I.B.*, VIII, 646.
[54] Instructions to Tobolsk, 1664, *D.A.I.*, IV, 363; and others.
[55] Ogorodnikov, *op. cit.*, p. 79; Bakhrushin, "Iasak," p. 104; Fisher, p. 69.

sian administration. Every year, after the hunting season was over, the natives who lived near the ostrog either brought the iasak individually, "everyone for himself," or sent it by men representing the tribe, usually their chiefs and "best men." The voevoda of an ostrog, or the *prikashchik* (commandant) of an *ostrozhek* (a small ostrog), and his staff received the furs, which were immediately inspected, counted, and evaluated by the sworn men, especially by the "treasury sworn men." Furs of poor quality were rejected and proper substitutes demanded, the lists of natives were compared with the amount of furs delivered, the shortages were noted, and each native's payment was recorded in the iasak books. Then the natives were treated to a hearty meal and drink, were given some presents and the receipts signed by the voevoda or prikashchik, as the case might be, and graciously dismissed, with the exception of the few who remained as hostages. During the stay of the natives in the ostrog they were given an opportunity to see the hostages who were kept there, or to exchange them for new ones.[56]

If the natives lived at some distance from the ostrog, the ostrog officials chose "as many as were needed" of serving men and organized them into groups. To each group of serving men one or two sworn men were added. At least one member of the party had to be literate. These groups were sent to collect iasak from the distant natives. They were instructed to obtain a maximum of furs, without, however, resorting to cruelty.[57] The actual procedure of iasak collection in some regions was very primitive. Around 1629, for instance, the iasak collectors sent to certain nomadic tribes from Mangazeia would enter a zimov'e (usually a simple cabin with a stove adapted for wintering)[58] and there await the natives with the furs. The natives, two or three at a time, would in their turn approach the place and throw their furs through the window. The iasak collectors, also through the window, would show the hostages, whom they had brought along for this purpose from the ostrog, and throw back some beads, tin, and bread. Both sides regarded each other with extreme suspicion, because, as it is stated in one

---

[56] Ogorodnikov, *op. cit.*, p. 73; instructions to Iakutsk, 1651, *D.A.I.*, p. 304; instructions to Iakutsk, 1658, *D.A.I.*, IV, 103–104; instructions to Ilimsk, 1659, *D.A.I.*, IV, 159; instructions to Tobolsk, 1664, *D.A.I.*, IV, 362; and others.

[57] Instructions to Iakutsk, 1651, *D.A.I.*, III, 301; instructions to the iasak collector, 1660, *D.A.I.*, IV, 201; instructions to Iakutsh, 1670, *A.I.*, IV, 450.

[58] Description of a typical zimov'e is given in I. M. Trotskii, comp., "Kolonial'-naia politika moskovskogo gosudarstva v Iakutii" (to be cited hereafter as "Kolonial'naia politika"), p. ix, n. 1.

of the voevodas' reports: "the natives are afraid of being seized as hostages, while the serving men are afraid of being murdered."[59]

In regions already pacified, the procedure of iasak collection was more orderly, resembling the collection at the ostrog. Before the iasak collectors came, the natives were supposed to have the furs in the villages or other specified places ready for delivery. Upon their arrival, the iasak collectors examined the furs offered in payment of the iasak, accepting only those which satisfied the government requirements, and gave receipts for them as was the procedure in the ostrogs.[60] The iasak collectors were instructed to take pains to include in the iasak all the best furs gathered by the natives, so that these furs would not fall into the hands of private traders.[61] When short of sables, the natives were allowed to substitute for them other valuable furs[62] and, in exceptional cases such items as walrus tusks, horses, cattle, and metals.[63] At the time of the iasak collection the hostages were either shown or exchanged, and, to promote good will, presents were distributed among the natives.[64] When delivery was completed, the furs were taken by the iasak collectors to the ostrog.[65]

Sometimes the natives were asked by the voevodas to furnish some of their men to accompany the fur caravans. That was done in order to prevent the iasak collectors from appropriating some of the iasak and afterwards claiming that the natives did not deliver

---

[59] Butsinskii, *Mangazeia*, p. 22.

[60] "Collect for iasak black foxes and good sables, worth 15–30 rubles per forty; do not accept any sables worth less than 15 rubles per forty." Instructions to Surgut, 1594, Ogloblin, IV, 123.

"Collect good whole sables with paws and tails; do not accept defective, rotten, torn, mutilated ones or the skins of young animals ... the worst sable which you may accept must be worth at least 1½ rubles." Instructions to the iasak collector in Iakutsk, 1652–1653, *D.A.I.*, III, 377.

[61] "[We have heard] that the Iakut Salbuk has a rare sable, which he has refused to barter for a bull.... Find this sable, take it as iasak and make a special note of it in the books.... If Salbuk tells you that he has sold this sable already, find it without fail." Instructions to the iasak collector in Iakutsk, 1652, *D.A.I.*, III, 378.

[62] "Instead of a good sable the Iakuts are allowed to deliver either two red foxes, or one black-bellied fox." Instructions to Iakutsk, 1652–1653, *D.A.I.*, III, 377; also Mueller, *Opisanie*, pp. 194–195.

[63] Bakhrushin, "Iasak," p. 103; instructions to Iakutsk, 1652, *D.A.I.*, III, 352; Ogorodnikov, *op. cit.*, p. 74.

[64] Fisher, pp. 59–60.

[65] It is interesting to note that the iasak collectors of Iakutsk sometimes brought the furs to Ilimsk, instead of Iakutsk, if their district was between the two ostrogs, Ilimsk being nearer to European Russia. Instructions to Iakutsk, 1651, *D.A.I.*, III, 303.

it in full.[66] With a few exceptions, the iasak collectors were not allowed to acquire furs for themselves.[67] Therefore the voevodas used to send another party of their most trustworthy boiar sons, streltsy, and cossacks to meet the collectors on their way and to search them thoroughly. If the collectors were caught in possession of illegally acquired furs, such furs were confiscated and brought to the ostrog. The iasak collectors tried to avoid the search by having some natives keep their private furs until the inspection was over. In order to prevent this, the voevodas warned the natives along the route of collectors not to accept any furs from collectors, but to report the tricks of collectors to the voevoda.[68] If the iasak collectors managed to pass their private furs through the control of the party sent to meet them, they still had to explain to the voevoda and the diak where and how they had obtained their furs—whether they had been bought, or bartered, or received as gifts, or were the result of their own hunting. In Iakutsk, the iasak collectors were allowed to keep furs of inferior quality, which they acquired by hunting or by bartering their clothing and extra supplies. In other places the regulations were more strict. Everywhere, however, anyone possessing furs had to procure witnesses to testify that his furs had been neither given to him as bribes nor extorted from natives by force.[69]

In addition to the collection of the iasak, the Siberian officials obtained furs for the state from the natives in the form of the so-

---

[66] *Ibid.*, p. 301.

[67] Instructions to the customs heads, 1693, *P.S.Z.*, III, 166. The reasons for such a policy are found in earlier documents:

"The merchants and promyshlenniks ... choose as their friends the sworn men and interpreters and in secret from the voevodas hand over to them goods worth from 100 to 600 rubles. With these goods the sworn men and interpreters buy the best furs, especially beavers and sables, before collecting the iasak, meeting the natives before the latter reach the zimov'e [designated for the collection of iasak. As a result] the natives come to the serving men in the zimov'e with poor sables." Report from Mangazeia, 1623, Butsinskii, *Mangazeia*, pp. 46–47.

"The serving men who are sent either to explore new regions or to collect iasak in old volosts should not have with them any wine or goods and should not trade or barter with the natives for furs, so as not to diminish the iasak of the sovereign. In the past the ataman Galkin, and the boiar son Khodyrev, used to take along many goods when they were sent after the iasak, and bought and exchanged furs from the natives. As a result they came back with plenty of the best sables, foxes, and beavers and kept them, paying only 10 per cent tax, because the voevodas were in collusion with them. Of the iasak they brought little only." Instructions to Iakutsk, 1651, *D.A.I.*, III, 305.

[68] *Ibid.*, pp. 305–306.

[69] Instructions to Iakutsk, 1651, *D.A.I.*, III, 305–306.

called *pominki* (gifts of honor), which are regarded by some writers as a variety of iasak.[70] Pominki were given to the sovereign or to the officials and either accompanied the delivery of the iasak or were brought on special occasions.[71] When presenting them, the natives expected reciprocal gifts.[72] At first, the officials did not demand that the pominki be of any fixed value, relying upon the good will of the natives.[73] They accepted the pominki both for the sovereign and for themselves from the natives (and occasionally from the Russians as well), took them into the state fur treasury and made an appropriate record in the books.[74]

Gradually these purely voluntary gifts became a permanent fixture among the obligations of the natives, exacted at a definite rate varying with the locality[75] and differing from iasak only in name.[76] To make matters worse for the natives, in addition to the official pominki brought in honor of the Siberian administrators and now included in the fur quota for the natives and paid into the state treasury, the voevodas also extorted other and unofficial

---

[70] The word *pominki* has its origin in the verb *pomnit'*, to remember. Pominki therefore were gifts, whereby the donors expected to be remembered by a person in whose honor they were given.

[71] "[In addition to the iasak] the natives brought pominki in your honor, O sovereign, including 354 sables, and also beavers, foxes, and fur caps worth altogether 40 sables. Besides, the chief Bosha presented 40 sables on account of his being elected chief . . . and 30 sables on account of his marriage." Report from Pelym, 1597–1598, *R.I.B.*, II, 141.

[72] "The natives should be given a small quantity of tin, copper and beads, according to the value of their pominki." Instructions to Iakutsk, 1651, *D.A.I.*, III, 301.

[73] "Whatever amount the natives of various volosts should bring, such amount should be taken into the treasury." Early document of Berezov, quoted without date by Bakhrushin, "Iasak," p. 105.

[74] "You [the voevodas] must not take any pominki for yourselves, but if anybody should honor you with furs, after delivering the iasak, you must take them and put them into our treasury." Instructions to Surgut, 1601, Bakhrushin, "Iasak," p. 106.

"If the iasak natives or the Russian merchants and promyshlenniks should bring sables, foxes, beavers, or other furs as pominki to the voevoda and diak, the latter are prohibited from taking these furs for themselves. Such furs are to be taken, appraised, registered, and sent to Moscow." Instructions to Iakutsk, 1651, *D.A.I.*, III, 307.

[75] Pominki varied as follows:

The natives of Verkhoturie, in 1620, paid 555 rubles worth of iasak and 7 rubles worth of pominki; in 1628, paid 658 rubles worth of iasak and 17 rubles worth of pominki. The natives of Turinsk, in 1628, paid 334.21 rubles worth of iasak and 7.60 rubles worth of pominki. (Butsinskii, *Zaselenie*, pp. 5–7.)

Some natives of Timen, in 1638, paid 158.40 rubles worth of iasak and 8.51 rubles worth of pominki. (Ogloblin, I, 101–102.)

The natives of Tobolsk paid 140.40 rubles worth of iasak and 16.78 rubles worth of pominki. (Bakhrushin, "Iasak," pp. 105–106.)

[76] Fisher, p. 60.

pominki for themselves, which they put into their own coffers.[77] In
this respect they followed the practice of their European colleagues
who, still remembering the abolished system of kormlenie, oppressed the population of their towns by demands that they be
honored with gifts.[78]

Frequently after the iasak and pominki had been collected, the
natives still had some furs of good quality left over. The government agents bartered for such furs. In 1651 the voevoda of Iakutsk,
Lodyzhenskii, brought eight pieces of colored cloth, 15 *puds*[79] of
tin plates, 15 puds of copper wire, 15 puds of beads, 100 buckets
of hard liquor and 20 buckets of sweet mead to be used, some as
gifts, but mostly for barter with the natives.[80] As Fisher has pointed
out, such barter bore a resemblance to the procedure whereby the
natives were rewarded with presents upon delivery of iasak. The
essential difference, however, was that no compulsion underlay
barter, which consisted in the exchange of merchandise as such at
current market prices, whereas the gifts given to the natives were
usually of negligible value.[81] Altogether, by means of iasak, pominki, and barter, an enormous volume of furs was drawn annually
into the local state treasuries.[82]

THE CUSTOMS ADMINISTRATION IN SIBERIA

Customs offices.—Had it been possible, the government would
probably have preferred to maintain the privilege of exploiting
Siberian fur resources in its own interests exclusively. It had, however, no means at its disposal to prevent the coming of enterprising
men, rich and poor, who rushed from all corners of Russia to
Siberia, excited by stories of Siberian wealth. The prosperous
merchants sent expeditions in charge of *prikashchiks* (local managers) ; the poor men banded together in groups called *vatagi*. The
prospectors not only followed the march of the government troops

[77] In 1647 the chief Lodereiko complained that the voevoda of Mangazeia
demanded for himself 4 sables from every man in addition to other extortions.
In 1661 there was a report in Tobolsk that the Tungus hostages had to pay 11
sables each into the private treasuries of the voevodas. Bakhrushin, "Iasak,"
pp. 106–107.

[78] V. O. Kliuchevskii, *Kurs russkoi istorii*, III, 190.

[79] One *pud* is approximately equal to 36 English pounds.

[80] Instructions to Iakutsk, 1651, *D.A.I.*, III, 297.

[81] Fisher, pp. 65–66; Bakhrushin, "Iasak," pp. 120–126; Ogloblin, I, 42–44,
243; III, 79, 81; Butsinskii, *Mangazeia*, p. 19; instructions to the iasak collector, 1660, *D.A.I.*, IV, 216.

[82] Fisher, p. 67.

but indeed often preceded it.[83] These private enterprisers threatened the government with serious and annoying competition. Not being able to stop them, the government, taking advantage of its political power, tried at least to reach the profits which went into private hands and to take from private traders the most valuable furs.

In order to accomplish these objectives, an elaborate system of internal and border customs service[84] was instituted. Customhouses in charge of customs heads were established in towns and ostrogs.[85] In addition to these, small subsidiary customs stations were placed along the route of the merchants and promyshlenniks, in the Russian and native villages, in ostrozheks and zimov'es. These subsidiary stations were in charge of ordinary sworn men, who themselves were subordinated to the customs heads of the nearest town.[86]

The border customs officials watched over the traffic to and from Siberia. In order to make their efforts more efficient the government by decrees closed certain routes to Siberia. Thus in 1619 the "sea route" to Mangazeia was closed, and, to prevent any further transportation there, an ostrozhek with a garrison of 40 to 50 men was erected near the portage between two rivers on the peninsula separating the Kara Sea from the Gulf of Ob'.[87] In 1695 all the routes radiating from Kazan were closed except the one through Verkhoturie.[88] Among the most important routes were two passing through the uezd of Berezov and one passing through Verkhoturie. The Berezov routes were guarded by the Sobskaia and Obdorskaia barrier, near the mouth of the Soba, in charge of the local customs heads, and by the Kirtas barrier overlooking the traffic along the river Sosva, supervised by the customs heads of Berezov.[89] Verkhoturie, being a town, had its own customhouse, which handled most of the traffic crossing the Siberian border. Roads which did not pass through these points were patrolled by customs guards recruited

[83] G. V. Vernadskii, "Gosudarevy sluzhilye i promyshlennye liudi," *Zh.M.N.P.*, New Series, LVI (April, 1915), 339.

[84] In Russia, internal and border customs service had existed since the days of the earliest principalities.

[85] Fisher, p. 62; Ogloblin, II, 3–4.

[86] Instructions to the customs sworn man in Iakutsk, 1645, *D.A.I.*, III, 41–42; Ogloblin, II, 27.

[87] There was also fear that foreign merchants might use the Mangazeia route and export Siberian furs. Butsinskii, *Zaselenie*, pp. 173, 175–176.

[88] Boiars' decision, 1695, *P.S.Z.*, III, 206–207.

[89] Butsinskii, *Zaselenie*, 178–179; Ogloblin, II, 27.

from the serving men and the sworn men, who had to see that no one crossed the frontier without inspection and payment of the proper dues.[90]

The customs administration as the agency of control over private business.—Through the network of its customs agencies the government attempted to trace the character and extent of the operations of private enterprisers and to follow their movements step by step. All merchants arriving at the Siberian border had to declare their capital and goods. The customs officials inquired where the goods were going and who was to accompany them. Unless the merchants intended to trade with local people, upon a payment of a fee equal to 4 per cent of the value of the goods, they were given the *proezzhaia gramota* (passport), which contained a detailed description of their goods and their values. Information similar to that which was contained in the proezzhaia gramota was sent by border officials to the customs head of the town which was indicated by the merchants as their place of destination.[91]

Upon arrival at the town where the merchants expected to do business, they had to present their proezzhaia gramota and goods to the local customs official for inspection and appraisal.[92] If everything was in order, the merchants were required to pay at the customs house 10 per cent of the value of the goods offered there for sale, either in money or in kind. As a consequence, the treasuries of the Siberian towns often hoarded many strange items such as shoes, coats, shirts, new and secondhand, copper and tin utensils, buttons, needles, and even dog food. These goods were later used by the town officials in place of salaries for the serving men, as gifts for the natives, or as articles for government trade. After the 10 per cent tax had been paid the merchants were allowed to open their business.[93]

If the merchants did not dispose of all their goods in one town

[90] Instructions to Verkhoturie, 1635, *D.A.I.*, III, 336–337; Bakhrushin, *Ocherki*, pp. 104–107.

[91] Instructions to Verkhoturie, 1692, *P.S.Z.*, III, 135, 137; Butsinskii, *Zaselenie*, p. 181; instructions to Tobolsk, 1697, *P.S.Z.*, III, 357–358.

[92] "The customs heads should not appraise the goods above the market price, while merchants of all descriptions should not conceal their goods or money which is to be used to purchase goods; they should not lower the price of goods, but declare goods, money and sale prices truthfully, without any craftiness." Instructions to customs heads, Eniseisk, 1687, Ogloblin, II, 71–72.

[93] Slovtsov, I, 151; Ogloblin, II, 20–23; Butsinskii, *Zaselenie*, pp. 181–182; Ogloblin, III, 79, 81.

and wished to proceed to another, they had once more to obtain the
proezzhaia gramota, which stated what goods they had, how much
these goods were worth and whether or not the 10 per cent presale
tax had been paid on these goods. Otherwise, the officials of the
next town where they intended to trade, and where they had to
pass another customs inspection, might ask again for the payment
of the 10 per cent tax.[94] Thorough inspection of goods at the customhouse of every town visited by the merchants made the avoidance
of the payment of the 10 per cent presale tax extremely difficult.
The inspection also afforded a means of enforcing such regulations
of the trade itself as protected the government fur business from
encroachment by private enterprisers.

In dealing with the natives, the merchants, who could offer
attractive wares, had a great advantage over the government, which
simply took the natives' furs as iasak. The government, however,
prohibited a number of articles from being sold to natives, such
as knives, axes, and other metal tools, which could be used by the
natives as weapons. The list of prohibited goods also included wine,
tobacco, and gambling devices, which would demoralize the natives
and lower their ability to deliver the iasak. Forbidden articles, if
found during the customs inspection, were confiscated, although
some of them, especially metal tools, later found their way to the
natives as gifts or objects of government barter.[95]

Government instructions to the Siberian officials continually
reminded them that merchants had been visiting the natives and
had been able to obtain the best furs in exchange for their goods,
before the government agents collected the iasak. As a result, the
remaining furs, which the natives brought as iasak, were of inferior
quality. In order to get first choice, the government prohibited the
merchants from trading with the natives until the delivery of the
iasak had been completed. Furthermore, all trade was forbidden in
native as well as in Russian villages where the merchants could
escape official supervision. A special *gostinnyi dvor* (merchants'
hall) was constructed in every town, and merchants had to do
business either there or in the *torg* (the town market place).[96]

---

[94] Ogloblin, II, 22, 51; instructions to Tara, 1631, *P.S.Z.*, III, 554; instructions to Iakutsk, 1651, *D.A.I.*, III, 307.
[95] Charter to Pinega promyshlenniks, 1600, *A.I.*, II, 28; instructions to Mangazeia, 1601, *R.I.B.*, II, 824, 830.
[96] Instructions to Tara, 1631 and 1633, *P.S.Z.*, III, 561, 569; instructions to
Iakutsk, 1651, *D.A.I.*, III, 308; instructions to Pelym, 1598, *R.I.B.*, II, 143–

Forbidden trade outside the town was detected by a comparison of the goods declared in the customhouse with the items specified in the proezzhaia gramota of merchants, which they obtained at the customhouse of their last stopping place.

Merchants from European Russia were chiefly attracted to Siberia by Siberian furs. They acquired them, in exchange for their goods, from native and local Russian hunters, or themselves organized hunting expeditions. At the very first they were comparatively free in their movements and private hunting was unrestricted.[97] Very soon, however, with the strengthening of governmental control over the fur trade, the activities of Russian hunters were prohibited in certain areas,[98] and special permission to hunt fur-bearing animals was required.[99] The hunters were searched before they left, for money and goods which they might use in trade with the natives,[100] and they were required to return through the same town in which they had obtained their hunting license.[101] If they failed to do so, their furs were likely to be confiscated in the first customhouse which they chanced to pass on their way back to Russia.[102]

Whether acquired by trade at the local market or by hunting, all furs had to be brought to the customhouse, and the customs officials, after having sorted the pelts into bundles according to their quality, collected the best pelt out of every ten for the government fur tithe. Furs hidden in order to avoid the payment of this tax were to be confiscated.[103]

144; instructions to Berezov, 1607, *R.I.B.*, II, 166–169; instructions to Kuznetsk, 1625, *A.I.*, III, 220; instructions to Tobolsk, 1664, *D.A.I.*, IV, 353–354; instructions to Iakutsk, 1694, *A.I.*, V, 435; instructions to Tara, 1631 and 1633, *P.S.Z.*, III, 561, 569.

[97] Instructions to Berezov, 1607, *R.I.B.*, II, 166–169; instructions to Pelym, 1598, *R.I.B.*, II, 143–144.

[98] Instructions to Iakutsk, 1685, *A.I.*, V, 204; instructions to Iakutsk, 1694, *A.I.*, V, 435.

[99] Ogloblin, II, 47.

[100] *Ibid.*, II, 46.

[101] Instructions to Iakutsk, 1651, *D.A.I.*, III, 308.

[102] Ogloblin, IV, 115.

[103] "The serving men, the merchants, the promyshlenniks and all other men have to pay the sovereign's customs tithe. The sables should be sorted in tens, the best with the best, the medium with the medium, and this should be done with other animals also. The best of every ten should be taken, whether it is a sable, or fox, or beaver, or any other animal, and whether it was acquired by hunting or by purchase." Instructions to a Iakutsk official, 1660, *D.A.I.*, IV, 209; also see the charter to the promyshlenniks from Pinega, 1600, *A.I.*, II, 27; instructions to the sworn man in Iakutsk, 1645, *D.A.I.*, III, 40; Ogloblin, II,

Merchants were forbidden to buy the most valuable furs from the natives. Also, if they came into possession of such furs by hunting, they had to surrender them to the government under fear of confiscation of all their furs and severe punishment as well. These furs were appraised by the customs officials according to the current local prices and bought for the government.[104] Unless one-tenth of these best furs had already been taken, the merchants were paid nine-tenths of the estimated value of the furs, the remaining tenth being considered the tax payment.[105]

Through the concentration of private trade in towns and ostrogs, where it could be supervised,[106] and by acquiring there the best furs from private hands, the government might have succeeded in obtaining the best furs for itself, provided the customs officials were honest and the regulations carefully observed. As that was not always the case, the government felt the need to supervise carefully the return journey of the merchants, who were made to appear with their papers, furs, and other goods at the customhouses along their route. Customs officials inspected the documents and goods, with the purpose of finding out whether or not the tithe had been properly paid. If the papers referred to furs of poor grades and the merchants had furs of high quality, indicating substitution, such furs were confiscated. Similar action was taken with respect to furs and goods not mentioned in the merchants' documents.[107]

Altogether the 10 per cent tax (fur tithe) and the confiscated goods provided a great many furs for the government, although not nearly so many as did the collection of the iasak. On the basis of available data, Fisher, in his study of the Siberian fur trade,

---

43–45; instructions to customs sworn man in Iakutsk, 1645, *D.A.I.*, III, 40; instructions to Iakutsk, 1651, *D.A.I.*, III, 307.

[104] "The visiting merchants, or promyshlenniks, or any other people are strictly forbidden to buy from the natives the black and black-gray foxes [in other instructions also grey foxes and other valuable animals]. If they obtain such furs themselves by hunting they must bring them [to the authorities].... The voevoda will give them the money, according to the straight value.... But if they hide such furs and are detected, then the furs will be confiscated, and their owners will be punished." Instructions to Tara, 1631, *P.S.Z.*, III, 559–560. Also, instructions to Tobolsk, 1664, *D.A.I.*, IV, 365; Ogloblin, quoting instructions to Tara, 1599, and to Tobolsk, 1598, IV, 130–132; instructions to Tobolsk, 1697, *P.S.Z.*, III, 369.

[105] Ogloblin, II, 39–40.

[106] Here the government followed a practice already in use in European Russia. Instructions to Novgorod, 1622, *A.A.E.*, III, 180.

[107] Ogloblin, II, 45; instructions to the customs official in Iakutsk, 1645, *D.A.I.*, III, 42; instructions to Verkhoturie, 1692, *P.S.Z.*, III, 136.

estimates the proportion of fur revenue contributed by different sources as follows: "65 to 80 per cent for iasak, 15 to 30 per cent for the tithe, and a residual 5 per cent or less for the other sources."[108] These figures show that together with the customs dues on other goods the customs must have supplied the government with considerable revenue.

The customs administration as the agency of control over Siberian officials.—In addition to the functions described above, the customs administration in Siberia rendered another valuable service to the government. The profits of the government were endangered not only by the merchant class, which the government watched closely and deprived of the best share of furs, but very often by its own officials. The Siberian voevodas and the members of their staffs were strictly forbidden to trade. For that reason, like the merchants, they were inspected on their way to Siberia and any goods which they took along with them for the purpose of trade were to be confiscated.[109] In Siberia they were allowed to buy merchandise only for their personal use, and if they needed furs for their own clothing, they had to buy the less expensive pelts. All their purchases had to be made at the gostinnyi dvor at market prices.[110] Nevertheless, the voevodas who regarded their appointment to Siberia as a lucky turn of fortune and who amassed great wealth by briberies and extortions, were also active as traders and businessmen, usually to the detriment of the state revenues.[111] In 1634, for instance, two large boats laden with the goods of the voevoda of Tobolsk, Suleshov,[112] passed through Mangazeia. These goods

---

[108] Fisher, p. 118.

[109] Instructions to Verkhoturie, 1679, *A.I.*, V, 77–78.

[110] Instructions to Mangazeia, 1601, *R.I.B.*, II, 832; instructions to Kuznetsk, 1626, *A.I.*, III, 222–223; instructions to Tara, 1633, *P.S.Z.*, III, 554, 560; instructions to Tobolsk, 1664, *D.A.I.*, IV, 354, 361; instructions to Iakutsk, 1658, *D.A.I.*, IV, 111 ff.

[111] "The voevodas, forgetting their oath and spurning strict decrees . . . carry ample supplies of wine and other goods to Siberia, and also manufacture wine there and [with these goods and wine] make large profits. They smuggle wine and goods to Siberia without paying the customs dues. . . . They take bribes from men whom they send to collect iasak. . . . [From the collected furs] they take the best furs for themselves and leave the poor furs in the treasury. . . . They decrease the sovereign's revenues in iasak, in the 10 per cent tax from furs, in customs dues, in the sovereign's sale of wine, and in a short time build enormous fortunes, while the serving men and the natives suffer from their injustice, outrages, and extortions." Decree, 1695, *P.S.Z.*, III, 203; cf. instructions to Verkhoturie, 1692, *P.S.Z.*, III, 130–131; instructions to Tobolsk, 1697, III, 347.

[112] Probably an error and it should be 1624, when Suleshov was in Siberia.

were appraised in the local customhouse at 1196.71 rubles, which was a considerable amount in the seventeenth century. The customs dues were taken according to the appraisal. Ogloblin, however, expressed his belief that the goods were evaluated in the interests of the voevoda, with a corresponding loss in the customs revenue, and that they were worth at least twice as much.[113]

Commercial interests and a common desire to evade the regulations of the Muscovite government often brought about a sort of alliance between the local officials and the merchants. The voevodas protected the merchants from the demands of the customs officials, helped to hide their furs, and aided them in escaping payment of the 10 per cent fur tax. The merchants, in return, supplied goods for the private trade of the voevodas and carried furs belonging to the voevodas to Russia.[114] As a result of this coöperation the customs officials along the border had special instructions to watch for attempts on the part of the merchants to smuggle the furs of the voevodas.[115]

Sometimes the voevodas tried to smuggle their furs to Russia through the aid of the settlers around Verkhoturie,[116] or by sending their servants or relatives by side roads. The customs patrols, however, were on the lookout for such maneuvers and if they succeeded in detecting them, brought the voevodas' agents to Verkhoturie.[117] The voevodas and diaks themselves, when passing through Verkhoturie, had to undergo a minute and rigorous inspection. Passing officials, irrespective of their standing, had to get out of their carriages, and not only was their baggage carefully examined, but also their persons. Returning voevodas were searched chiefly for concealed furs. Inspection often disclosed furs in various odd places, as for instance in 1635 when the voevoda of Berezov hid his furs inside his pillows, feather bed covers, mattresses, and even horse collars.[118] The baggage of voevodas going to Siberia was

---

[113] Ogloblin, II, 31–33; compare with the shipment of furs belonging to the boiar Cherkasskii in 1656 evaluated in Berezov at 983.81 rubles. Ogloblin, II, 59.

[114] Report from Iakutsk, 1645, *D.A.I.*, III, 35; petition of the *mir* (assembly of all inhabitants), Iakutsk, 1651, "Kolonial'naia politika," pp. 29, 39, 44–45; instructions to Iakutsk, 1694, *A.I.*, V, 442.

[115] Instructions to Verkhoturie, 1692, *P.S.Z.*, III, 132; instructions to customs head, 1678, *A.I.*, V, 44.

[116] The officials in their travel to and from Siberia had to pass through Verkhoturie. Bakhrushin, *Ocherki*, pp. 104–105.

[117] Instructions to Verkhoturie, 1635, *A.I.*, III, 336–337; instructions to Verkhoturie, 1692, *P.S.Z.*, III, 134.

[118] Ogloblin, II, 57; Slovtsov, I, 150.

examined for goods intended for barter or sale in Siberia, and, in addition, the amount of food, wine, and other things which they were allowed to bring for their own needs was checked.[119]

The worldly goods which the voevodas and members of their staff took to Siberia were compared with those which they had on their return.[120] The government allowed the chief voevodas of Tobolsk, Tomsk, and Iakutsk (the principal towns of the Tobolsk, Tomsk, and Lenskii razriads) to bring 500 rubles from Siberia, and other voevodas and diaks were allowed to bring 300 rubles apiece, but all the money and furs in excess of this sum were to be confiscated.[121]

The voevodas, however, on their way to Siberia would declare money and property which they really did not possess at that time, in the hope that they would accumulate its equivalent in Siberia, so that on their way back the inventories would not show any difference. For that purpose the voevodas traveling in a group used to coöperate by loaning each other money, clothing, and other property. In order to stop this practice the government recommended that customs officials, after inspection, put seals on all possessions of any passing voevoda, who was not allowed to break them until well under way from Verkhoturie.[122]

To summarize the discussion of the customs administration in Siberia: the customs agencies not only procured furs as well as other goods for the government, but also were instrumental in the regulation of private trade in the interests of the government and in curtailing the illegitimate profits of local Siberian administrators.

The Siberian Tax System

In addition to the revenues from Siberia already described, different local taxes were collected in every Siberian town. These taxes

---

[119] Ogloblin, II, 62.

[120] "When the voevodas and other officials travel through Verkhoturie to the Siberian towns, check their property in goods and money in Verkhoturie. Send to Moscow the inventory signed by the customs and barrier heads and by the sworn men, and leave a copy of it in Verkhoturie in case of future disputes....

"When these voevodas are replaced and come back, check again their property and money. Make an inventory of whatever may be found in excess [of what they had on their way to Siberia] and dispose of it in accordance with the orders of our great tsar." Instructions to Verkhoturie, 1667, *A.I.*, IV, 309.

[121] Instructions to Tomsk, 1648, I. P. Kuznetsov-Krasnoiarskii, comp., *Istoricheskie akty XVII st.*, Vol. I, p. 13; instructions to Iakutsk, 1658, *D.A.I.*, IV, 118; Ogloblin, II, 54–57; instructions to the customs head, 1678, *A.I.*, V, 44

[122] Instructions to Verkhoturie, 1697, *P.S.Z.*, III, 386.

varied in kind and number. In the small ostrog of Ketsk, the revenue books of 1629 mentioned only three types of taxes, namely, a 10 per cent tax collected from goods offered for sale, a yearly *obrok* from the *guliashchie liudi*,[123] and court dues.[124] In larger towns there were a great many taxes, varying according to the inspiration of the local voevodas who were given a free rein in increasing "the profit of the great sovereign."[125]

Different taxes already existing in European Russia provided the source of inspiration, and a comparison of European and Siberian taxes does not reveal any particular innovations in Siberia.[126] The absence of any general system of devising and introducing new taxes caused the same tax to appear in many towns under different names, while the same name was used in various towns for taxes of different kinds. The amounts of the charge also varied from town to town. Only at the end of the century were efforts made to bring order and uniformity into the system of taxation.[127]

Some insight into the working of the tax system in Siberia might be obtained by imagining the arrival of a merchant in a Siberian town. In the first place, if he had arrived by river, he would pay for permission to moor his boats, in Tobolsk according to the length, in Mangazeia according to the type of the vessels.[128] An additional charge was collected from every member of the crew on the boat.[129]

---

[123] Obrok was usually a rent paid for a short-term contract. The term was also used to designate a single small tax imposed upon those who were exempt from *tiaglo*, which was a total sum of different taxes and labor obligations imposed on the tax-paying population of a town or village. A. A. Lappo-Danilevskii, "Organizatsiia priamogo oblozheniia," *Zapiski istoriko-filologicheskago fakul'teta S.-Peterburgskago universiteta*, XXIII, 18, 22–23. For obrok payable in grain, see *infra* p. 169.
  Guliashchie liudi were the people not attached to any *tiaglo*, and therefore free to move from place to place; usually they were itinerant workers. Ogloblin, III, 161.

[124] Ogloblin, II, 21.

[125] "The voevodas must use the most expedient means to increase the profit of the sovereign, in so far as the wisdom granted to them by the Lord will allow it, without, however, oppressing the local population." This quotation represents a typical formula in practically all instructions to the voevodas. Instructions to Mangazeia, 1603, *R.I.B.*, II, 841; instructions to Kuznetsk, 1625, *A.I.*, III, 223; instructions to Tobolsk, 1664, *D.A.I.*, IV, 349 ff.

[126] K. Lodyzhenskii, *Istoriia russkago tamozhennago tarifa*, pp. 1–5; M. A. Diakonov, *Ocherki*, pp. 181–190; customs instructions to Belöozero, Ves'egonsk, Troitsko-Sergiev monastery, Novgorod, Kholmogory, Gorokhovets, 1497, 1551, 1563, 1571, 1586, 1633, *A.A.E.*, I, 99–101, 222–226, 295–297, 320, 398, 400, 408–411, III, 359–363.

[127] Instructions to customs heads, 1693, *P.S.Z.*, III, 160–167; Ogloblin, II, 19; IV, 76.

[128] *Posazhennaia poshlina s sudov.* Ogloblin, II, 24, 26.

[129] *Privalnaia.* Ogloblin, II, 34–35.

If a merchant arrived in winter, then he had to pay a duty imposed upon horses carrying goods.[130] Upon his arrival, the merchant had to visit the local customhouse and to pay there the customs dues already mentioned. He was also charged for the official measuring and weighing of declared goods.[131] When the goods had been transported to the gostinnyi dvor, charges were collected for a place where the merchant could store his goods and for a place where he could do business.[132] During his stay in town the merchant paid a sort of poll tax[133] and a residence tax, and upon leaving the town, he paid the departure tax, in addition to charges for the examination and release of his passport.[134]

Most of the Siberian taxes fall in one of the following groups: poll taxes, taxes on property and business, taxes on produce, taxes for business transactions and court charges. The poll taxes were imposed either on some special groups, such as travelers passing through the town[135] or the guliashchie liudi,[136] or were collected from all the residents, usually for some special purpose such as maintenance of the government buildings, the upkeep of the hostages, or other local expenditures.[137] The property taxes were imposed on house owners,[138] or owners of business establishments such as tanneries, slaughterhouses, saltworks, or places where they made soap, shoes, or other commodities.[139] The most burdensome of the property taxes was the one collected for the purpose of paying the salaries of the serving men. This tax was introduced in 1655 and amounted to 10 per cent of the value of the property.[140] Instead of the tax being levied upon the business, it was often imposed upon the

---

[130] *Polozovoe.* Ogloblin, II, 22, 35.

[131] *Veshchee* and *pomernoe.* Ogloblin, II, 17, 22–23; instructions to Iakutsk, 1685, *A.I.,* V, 208.

[132] *Poanbarnoe, anbarnoe* or *teplovoe* and *lavochnoe, polavochnoe* or *polkovoe.* Report of revenues and expenditures in Siberia for 1698–1699, *R.I.B.,* VIII, 695; account of the customhouse in Iakutsk, 1658, "Kolonial'naia politika," p. 174; instructions to the customs head in Iakutsk, 1685, *A.I.,* V, 208; Ogloblin, II, 22.

[133] *Iavchaia* or *iavchaia golovshchina.* Ogloblin, I, 255–256; II, 17, 22, 24, 26; III, 68.

[134] *Izbnaia,* "from the time of arrival to the time of departure." Ogloblin, II, 18; account of the customhouse in Iakutsk, 1658, "Kolonial'naia politika," p. 174; *privorotnoe* and *ot'ezzhee.* Ogloblin, II, 17, 22, 36.

[135] *Iavchaia.* Ogloblin, II, 17, 24.

[136] *Obrok.* Ogloblin, II, 21, 24.

[137] *Pogolovnaia.* Ogloblin, II, 29, 31, 65–67.

[138] *Podymnoe* and *povorotnoe.* Ogloblin, I, 152, 228.

[139] *Pozhivotovoe.* Ogloblin, I, 161–163; II, 65–66.

[140] *Desiataia denga.* Ogloblin, I, 161–163.

produce. Just as the hunter had to deliver one-tenth of his furs, so the fisherman had to yield one-tenth of his newly caught fish, the soapmaker one-tenth of his soap, and the salter one-tenth of his salt.[141] Among the taxes on business transactions there were numerous sales taxes, paid either by the seller or by both the vendor and the buyer. These taxes usually were called by the name of the article which was traded.[142] The court charges included the charges for a lawsuit, contract deeds, bondage deeds, and court fines.[143]

Most of these taxes were collected regularly, but at certain times, such as during grave national financial crises, the government exacted also special extraordinary taxes. In 1662 and 1676, for instance, the government collected a tax which amounted to 20 per cent of the value of the capital or property.[144] Sometimes the local voevodas also collected an extraordinary local tax. Thus in 1698 and 1699 the townsmen and peasants of Tobolsk had to collect money to pay the salaries of the dragoon troops;[145] and in 1658 the people of Surgut had to pay a special local assessment to equip a government-owned bathhouse.[146]

A comparison of taxes in Siberia with those in European Russia shows, according to Slovtsov, the absence in Siberia of the stage tax and the tax levied for the payment of ransom for Russian captives seized by the Tatars, the two taxes which were collected everywhere in Russia.[147] The findings of the present study confirm this statement, so far as the ransom collection is concerned, but the stage tax is mentioned in a few documents.[148]

THE WINE MONOPOLY

In developing its financial activities in Siberia, the government went further than the collection of the fur tribute, customs dues, and taxes. It assumed the role of a large business enterpriser and

---

[141] Ogloblin, II, 23, 26, 29–30, 35, 37–38, 40, 73, 77.

[142] *Porublevoe, perekupnoe, posherstnoe, porogovoe, skotinnoe, pogolovnoe,* and others. Ogloblin, II, 17, 24, 26, 36, 42; instructions to Iakutsk, 1685, *A.I.,* V, 207–208; account of the customhouse in Iakutsk, 1658, "Kolonial'naia politika," p. 174.

[143] Butsinskii, *Zaselenie,* pp. 57–58; *idem, Mangazeia,* pp. 25–26; Ogloblin, I, 173.

[144] Slovtsov, I, 182; Ogloblin, III, 67; instructions to Berezov, 1663, *D.A.I.,* IV, 316.

[145] Report of the revenues and expenditures . . . in Siberia, 1698–1699, *R.I.B.,* VIII, 698–699.

[146] Ogloblin, II, 37; for other similar collections, see *ibid.,* I, 223.

[147] Slovtsov, I, 153.   [148] Ogloblin, I, 165.

actively participated in trade, with a partial or complete monopoly over certain goods. One of the most important business undertakings of the government was the manufacture and sale of wine[149] and other alcoholic beverages.

In the beginning of the seventeenth century the so-called "sovereign's wine treasury" was entirely in the hands of the voevodas. The wine was for the most part imported from European Russia and sold under the direction of the voevodas by the sworn men. Before long, however, local distilleries were established in almost all Siberian towns. Apparently the distilling and manufacture of liquors was profitable, because the management of the distilleries was regarded as a privilege and granted as a reward to serving men of upper rank or to clerks of the voevoda's office.[150]

The voevoda could employ these men as managers of distilleries, because the manufacturing of wine did not require any particular skill. In fact, it was so simple that practically anybody could prepare wine, and the people were allowed to do so, upon payment of a small tax, although only for their own needs and not for sale. Permission to make home brew and beer was granted on occasions such as the baptism of a child, a marriage ceremony, the celebration of a patron saint's day, or Christmas.[151]

The comparative simplicity of making wine accounts for the practice in Verkhoturie of allowing private individuals—serving men, townsmen, and peasants—to manufacture wine on a large scale and to supply it to the government *kabak* (saloon or pothouse) on a contractual basis. This practice was discontinued because the manufacturers retained too much wine and secretly sold it for their own profit. Thereupon, in 1627, the voevoda confiscated all private equipment and himself started distilling wine in the ostrog. As a result of the removal of competitors, the government wine income rose from 455 to 1,071 rubles, a significant addition to the total money collected in this town, which amounted to 4,484 rubles in that year.[152]

---

[149] Alcoholic beverages in Siberia included a strong liquor prepared from grain to which the documents refer as wine or hot wine—corresponding to the modern vodka. Ogloblin, II, 82. In this study the word wine will be used in the same sense as it was used in the documents. Other beverages were beer and mead.

[150] Ogloblin, II, 80–81, 83; instructions to Verkhoturie, 1623, *A.I.*, III, 187–188.

[151] Ogloblin, II, 83, 96–98.

[152] Butsinskii, *Zaselenie*, 60–61; instructions to Verkhoturie, 1628, *A.I.*, III, 251–252.

When the financial functions of the voevodas were curtailed the preparation and disposal of wine was transferred to special officials, sworn men of higher rank, called *kruzhechnye golovas* (head wine keepers). Infrequently the head of the customhouse combined his duties with the supervision of the wine business. The voevodas ceased to interfere with the actual management and were left only the general supervision and control.[153]

Because considerable profit could be derived from the liquor business, the government decided to make it a state monopoly. Private distilleries, tolerated at first, were to be confiscated and merchants selling wine were to be severely punished.[154] But, although the prohibition of the private sale of wine was insisted upon even in the earliest instructions,[155] violations were frequent; for instance in Mangazeia and the Turukhansk zimov'e, the liquor trade, in which the merchants, promyshlenniks, serving men, and the voevodas themselves took part, flourished until 1620. At that time the voevoda of Tobolsk was informed that the voevoda of Mangazeia, Birkin, had made a fortune of 8,000 rubles for himself by selling wine in Turukhansk. The voevoda of Tobolsk, in his report to Moscow pointed out the desirability of opening in Turukhansk a state-owned kabak. He claimed that by selling 150 buckets of wine and 50 puds of mead there, the government would receive 2,210 rubles clear profit, and were the liquors to be bartered for furs the profit would probably double. The government followed the suggestion and sent to Mangazeia the pod'iachei, Chaplin, from Tobolsk with wine and the proper instructions. These instructions disclose the government attitude toward the question of wine revenues. Chaplin was instructed to open his establishment for merchants and traders, but only after they had paid all their taxes, and for natives, but not before they had delivered the iasak. The serving men were to be kept out of the kabak altogether, "so they would not lose their possessions through drunkenness."[156]

Another illustration of the government policies is found in the correspondence of Bariatinskii, the voevoda of Verkhoturie, with

---

[153] Ogloblin, II, 81, 83, IV, 42–43.
[154] "If any of the serving men, merchants, or promyshlenniks ... have for sale alcoholic liquors, ... such men should be punished without mercy." Instructions to the supervisor of the manufacture and sale of liquors at Iakutsk, 1652, *D.A.I.*, III, 373; instructions to Iakutsk, 1651, *D.A.I.*, III, 313.
[155] Instructions to Mangazeia, 1601, *R.I.B.*, II, 831.
[156] Butsinskii, *Mangazeia*, pp. 27–28.

Moscow. Bariatinskii was worried "because the serving men, . . . the *iamshchiks* [government drivers], and peasants have spent everything in the kabak and then have had to quit the service in debt and misery." Bariatinskii recommended closing the kabak, as had been done in Tobolsk. Moscow, however, sharply reprimanded the prohibitionistic leanings of the voevoda and accused him of lacking sufficient zeal for the sovereign's profits. The general formula seemed to be: to keep the local men in government employ from drunkenness, but to encourage the sale of wine to outsiders, merchants, and traders. Such a policy explains why the government closed the kabak in Tobolsk with its large population of serving men, and did everything possible to increase the sale of wine in Verkhoturie, which controlled most of the traffic to Siberia. The letter to Bariatinskii stated: ". . . if you see that the kabak in Tobolsk is closed, that is not an example for you."[157]

The prices for wine were not fixed, but left to the discretion of the local administration. Once the voevoda of Eniseisk was asked to send 2,000 rubles to Iakutsk. In order to raise this sum, he arbitrarily doubled the prices of local wine from 3 to 6 rubles per bucket.[158] In general, the profits made in wine were among the larger money collections in Siberia. Since it made large profits in the wine trade, the government could afford to dispense some of it without charge. As was mentioned in a previous chapter, the native chiefs on certain occasions were entertained with feasts where free wine was served. Wine was sometimes distributed among the serving men when they had to undertake long trips for iasak collection, or given to them as a reward for some exploit. On the days of state holidays or the local saint's day, everybody in town was given a free drink.[159]

GOVERNMENT TRADE

In addition to wine there were other articles among the "prohibited merchandise" which were excluded from private trade and preserved for the exclusive trade of the government. One of them was tobacco, 120 puds of which, estimated at 45,000 rubles, the government imported to Siberia in 1648, although the pressure brought

---

[157] Butsinskii, *Zaselenie,* pp. 59–60; instructions to Verkhoturie, 1623, *A.I.,* III, 187–188.

[158] Communication from Eniseisk to Tomsk, 1652, *D.A.I.,* III, 345.

[159] Ogloblin, II, 91–94.

about by the church interfered with its disposal.[160] In the middle
of the seventeenth century the government became interested in
rhubarb (used for medicinal purposes?). In 1653 a caravan from
Bokhara arrived in Tara with 625 puds of rhubarb, and after 33¾
puds had been taken as a tax, the rest of it was bought by the officials
for the government treasury.[161] In 1657, rhubarb was added to the
prohibited list and became a government monopoly.[162] Silver and
gold as well as precious stones were also included in the government monopolies, and at the end of the century Nerchinsk became
the main channel for gold coming from China.[163] The trade in salt
might be used as an example of a partial monopoly of the government. Salt was indispensable in the preservation of food, especially
fish, an essential item in the diet of Siberian service men. Consequently, although private individuals were not prohibited from
selling salt, the government owned and operated the largest and the
best saltworks in Siberia.

Government merchandise was sold to the serving men, traders,
Russian colonists, and natives by sworn men appointed for this
purpose and supervised at first by the voevodas and later in the
century by the customs heads. An important aspect of government
business enterprise was the barter with the natives to which reference has been made earlier in this chapter; the government also
bartered with the Russian serving men and merchants who chanced
to be in possession of finer furs.[164] The government caravan trade
with China was another important venture. Although commercial
relations with China existed as early as 1653,[165] they acquired
special significance only at the end of the seventeenth and at the
beginning of the eighteenth centuries, when the government took
a series of steps to put them on a solid basis.[166] As a result, the
caravans of 1706 and 1709 yielded respectively 261,778.75 and
223,550.59 rubles of clear profit to the government.[167]

[160] Slovtsov, I, 62; communications from Tobolsk to Turinsk, 1649, *D.A.I.*,
III, 139–141.

[161] Ogloblin, II, 103–137; III, 81.

[162] Slovtsov, *loc. cit.;* instructions to Verkhoturie, 1680 and 1681, *A.I.*, V,
91, 100–101.

[163] Decree, 1698, *P.S.Z.*, III, 497, 504–505; report of revenues and expenditures . . . in Siberia, 1698–1699, *R.I.B.*, VIII, 826.

[164] Ogloblin, II, 75.

[165] *Ibid.*, III, 195, 340; G. Cahen, *Histoire des relations de la Russie avec la
Chine* . . . , p. 57.

[166] Slovtsov, I, 152.

[167] N. Abramov, "O dvorianakh i detiakh boiarskikh . . . ," pp. 14–15.

LOCAL GOVERNMENT ENTERPRISES

The financial activities of the government described so far have been more or less general, having to do with Siberia as a whole. But it must be remembered that every voevoda, in addition to his other duties, was a sort of business manager of the little colony represented by his town and uezd. Most of the ostrogs were built in a comparative wilderness, and the newcomers faced the lack of even rudimentary commodities. The voevodas had to take care of the needs and welfare of their garrison and of the colonists. Accordingly, in order to secure food supplies and to avoid the expense of importing them, the voevodas set apart for the state some of the convenient land and grass meadows, settled colonists on them "to till the soil for the sovereign,"[168] and erected flour mills to grind grain.[169] As salt was an indispensable article used in large quantities for the preservation of food, the voevodas searched for salt deposits and established saltworks, the largest of which were in the Tobolsk, Ilimsk, and Eniseisk regions.[170] In order to maintain communication, which was mostly by water, the voevodas constructed boats[171] and planted hemp for making the ropes used in dragging the boats upstream and across the portages.[172] Within the town they built public bathhouses[173] and started soap and candle making.[174] This work was done by carpenters, smiths, and other workmen imported by the government from Russia and assisted in their labors by local men.[175]

When Russian immigrants began to settle in Siberian towns, the voevodas, rather than operate various government enterprises themselves, preferred to lease them to private bidders, the rent thus collected being called *otkup*.[176] The voevodas also collected money for permission to fish in lakes and rivers, for the use of government meadows, for the use of rafts on the river, and for

[168] The agricultural efforts of the government will be discussed at greater length in the next chapter.

[169] Ogloblin, I, 121, 291; II, 223; III, 57, 74, 318.

[170] Account of the revenues and expenditures ... in Siberia, 1698–1699, *R.I.B.*, VIII, 707, 794, 814.

[171] Ogloblin, III, 70, 81.

[172] *Ibid.*, I, 28; III, 81.

[173] *Ibid.*, II, 37.

[174] *Ibid.*, I, 374, 376; II, 136.

[175] Instructions about the building of Verkhoturie, 1597, *R.I.B.*, II, 59; instructions to Verkhoturie, 1603, *A.I.*, II, 54; Ogloblin, II, 82.

[176] Ogloblin, I, 374, 376; II, 136; Butsinskii, *Zaselenie*, pp. 57–58.

openings cut in the ice where the town washing was done. All these fees, as well as money received for licenses issued to persons engaged in certain occupations such as that of public scribe, were also known as otkup[177] and were collected in most of the Siberian towns.

In concluding the discussion of the financial and business activities which were carried on in Siberia by the Muscovite government and its local agents, some more or less successful attempts to exploit the mineral wealth of Siberia should be noted.[178] The most important of them was the sending to Siberia in 1696 of a Greek "mining master," Levandian, who was instructed to organize a system for the extraction of precious metals.[179]

SIBERIAN EXPENDITURES

All Siberian revenues were divided into two parts. Furs obtained as iasak or by any other means were shipped to Moscow to be disposed of there by the Siberian Prikaz, while collections of money and goods were kept in Siberia for local needs.[180] The greater part of this local money was spent to pay the salaries of government employees and serving men.[181] However, the highest-paid members of the Siberian administration, the voevodas, diaks, and pismennye golovas apparently were paid in Moscow,[182] or at least in European Russia,[183] since the documents examined in the preparation of this

[177] Butsinskii, *Zaselenie, loc. cit.*, also *idem, Mangazeia*, p. 25; N. N. Ogloblin, "Proiskhozhdenie provintsialnykh pod'iachikh," p. 144.

[178] Ogloblin, III, 82–83.

[179] *Ibid.*, I, 249.

[180] Butsinskii, *Mangazeia*, p. 26.

[181] The table below illustrates the percentage of money spent for payment of salaries, in some towns selected at random.

Town	Year	Total expenditures (in rubles)	Salaries (in rubles)	Per cent
Surgut	1625	1,304	1,175	90
Tobolsk	1625	5,500 (*ca.*)	4,234.93	77
Tobolsk	1626	5,500 (*ca.*)	4,735.24	86
Tobolsk	1698	15,515	13,814	90
Tobolsk	1699	16,319	14,031	88
Mangazeia	1626	600 (*ca.*)	500 (*ca.*)	83
Tiumen	1698	5,449	5,203	95
Verkhoturie	1698	1,496	701	47
Tomsk	1698	6,349	5,807	91
Eniseisk	1698	2,172	1,836	84

Butsinskii, *Mangazeia*, p. 28; *idem, Zaselenie*, pp. 137, 142; report of revenues and expenditures in Siberia . . . 1698–1699, *R.I.B.*, VIII, 699–702, 713–714, 725–728, 741–744, 786–788.

[182] "Otnosheniia voevod i diakov," *Chteniia*, Vol. CCXXXIII (1910), Bk. 2, pt. 2, p. 15; Ogloblin, III, 24; IV, 168.

[183] Instructions to Verkhoturie, 1613, *A.I.*, II, 407.

study mention only two occasions on which the voevodas were paid
from the local treasuries in Siberia; one was a reappointment
(which was rare),[184] and as for the other it is not clear whether 100
rubles received by the voevoda from a local treasury was his salary
or a special reward.[185]

The salaries of the serving men in Siberia varied with their rank.
The cossacks and streltsy on foot received on the average from 4.25
to 5.00 rubles per year; the streltsy, cossacks, and Litva on horse
from 7.25 to 7.75, the boiar sons from 10 to 12, and the officers 20 to
30 rubles. Some of the serving men received a few rubles more than
the average as a reward for excellent service. Higher salaries went
also with promotion, but if the men were later demoted, usually as
a punishment or because the Muscovite government did not ap-
prove their promotion, they had to pay back all extra money
received during the period of promotion.

In addition to the serving men, the Siberian pay rolls included
ruzhniks (churchmen : monks, priests, deacons, sextons) and *obroch-
niks* (men whose relation to the government was based on contract :
clerks, interpreters, smiths, millers, gate- and jail-keepers, watchmen, executioners, and, strange to say, gunners).[186] In comparison
with the rates of salaries for the serving men in European Russia,
as given by Miliukov,[187] the Siberian rates are somewhat higher.

Few Siberian towns, and then not all the time, were able to pay
the salaries of their serving men in full out of the local treasury.
Among such towns were Mangazeia (in the first half of the seventeenth century),[188] Verkhoturie (apparently throughout the seventeenth century),[189] and Berezov (during the 'forties of the same
century) ;[190] in other words, the towns which gathered large customs
revenues. In most of the Siberian towns the local money resources
were inadequate. Tiumen, Turinsk, and Tara seemed to have had

---

[184] Instructions to Eniseisk, 1655, *D.A.I.*, IV, 41.

[185] Report of revenues and expenditures ... in Siberia, 1898–1699, *R.I.B.*,
VIII, 727–728.

[186] P. M. Golovachev, ed., *Tomsk v XVII veke.* The lists of the serving men
and the schedules of their salaries, 1626, 1633, 1680, 1699, 31–45, 47–48, 54–
135; several documents in *R.I.B.*, II, 51–52, 110, 332, 352 ff; Ogloblin, I, 121;
instructions to Berezov, 1608, *R.I.B.*, II, 170–171; instructions to Verkhoturie,
1676, *A.I.*, V, 12–13.

[187] P. N. Miliukov, "Gosudarstvennoe khoziaistvo Rossii ... ," *Zh.M.N.P.*,
CCLXXI, Sept., 1890, 48–49.

[188] Butsinskii, *Mangazeia*, p. 26.

[189] *Idem, Zaselenie*, p. 61; report of the revenues and expenditures of Verkhoturie, 1698–1699, *R.I.B.*, VIII, 727–728.

[190] Butsinskii, *Zaselenie*, p. 183.

an especially hard time, the first two because, in addition to their serving men, they had the numerous iamshchiks (government drivers) who received salaries from the state, and the third, because it had a numerous garrison and very small revenues.[191] To such poor towns money had to be sent from Russia, and until 1637 it was usually sent from Kazan.[192] The shortage of money in Siberia for the payment of salaries can be illustrated by the fact that around 1690 the total of money collection in Siberia was approximately 18,000 rubles, while the total pay roll was 53,995 rubles.[193] Again in 1698 the total money collection was 40,208 rubles and the total money which was paid out as salaries was equal to 54,445 rubles.[194]

COLONIAL PROFITS

In order that the local administrators could meet their expenditures, the Muscovite government had to send a certain amount of cash money to Siberia every year. The preserved records of 1596, 1632, and 1691 indicate shipments of 5,340 rubles,[195] 20,453 rubles,[196] and 15,000[197] rubles respectively. But even with these subsidies the serving men were not paid according to the salary schedules. The Muscovite government, which was in continuous financial difficulty during the seventeenth century, adopted the profitable practice of withholding some of the money. As a result, in 1681 it owed the serving men 31,996 rubles[198] and in 1691 this sum reached 143,000 rubles.[199] In both 1698 and 1699 the serving men were supposed to receive 67,657 rubles, but they were paid only 54,445 rubles in 1698 and 54,086 rubles in 1699.[200]

Because the Muscovite government needed cash money in European Russia, on several occasions it sent goods to Siberia to be used at least in partial payment of salaries. In 1668 the men in Surgut were given different kinds of cloth. In 1676 the government sent to

---

[191] *Ibid.*, pp. 78–79, 100–101, 159; report of the revenues and expenditures ... in Siberia, 1698–1699, *R.I.B.*, VIII, 713–714, 843–846.

[192] Ogloblin, III, 66; instructions to Verkhoturie, 1632, *R.I.B.*, II, 509.

[193] Ogloblin, IV, 113.

[194] Report of the revenues and expenditures ... in Siberia, 1698–1699, *R.I.B.*, VIII, 887–888.

[195] List of supplies and money sent to Siberian towns, 1596, *R.I.B.*, II, 132.

[196] Instructions to Verkhoturie, 1632, *R.I.B.*, II, 509.

[197] Ogloblin, IV, 113.

[198] *Ibid.*, IV, 161.

[199] *Ibid.*, IV, 113.

[200] Report of revenues and expenditures ... in Siberia, 1698–1699, *R.I.B.*, VIII, 987–988.

Verkhoturie cloth, *kumach* (red fustian stuff) worth 846, and wax worth 34 rubles to be distributed among the local men in place of salaries. In 1678 the same garrison received copperware, cloth, leather, silk thread, and other goods, "some of them spoiled." In 1685, belts, hats, and wine were distributed among the men in Tomsk.[201]

The serving men were dissatisfied with this method of paying salaries and repeatedly complained of it to the local voevodas and to Moscow. They contended that the goods were appraised too high and that they were cheated by substitution.[202] Besides, the articles received on some occasions were utterly useless. In 1703–1704, for instance, the government sent to Verkhoturie over half a ton of iron wire to be used by the artillery men (for wrapping guns?). The wire proved to be of such poor quality that the "master gun-makers" refused to accept it. The local voevoda, in order, "to prevent damage and detriment for the sovereign" distributed this wire among the local serving men in place of salaries at the estimate of 3½ rubles per pud.[203]

The unsatisfactory methods of paying salaries in Siberia in no way indicate that the government colonial enterprise was unprofitable. They merely mean that the government tried to economize in Siberia in order to spend the Siberian income elsewhere. This holds true in spite of the government decree in 1697 which recommended improvement on the methods of acquiring furs and put the blame for the existence of salary arrears in Siberia on the mismanagement by local administrators.[204] A basis for speculation on the extent of the profits derived from the Siberian colony is provided by the following tabulation of the scarce data available and of estimates concerning the state of Siberian finances, which urgently need to be supplemented by further information still hidden in the archives of the Siberian Prikaz.

Before using the figures given in the table on the following page, meager as they are, certain precautions must be taken. First of all, it should be remembered that there is no indication whether the salaries of the voevodas—a considerable item—were included in the

[201] Ogloblin, I, 131; instructions to Verkhoturie, 1676, *A.I.*, V, 1; report from Verkhoturie, 1678, *A.I.*, V, 46–47.

[202] Ogloblin, IV, 113; instructions to Tobolsk, 1697, *P.S.Z.*, III, 357–358.

[203] Ogloblin, II, 26.

[204] Decree of 1697 and instructions to Tobolsk, 1697, *P.S.Z.*, III, 359, 383.

expenditures. Secondly, the expenditures show only money actually spent by the government during a specified year and do not take into account the money due to the serving men but not paid. The

SIBERIAN REVENUES AND EXPENDITURES

Year	Income in furs (rubles)	Money collected (rubles)	Expenditures (rubles)
1589.......	12,000[a]	......	......
1596.......	......	......	5,340[b]
1605.......	36,000[c]	......	......
1606–1624..	25,000–45,000[c]	......	......
1625–1634..	45,000–60,000[c]	......	......
1632.......	......	......	20,453[d]
1635.......	63,518	7,442	59,900[e]
1640.......	81,648	35,030	111,152[e]
1644.......	102,021	......	103,889[e]
1645–1655..	100,000–125,000[f]	......	......
1656–1679..	125,000–100,000[f]	......	......
1680.......	102,026[g]	......	......
1681.......	113,042[h]	......	......
1690.......	58,762[i]	......	......
1691.......	77,365	18,000 (*ca.*)	69,203[i]
1698.......	103,467	40,208	60,728[j]
1699.......	74,982	56,538	59,939[j]
1701.......	90,000 (*ca.*)	38,110 (*ca.*)[k]	
1706.......	145,440, total income in furs and money[k]		

a Fisher's estimate,"The Russian Fur Trade," p. 114.
b This amount represents only money sent from Russia, to supplement local collections in covering the expenditures. List of supplies and money sent to Siberia, 1596, *R.I.B.*, II, 132.
c Fisher's estimates, p. 114.
d This amount represents only money sent from Russia to supplement local collections in covering the expenditures. Instructions to Verkhoturie, 1632, *R.I.B.*, II, 509.
e Miliukov,"Gosudarstvennoe khoziaistvo . . . ," *Zh.M.N.P.*, CCLXXI, Oct., 1890, 345.
f Fisher's estimates, p. 114.
g Miliukov, p. 346.
h Ogloblin, IV, 161.
i *Ibid.*, IV, 113.
j Report of revenues and expenditures . . . in Siberia, 1698–1699, *R.I.B.*, VIII, 887–888.
k Miliukov, pp. 346–347.

payment of salaries in full, for instance, would increase the expenditures for 1698 and 1699 by 13,212 and 13,571 rubles respectively. Thus the expenditures, as shown in the table, do not give a true picture. On the other hand, the fur income is estimated in the table according to Siberian prices while at Moscow the prices were at least 20 per cent higher.[205] A proper correction would change the fur income for 1698 and 1699 from 103,467 and 74,982 rubles to approximately 125,000 and 90,000 rubles respectively.

Although the figures in this table are insufficient to make a definite, positive statement about the economic advantages derived by the government from Siberia, they throw doubt on the reliability of the evidence of Kotoshikhin, who wrote in 1666–1667 that the Siberian fur revenue of the state amounted at that time to 600,000 rubles.[206] This figure has been accepted in some investigations, one of which estimated that the fur income of the Muscovite state must have constituted more than one-fourth of the total income of the state.[207] Kotoshikhin himself, however, admitted that he could not trust his memory in this matter and merely made a tentative guess. Miliukov lowers the figure of the average income of the Siberian Prikaz to hardly more than 150,000 rubles,[208] and Fisher reduces the share of fur revenue in the state income to one-tenth.[209] The problem of exact financial returns from Siberia can be solved only by further archival research.

Although at present the lack of published sources prevents an accurate judgment of the profitableness of the Siberian enterprise, there is no doubt that the income from furs, collected in the form of iasak and customs duties, was alone sufficient to cover the costs of administration and still return a comfortable profit to the state— a profit further increased by other forms of state revenue derived from taxes and government business ventures. Moreover, the fur income was, as Fisher shows, a particularly useful form of wealth. The findings of this study further confirm conclusions that the conquest and occupation of Siberia more than rewarded the Muscovite government for its efforts.[210]

[205] Fisher, p. 114, n. 19.

[206] "Every year they send from Siberia ... sables, ... martens, ... [there follows enumeration of other furs]. It is impossible to write from memory [*Togo opisati ne v pamiat'*] what is the yearly value of this precious shipment, but I suppose [*chaiat'*] that it is worth more than 600,000 rubles." Kotoshikhin, p. 104.

[207] G. V. Vernadskii, "Protiv solntsa," *Russkaia mysl'*, January, 1914, p. 63.

[208] "The statement of Kotoshikhin [quoted above] ... should be recognized as completely wrong," Miliukov, *op. cit.*, CCLXXI, October, 1890, 346.

[209] Fisher, p. 122.

[210] Fisher, pp. 120–122.

CHAPTER VIII

GOVERNMENT COLONIZATION OF SIBERIA

AN OFT-QUOTED statement on Russian history is that of Kliuchevskii, who said that the history of Russia, from its beginning, has been the history of the colonization of the Russian people.[1] The absence of natural barriers in the Russian plain as well as the peculiar advantages offered for transportation by the river systems[2] simplified the migrations of even large groups of colonists. The rise of Moscow interfered with this process. The appearance of the unified Russian state, which grew out of a loose federation of principalities, effectively checked the greatest colonizer of the Russian northeast, namely, the republic of Novgorod. The consolidation of Russia, accompanied by the development of centralized administration and governmental control which penetrated into all activities of the Russian people, tended to stabilize the population. The opening up of Siberia, however, revived for more than a century the intensive colonizing advance of the Russians.

The initiators of the new wave of colonization were the adventurous fur traders who went into Siberia without any intention of settling there; rather, they expected to remain there only long enough to make a fortune and then to return with it to European Russia. But following closely upon these first immigrants came settlers who were to constitute a body of permanent colonists.

Monasteries, which during the earlier history of Russia had been active in leading and developing colonization in Europe,[3] appeared in a similar role at various places in Siberia. Merchants and businessmen found it profitable to establish themselves in Siberian towns. The bulk of the permanent Russian population in Siberia, however, was made up of peasants who went there to seek free land, to escape creditors and government regulations, to flee from the menace of servitude, and, in many cases, from the punishments of a severe Muscovite justice. Taken as a whole, during the first century of expansion the colonizing activities of the monks, business-

---

[1] V. O. Kliuchevskii, *Kurs russkoi istorii*, I, 24.

[2] R. J. Kerner, *The Urge to the Sea: The Course of Russian History*, passim. S. M. Solov'ev, *Istoriia Rossii*, Vol. I (I), pp. 12–28.

[3] Kerner, *op. cit.*; Kliuchevskii, *op. cit.*, II, 312–318, 323–337; S. F. Platonov, *Proshloe russkogo severa*, pp. 35–38.

men, and peasants, as private individuals, seem to have been much more extensive than the official colonization conducted by the government.[4]

The fact that there was considerable private colonization must be kept in mind for a proper understanding of the extent of government colonization and of the manner in which it was carried on. The government created several towns and ostrogs, which served as bases for the exploitation of the fur resources of the country. The building and maintenance of these towns involved, among others, problems of defense, communication, and supplies. To solve these problems the government needed more men than it alone could bring to Siberia. Consequently, a study of the colonizing efforts of the government will include the importation of government colonists and the utilization of different elements which on their own initiative made their way to Siberia.

Nonagricultural Colonization

One of the major problems which confronted the government in Siberia was the creation there of a military force. Because of the great distances between the Siberian and European towns, it became necessary to establish a permanent army in Siberia. In order to fulfill this need the government sent to Siberia numerous military colonists—the serving men. Although the chief officers among them were appointed to Siberia only for short terms, the rest of the serving men remained there for good. The composition and importance of this group of colonists has already been discussed above.[5]

Another important problem was the financial organization of Siberia. To collect its revenues, the government used principally serving men at first, but soon in addition to them it engaged in its financial service several businessmen in the capacity of golovas and tselovalniks. In the beginning of the century, probably because of the shortage of employees, the government on some occasions hastened the migration of this type of colonist. In 1600, for instance, 30 merchants from northern towns of European Russia were brought to be settled in Verkhoturie, as shown in their request for permission to leave their families behind until they

---

[4] N. M. Iadrintsev, *Sibir' kak koloniia,* p. 190.
[5] See chapter v.

became established in the new place.[6] But the extensive importation of businessmen was not necessary, inasmuch as a great many of them came to Siberia voluntarily.

As competitors in the quest for furs these representatives of the Russian seventeenth-century bourgeoisie caused some concern to the government. However, as shown in the preceding chapter, the government soon circumscribed private trade and made the merchants and other businessmen serve the interests of the state. In 1634, for example, out of 61 townsmen of Tobolsk 43 were more or less regularly employed by the government, while the remaining 18 were often used for various occasional commissions.[7] In 1641, in the same town, out of 56 townsmen 46 were assigned official duties for terms ranging from three months to ten years. The burden of these duties might have been responsible for the decrease of the number of townsmen.[8]

Agents of the church could not be dispensed with at a time when death without absolution meant the perdition of the soul, and when religious rites were closely interwoven with all the important events in a man's life. The necessity of satisfying the religious needs of its colonists forced the government to bring priests and monks to Siberia and to assist the founders of monasteries. A further discussion of the government activities in this respect, however, will be postponed until the next chapter which will take up in detail the relations between the state and the church in Siberia.

From the very beginning of the conquest the government needed skilled workers in Siberia, especially carpenters. Instructions to Pelym in 1597 and 1600 reveal the shortage of men skilled in boatbuilding, repairing firearms, and erecting houses and fortifications.[9] Originally the serving men carried on all the construction of towns and ostrogs, but this proved to be a burdensome duty and evoked so many complaints that the government began sending

---

[6] Instructions to Verkhoturie, 1600, *A.I.*, II, 27.

[7] In 1634, among 43 regularly employed townsmen, 14 golovas and sworn men handled money operations in connection with the local customhouse, the sable treasury, the archbishop's court, the jail, or were attached to storehouses of ammunition, grain, salt, and wine, 29 were commissioned to accompany shipments of money or act as government purchase agents outside of Tobolsk. N. N. Ogloblin, *Obozrenie stolbtsov* (cited hereafter as Ogloblin), III, 357–358.

[8] In 1641, 2 townsmen were employed in the customhouse in Tobolsk, 7 were sent as sworn men to Obdorsk, and 1 to Mangazeia, all serving for three years or more, 4 were sent as sworn men to Tiumen, Pelym, Turinsk, and Surgut respectively for one year. P. N. Butsinskii, *Zaselenie*, pp. 252–253.

[9] G. F. Mueller, *Opisanie*, p. 192; instructions to Pelym, 1597, *R.I.B.*, II, 139.

workers from Russia. In 1597, a request was made to the people of Perm to provide a number of carpenters, who were to be sent to Siberia.[10] In 1603 two parties of carpenters, each consisting of 80 men, and in 1609 a party of 50 more carpenters were sent to Verkhoturie.[11] In 1622 and 1623 the voevoda of Cherdyn had to send a total of 40 carpenters for the Siberian service.[12] This importation of skilled workers continued until the Siberian population had increased sufficiently and provided its own men for the needs of the government.

An early document illustrates how the government obtained men. In 1597 two officials, Golovin and Voieikov, came to Perm to engage workers in connection with the foundation of the new town of Verkhoturie. They were authorized to use for this purpose 300 rubles from the treasury of Perm. At first the two officials called for volunteers, but only a few consented to go, and these demanded higher wages than the officials were prepared to pay. Being in doubt, Golovin and Voieikov asked the government for additional money and further instructions. From Moscow they received a curt comment upon their inefficiency and the advice, in the absence of a sufficient number of volunteers, to impress the carpenters of the local population. Furthermore, the officials were instructed to pay wages according to the schedule sent from Moscow, regardless of whether or not the men considered the remuneration sufficient. Since the place where the carpenters were going was "new, empty, and distant, and to go without supplies might mean starvation," the payments (from .90 to 1.20 rubles) were to be made in advance.[13] The documents mention the importation of carpenters more often than that of other skilled workers, but in addition to them the government brought to Siberia men who had had experience in finding and refining metal ores, as well as blacksmiths, gunsmiths, and others.[14]

One of the most pressing problems facing the Muscovite government was that of the organization of the transportation service in Siberia. Travel there could be carried on only with great difficulty.

[10] Instructions about building of Verkhoturie, 1597, *R.I.B.*, II, 59.

[11] Instructions to Verkhoturie, 1603, *A.I.*, II, 54–55; instructions to Ustiug, 1609, A. M. Gnevushev, comp., *Akty vremeni pravleniia tsaria Vasiliia Shuiskago*, p. 39; tsar's message to Perm, 1609, *A.A.E.*, II, 198.

[12] Instructions to Cherdyn, 1622 and 1623, *A.I.*, III, 168, 176.

[13] Instructions on the building of Verkhoturie, 1597, *R.I.B.*, II, 57–61.

[14] Ogloblin, III, 82–83.

During the summer season traffic moved, for the most part, along the rivers and portages. Therefore, at various places along the water routes, facilities had to be provided for the construction and repair of boats; also means had to be found for transferring boats and their cargoes over portages and around rapids and shallow places. To a lesser degree horse-driven carts and wagons were used for summer travel and this method of transportation involved even more difficulties, because the roads were few and little more than trails; there were rivers to ford and swamps to cross. In winter, conditions were somewhat better since frozen rivers served as excellent highways for sleighs. For all these methods of transportation the employment of a considerable number of men was required. There was also a need for post stations where supplies for men and horses could be obtained and repairs, inevitable because of the condition of the roads, could be made.

Transportation service in Siberia was imposed upon the so-called *iamshchiks* (drivers). In the beginning of the conquest the Russians demanded that the natives assist in transportation. By 1600, however, a Russian *iam* (post station) was established in Epanchin (later called Turinsk) with 50 Russian iamshchiks. In 1601 another iam was established in Tiumen and organized in 50 *pais* (shares).[15] Each pai represented a unit operated either by a man with his family, or by a group of from 2 to 4 single men, who could take turns in performing the task. The iamshchiks of Tiumen were supposed to provide transportation from Tiumen to Tobolsk or Turinsk, or any other place which might be indicated in government orders. Each pai was to be provided with at least three good horses, sleighs for winter use, saddles and carts for the summer, and in addition rowboats, oars, ropes, and other equipment.[16]

The importance of the transportation service to the government may be judged by comparing the numbers of serving men and iamshchiks. According to the estimates of Slovtsov, in 1622 there were 6,500 serving men in Siberia and 1,000 iamshchiks; in 1662 there were 13,000 serving men in actual service or retired, whereas there were 3,000 iamshchiks.[17] The figures given by Slovtsov are

---

[15] G. F. Mueller, "Sibirskaia istoriia," *Ezh. soch.*, January, 1764, 9–10; instructions to Tiumen, 1600, *R.I.B.*, II, 66; Butsinskii, *op. cit.*, p. 85.

[16] Butsinskii, *op. cit.*, p. 89; report from Tiumen, 1630, *R.I.B.*, VIII, 640–641, 649.

[17] P. A. Slovtsov, *Istoricheskoe obozrenie*, I, 83–85.

not very reliable, but the relative ratio of the two groups is probably correct.

The service was open to all men, townsmen, and peasants; permission was readily granted even to streltsy and cossacks who wished to become iamshchiks.[18] For their service the iamshchiks received certain privileges, salaries, and land; the salaries, however, being paid not to the individual men but to each pai.[19] Nevertheless, the service was so hard that the government had difficulty in finding volunteers, and often had to impress any available men. Some of them were brought from Russia, as in 1635 when 50 iamshchiks were sent to Tobolsk from the region of Pomorie.[20] Others were enrolled from among Siberian colonists, as in Tiumen, where in 1630 the local voevoda put into the iamshchik service 100 local men who did not cultivate land of their own.[21]

As a partial solution of the problem of transportation, a special duty known as *sudovoe delo* (boat duty) was imposed not only upon iamshchiks, but upon the Siberian population in general, including serving men, townsmen, and peasants. This duty consisted of providing boats for governmental needs. Orders were given that a certain town and its uezd must either supply a fixed number of boats or provide carpenters to build them.[22] The government paid for the boats or labor, but never enough to cover the actual expenses of the colonists.[23]

The boats were continually needed for the transportation of grain, salt, ammunition, and men to Siberia. In 1596 a single caravan from Perm brought to Siberia 8,041 chets of rye flour, 1,258 chets of barley and 1,258 chets of dried oatmeal, or about 60,900 bushels of foodstuffs.[24] In 1640 the government transported to Siberia about 80,000 chets or 411,000 bushels of grain alone.[25] The food supplies from Perm, Viatka, Vym, Sol'-Vychegodsk, Velikii

---

[18] Instructions to Verkhoturie, 1600 and 1601, *A.I.*, II, 33–34.

[19] Report from Tiumen, 1630, *R.I.B.*, VIII, 641, 652; Ogloblin, I, 166.

[20] Instructions to Verkhoturie, 1635, *R.I.B.*, II, 761.

[21] Report from Tiumen, 1630, *R.I.B.*, VIII, 639–640; Butsinskii, *op. cit.*, p. 88.

[22] Butsinskii, *op. cit.*, pp. 272, 274.

[23] "We were paid 15 rubles for smaller boats and 25 for larger ones, while the smaller boats cost us 35–40 rubles and the larger boats 50–60 rubles. The voevoda also impressed ten carpenters, and we had to give them each 15–20 rubles above their wages." Complaint of the peasants of Turinsk, 1640, quoted by Butsinskii, *op. cit.*, p. 275.

[24] List of supplies sent to Siberia . . . , 1596, *R.I.B.*, II, 126–137.

[25] Butsinskii, *op. cit.*, p. 277.

Ustiug, and other places[26] were assembled at Verkhoturie. From there they had to be shipped further to various Siberian towns, and how to accomplish the task was always a serious problem for the voevoda of Verkhoturie. In 1639, 110 boats were built in this town, but in the following year the voevoda reported to Moscow that he needed many more in order to dispose of the large supplies of grain which he had on hand.[27]

Because of the inadequacies in the transportation system, the importation of grain from Russia was an expensive and difficult undertaking. For the population along the route of shipment it meant many hardships in connection with the *sudovoe delo* mentioned above. But, so long as the Siberian colonists did not raise enough grain, it had to be imported, especially in the early stages of the conquest when the failure of food supplies to arrive would mean starvation.[28] Thus, famine threatened Verkhoturie in 1602 and in 1608,[29] following the interruption of grain shipments from Russia. In 1610–1611 the civil war stopped the grain shipments from European towns again, and the government advised the voevoda of Verkhoturie to confiscate the private supplies of any merchant who might arrive there.[30]

If Verkhoturie, the town nearest Europe, suffered several food crises, one can only imagine what was being experienced in the rest of the Siberian towns. The "Time of Troubles" in European Russia was a period of starvation in Siberia, when the serving men in despair planned desertion and a wholesale exodus back to Russia.[31] To bring relief, the government in 1609 abrogated the

---

[26] Instructions to Verkhoturie, 1603, to Perm, 1607 and 1609, to Verkhoturie, 1612, to Cherdyn, 1622, *A.I.*, II, 54, 110, 313, 402–403; III, 168–169; instructions to Perm, 1609, *A.A.E.*, II, 198.

[27] Butsinskii, *op. cit.*, p. 277.

[28] G. V. Vernadskii, "Protiv solntsa," *Russkaia mysl'*, January, 1914, p. 65; Mueller, *Opisanie*, p. 192; report from Tobolsk, 1609, *A.I.*, II, 314.

[29] Instructions to Verkhoturie, 1603, *A.I.*, II, 54; Butsinskii, *op. cit.*, pp. 25–26.

[30] Instructions to Verkhoturie, 1612, *A.I.*, II, 337.

[31] "Before this time you have sent to all Siberian towns grain supplies which were to be used in payment of salaries to the serving men. [These supplies] came from Ustiug Velikii, Sol'-Vychegodskaia, Vym, Viatka, and Perm. At present supplies are not being sent . . . and the serving men are dying from starvation, and, because of famine, they want to desert the Siberian towns and ostrogs and to migrate, together with their wives and children, back to Russia." Report from Tobolsk, 1609, *A.I.*, II, 314.

"In the year 1609 many serving men left their families and ran away to Russia . . . and the remaining men in Tobolsk and other Siberian towns came to

former prohibition of private trade in grain in Siberia[32] and resorted to building state warehouses, where supplies of grain could be stored for emergencies.[33] The real solution of the problem upon which (to a considerable extent) depended the success of the entire Siberian enterprise, lay, of course, in developing local agriculture.

AGRICULTURAL COLONIZATION

Encouragement of agriculture.—The government was fully aware that it must make Siberia independent of imported grain. With this end in view, it tried to develop farming among different groups of the Siberian population. Some of the natives in Siberia were already familiar with the cultivation of land. Steps were taken to protect such agricultural practices as were in existence and to increase the number of native farmers. The voevodas were prohibited from distributing fields cultivated by the natives among the Russian colonists[34] and told to encourage the nonagricultural natives to settle as "tillers of the soil for the great sovereign." The natives had to deliver a part of their crops to the government, the quota being determined by the local voevodas.[35] This attempt to develop farming among the natives was not successful[36] as was pointed out in the chapter dealing with the administration of the natives.

In order to reduce the amount of grain imported for the payment of salaries, the government tried, whenever it was possible, to substitute for it grants of land to its serving men, iamshchiks, and other employees. It also encouraged farming among other colonists.[37] When a voevoda was appointed to build a new town, one of his first duties was to survey all the arable land nearby. The

us and asked for their salaries in money and grain, saying that if they got them, they would be ready to serve the sovereign unto death, but if salaries were not forthcoming, they would have to flee to Russia, away from privations and famine." Message from Tobolsk to Perm, 1610, *A.A.E.*, II, 261.

[32] Instructions to Perm, 1609, *A.A.E.*, II, 257.

[33] Mueller, *Opisanie*, 285; instructions to Verkhoturie, 1639, *A.I.*, III, 363.

[34] Instructions to Tiumen, 1600, *R.I.B.*, II, 66; instructions to Verkhoturie, 1599 and 1612, *A.I.*, II, 26, 407.

[35] Instructions to Pelym, 1594, *R.I.B.*, II, 111; instructions to Tiumen, 1630, *R.I.B.*, II, 647.

[36] Petition of natives of pelym, 1599, *R.I.B.*, II, 146; V. I. Ogorodnikov, "Russkaia gosudarstvennaia vlast' . . . ," pp. 80–81.

[37] "[The voevoda] must make a list of the serving men who want to settle here. . . . The landmarks must be fixed. . . . Land must be given to everybody, so in the future everybody will become a farmer, and there will be no need for the importation of grain." Instructions to Pelym, 1594, *R.I.B.*, II, 110; instructions to Tiumen, 1600, *R.I.B.*, II, 69.

best part of the land was set aside as the "sovereign's ploughing field," another part was assigned to the serving men, some land was given to the government-paid clergy and the rest was made open for other colonists.[38] There was no sale of public lands in Siberia; plenty of land was available, and the need of agricultural development was so great that the government welcomed anybody willing to become a farmer. The administration, however, exercised a certain discretion in determining the regions in which the colonists were to be settled and ruled that the cultivation of land was essential in establishing a claim of ownership.

As a result of such a policy, monasteries, as well as some serving men and private individuals, accumulated considerable tracts of land which they cultivated with the aid of hired labor—the serving men using also captured natives. Such landowners let out their land to poor peasants who lacked capital to start farms of their own. It was customary for the owner to provide the tenant with horses, seeds, and agricultural implements. The tenants often paid their rent with half of their produce, and usually they were called *polovniks* ("half" men).[39] The conditions of the contracts between polovniks and their masters varied with circumstances. Thus, in 1618, a polovnik hired by a former agent of a monastery was to clear a virgin plot of land for ploughing, to till this land, to build a house on it, and after eight years to turn everything over to the monastery with the exception of the cattle and grain.[40] In 1619 a polovnik employed by a serving man received land for ten years, and at the end of this term was supposed to receive one-half the property.[41] The use of serfs was very exceptional,[42] because of the ease with which the serfs could run away and settle elsewhere.[43]

At first the possession of land did not seem to involve any special obligations to the state, but in 1623–1624 the voevoda of Tobolsk, Suleshov, introduced regulations which exacted every tenth sheaf

---

[38] Instructions to Pelym, 1594, *R.I.B.*, II, 111.

[39] Ogloblin, I, 48, 50, 86, 295, 302–305, 361; Butsinskii, *op. cit.*, pp. 282–283.

[40] Ogloblin, I, 304.

[41] *Ibid.*, I, 302.

[42] *Ibid.*, I, 48; K. P. Mikhailov, "Krepostnichestvo v Sibiri," *Sibirskii sbornik*, Bk. I, p. 94.

[43] The serfs appeared in Siberia only after the middle of the eighteenth century, as a result of the growth of monastery estates, government and private factories and mills, and the conversion of the lands given to the government employees into regular *vótchinas* (hereditary estates). Slovtsov, *op. cit.*, II, 28; D. M. Golovachev, "Chastnoe zemlevladenie v Sibiri," *Sibirskie voprosy*, No. 1, p. 125; Mikhailov, p. 94.

from the harvest of the serving men. This law was accepted throughout Siberia and remained in force until the end of the century. Furthermore, those who cultivated more than 5 *desiatinas* (about 13½ acres) no longer received a grain salary from the government. Even those who cultivated smaller portions of land had their grain salary decreased, subject to the discretion of the local voevodas.[44] Later, when the government became aware that the serving men tended to accumulate large tracts of land for the purpose of speculation, it checked the acquisition of free land on the part of serving men by stipulating that they must cultivate all the lands they held, otherwise the lands would be confiscated and distributed among those who really needed them.[45] The clergy and townsmen, according to the regulations of Suleshov, had to turn over to the government "every fourth sheaf from a best crop, every fifth sheaf from an average crop, every sixth sheaf from a poor crop." In practice it meant that they had to deliver every fifth sheaf of their crop.[46]

Farming by peasants.—Although the government obtained a considerable amount of grain by encouraging agriculture among all classes of the Siberian population, the bulk of the locally raised food supplies was provided by the peasants, who either came to Siberia on their own initiative or were imported by the government. As has already been indicated, great numbers of peasants migrated voluntarily into the "Land of Promise." Most of them were *guliashchie liudi*, itinerant workers, poor peasants without capital or equipment to undertake independent farming.[47] Finding themselves without the means of existence, they were easily induced to work land for the government. Sometimes the government made use of these peasants even after they had found private employment. Thus in 1665, the voevoda of Tobolsk, Godunov, made "sovereign's tillers of the soil" of some peasants who held land from the local monastery.[48]

The enlisting officials ordinarily were instructed to ascertain that among the prospective government farmers there were no

---

[44] Butsinskii, *op. cit.*, p. 249; Ogloblin, I, 124.

[45] Instructions to Verkhoturie, 1625, *A.I.*, III, 226.

[46] Instructions to Kuznetsk, 1625, *A.I.*, III, 222; instructions to Tobolsk, 1697, *P.S.Z.*, III, 364; Slovtsov, *op. cit.*, I, 21.

[47] "These newly enlisted peasants [recruited from the guliashchie liudi, who came to Verkhoturie] are poor, without families, and have no agricultural implements." Instructions to Verkhoturie, 1632, *A.I.*, III, 315.

[48] Ogloblin, I, 28.

serfs or men in bondage.[49] It is more than doubtful, however, whether this requirement was strictly enforced when there was a shortage of men. Only at the end of the century were definite steps taken to prevent the migration of runaway peasants to Siberia by careful inspection of travelers at the Siberian border.[50]

Among the imported agricultural colonists, should also be mentioned the so-called *ssylnye* (exiles) composed of criminals and war prisoners. Butsinskii thought that between 1593 and 1645 at least 1,500 of them were sent to Siberia. During the years 1614–1624, for which the exact figures were available, he found that altogether 560 exiles arrived in Siberian towns; 169 of them, mostly foreigners, were enlisted as serving men and 348 were settled as farmers.[51]

A much larger group, forming the vast majority of the imported agricultural colonists, was composed of the regular peasants whom the government obtained chiefly from Perm and Pomorie,[52] the same regions which provided the greatest number of voluntary immigrants.[53] The government procured its prospective Siberian farmers in two ways: *po priboru*, by contract, and *po ukazu*, by order. When men were procured by contract, the local voevoda or special official contracting agents advertised the advantages of farming for the sovereign in Siberia and signed up volunteers. In procurement by order, usually in the absence of volunteers, a town or a district received a government notice with a definite quota of men which the community was to send to Siberia. The peasants in European Russia were organized for taxation in units called *sokhas*. The quota of required colonists was distributed among these units, and the colonists thus provided were called *pososhnye*. Sometimes the government obtained colonists by transferring to Siberia peasants from state villages, who were then known as *perevedentsy* (transferred).[54]

[49] Instructions to Verkhoturie, 1632, *A.I.*, III, 314.

[50] Instructions to Perm, Cherdyn, and Solikamsk, 1683, *P.S.Z.*, III, 551; instructions to Verkhoturie, 1683, *A.I.*, V, 175–176; instructions to Tobolsk, 1697, *P.S.Z.*, III, 361.

[51] Butsinskii, *op. cit.*, pp. 199, 203; Vernadskii, "Protiv solntsa," p. 66; instructions to Verkhoturie, 1633–1634, *R.I.B.*, II, 529–530.

[52] Instructions to Perm, 1609, *A.A.E.*, II, 246; Butsinskii, *op. cit.*, p. 231.

[53] Ogloblin, II, 49; Butsinskii, *op. cit.*, p. 231.

[54] Instructions for the building of Verkhoturie, 1597, *R.I.B.*, II, 57–61; instructions to Perm, 1609, *A.A.E.*, II, 246; Butsinskii, *op. cit.*, pp. 195–196; instructions to Cherdyn, 1634, *A.I.*, III, 325–336.

The peasants who moved to Siberia "by contract" usually entered into an agreement which stated how much land the peasant was to receive, how much he was to cultivate for the government or how much grain he was to deliver to the local treasury. The document further specified the government aid: transportation, money for traveling expenses, subsidy for starting a farm and the purchase of horses and necessary equipment, exemption from taxes, and government loans for a certain period of time. The peasant had to name some substantial persons who could give guarantees that he would fulfill his obligations.[55]

A few examples may illustrate government aid. In 1609 colonists from Perm were offered money to buy horses and to start farms; they were to be exempt from taxes for two years with the promise of further exemption if necessary.[56] The 217 guliashchie liudi, who in 1631 were placed on farms in Verkhoturie, were granted exemption from taxes for three years and received a subsidy of 3 rubles apiece and one-half ruble per *desiatina* (variable unit from 2.7 to 3.6 acres) of land which they undertook to cultivate. In addition to this, a fund of 704 rubles was used to loan them money for the purchase of horses. They were placed on land already cleared and under cultivation, replacing old colonists who were transferred to Tomsk.[57] A promyshlennik who had enlisted as a government peasant on the Lena River received a subsidy of 30 rubles, another 30 rubles as a loan, as well as seeds for planting. The colonists on the Lena River in general received a subsidy, a loan, seeds, and such implements as sickles, scythes, and ploughs.[58]

The *pososhnye* peasants were usually provided for by the communities from which they came. The government required that such peasants should have horses, cattle, domestic fowl, carts, and other equipment.[59] In 1590 the population of Sol Vychegodsk was asked to contribute 25 rubles for every family moving to Siberia. The community raised 110 rubles for each family. The government,

[55] Butsinskii, *op. cit.*, p. 259; instructions to Perm, 1609, *A.A.E.*, II, 246; instructions to Verkhoturie, 1621, *R.I.B.*, II, 383; report from Iakutsk, 1641, *D.A.I.*, II, 252.

[56] Instructions to Perm, 1609, *A.A.E.*, II, 246.

[57] Instructions to Verkhoturie, 1632, *A.I.*, III, 314–318.

[58] Report from Iakutsk, 1641, *D.A.I.*, II, 252–253.

[59] "Each man must have 3 good horses, 3 cows, 2 goats, 3 pigs, 5 sheep, 2 geese, 5 chickens, 2 ducks, grain supply for a year, a plough, a sleigh, a cart, and tools." Instructions to Sol Vychegodsk, 1590, quoted by Butsinskii, *op. cit.*, p. 195. Cf. instructions to Pelym, 1594, Mueller, *Opisanie*, p. 185, or *R.I.B.*, II, 110.

however, with its characteristic economy, thought the aid too generous, gave each family 50 rubles and kept the rest of the money for a similar occasion in the future.[60]

The *ssylnye*, the *perevedentsy*, and the peasants who became established in Siberia, and whom the government transferred later from one town ot another, also received assistance. For instance, in 1632, when 100 families were moved from Verkhoturie to Tomsk, each family received 10 rubles, as well as transportation and farming equipment.[61] But the methods of such transference were often utterly unsatisfactory. In 1697 a party of over 600 colonists was sent from Tobolsk to Nerchinsk; on the way one-fourth of them died from privations, some ran away, and only two-thirds of them reached their destination.[62]

Peasants' tenure of land.—The various government agricultural colonists, whether imported from Europe, transferred from other Siberian towns, or enlisted from the local guliashchie liudi, were settled on the land by the local voevodas. It has been mentioned above that the voevodas of new towns had to designate a certain section of land as "the sovereign's ploughing field." It was this land which the state peasants had to cultivate. Until the first quarter of the century it was customary to assign to a peasant a definite portion of the "sovereign's field" to be cultivated for the state, and, in addition, he was allowed to take as much unoccupied land as he could manage for his own use.[63] In other words, there was no relation between the size of the land cultivated for the state and the size of the peasant's own holdings.[64]

In 1623–1624 the voevoda of Tobolsk, Suleshov, prepared regulations for the manner in which the government peasants were to fulfill their obligations to the state. The land to be acquired by the peasants was divided into lots the size of which varied in different towns. For each such lot the peasant had to cultivate a given section

---

[60] Butsinskii, *op. cit.*, pp. 195–196.

[61] Instructions to Verkhoturie, 1632, *A.I.*, III, 314–318.

[62] "In the year 1697 the voevoda of Tobolsk informed us ... that a party of 626 men were sent from Tobolsk to Nerchinsk, under the command of Petr Meleshkin. ... When Meleshkin reached Nerchinsk, he reported that altogether 164 had died during the journey, 18 had run away and 41 had been left behind, as unfit to continue the journey ... the peasants testified that ... many of them had died as a result of flogging by Meleshkin." Instructions to Nerchinsk, 1701, *P.S.Z.*, IV, 144.

[63] According to the size of the family, capital, equipment.

[64] Butsinskii, *op. cit.*, pp. 258–259.

of government land. The ratio of the area a peasant cultivated for himself to that which he had to cultivate for the state varied also in different towns.[65] About the time of Suleshov in Verkhoturie the ratio was 5:0.8, in Turinsk and Tiumen, 5:1.125, in Tobolsk and Pelym, 5:0.9. In 1641 along the river Lena it was 5:0.5, in 1697 in Nerchinsk, 5:1.25.[66] The average ratio was five to one. The slight differences in ratios were due to local conditions, the quality of the soil, and the number of duties required of the peasants, as well as to the eagerness of local voevodas to win a reputation for efficiency.

The regulations of Suleshov established a new principle, namely that the size of a peasant's holding determined the amount of labor he owed to the state. Thus when the grain official, Baskakov, discovered that the Tiumen peasants had ploughed for themselves 201.5 desiatinas of land in excess of their allotments, he made them cultivate an additional 45 desiatinas for the government.[67]

Because of anxiety over the food problem in Siberia, government instructions to the voevodas stressed the necessity of increasing the cultivated area of state lands. That meant, of course, that the peasants would also be expected to cultivate more land for themselves. Increased grants of land, however, could hardly benefit those who were poor or had small families. New assignments of labor on the "sovereign's field" were usually followed by complaints from the peasants. Inhabitants of the village of Tagil' in the uezd of Verkhoturie, for instance, bitterly protested when during 1624–1633, 53 desiatinas were added to the 34 desiatinas which they had had to cultivate for the state in 1623. Butsinskii explains that during this period the number of households in this village had doubled because of the influx of new colonists, and therefore the number of workers correspondingly increased, thus justifying the enlarged demand for peasants' labor. Nevertheless, the older settlers were dissatisfied, because the newcomers were granted the usual exemptions and did not as yet contribute their share to the fulfillment of the village obligations to the state.[68]

The dissatisfaction and complaints of the peasants, coupled with the fact that some of them managed to add to their farms without assuming greater assignments of state land, led to the adoption of

[65] *Ibid.*, 259–260.
[66] *Ibid.;* report from Iakutsk, 1641, *D.A.I.*, III, 252; instructions to Nerchinsk, *P.S.Z.*, III, 238.
[67] Butsinskii, *op. cit.*, p. 262.
[68] *Ibid.*, p. 267.

a more practical method of securing grain for the state. Instead of cultivating the state land, peasants were asked to deliver a part of the harvest which they gathered on their own fields. The ruling which had already been applied to the clergy and townsmen was extended to the peasants; it stated that "every fourth sheaf from the best, every fifth sheaf from the average, every sixth sheaf from the poor crop" should go to the government.[69] Thus, for one-fifth of the labor, one-fifth of the produce was substituted. The peasants welcomed the change, as it seemed to promise more independence and relieved them from arbitrary additional assignments of labor on the state fields. The voevodas found the new arrangement satisfactory, as, on the whole, it brought, in the words of a voevoda of Tobolsk, "neither profit, nor deficit to the treasury."[70]

The grain delivered to the government under this system was called *obrok* and was collected from the peasants either by the local voevodas[71] or by special collectors sent from the chief town of the *razriad*.[72] Along the river Lena, where the government encountered difficulties in developing agriculture, the peasants delivered every tenth sheaf, or one-tenth of their produce.[73] This was in accordance with the former ratio of peasant and state lands, 5:0.5, which existed there before the introduction of obrok.[74] The obrok system was widely adopted, although in some places it was in operation side by side with cultivation of the "sovereign's field."[75] This combination was particularly common in remote regions where cultivation of state lands was practiced until the end of the century.[76]

The prevalent method of landholding among the peasants was based on private ownership, although some of the villagers had common ploughing fields. Private ownership was recognized in the regulations of Suleshov and in the contracts concluded with the individual settlers, rather than with the *mir* (community). Still the community ties were very strong. When local officials increased the cultivation of state land, they demanded an additional contribution of labor from the community as a whole. The share of the

---

[69] *Ibid.*, pp. 263–264.

[70] *Ibid.*, p. 115; Ogloblin, I, 308.

[71] Instructions to a serving man from Iakutsk, 1644, *D.A.I.*, II, 178–179.

[72] Instructions to Verkhoturie, 1648, *A.I.*, IV, 56, 119.

[73] Report from Iakutsk, 1641, *D.A.I.*, II, 252; instructions to a serving man from Iakutsk, 1644, *D.A.I.*, II, 178–179.

[74] Report from Iakutsk, 1641, *D.A.I.*, II, 252.

[75] Instructions to a serving man from Iakutsk, 1644, *D.A.I.*, II, 178–179.

[76] Instructions to Nerchinsk, 1697, *P.S.Z.*, III, 238.

peasants who died or ran away was imposed upon the remaining inhabitants of the village, who were bound to each other by a mutual guarantee. Nevertheless, even under such circumstances the peasant remained master of his own field, and responsibility for dead and fugitive peasants was usually removed upon report to Moscow.[77]

Absence of restrictions in the matter of acquiring land, together with governmental subsidies and loans, stimulated the development of considerable farming in Siberia. Not only did the government help the peasants to start their farms, but often it came to their aid in time of distress. Such assistance was usually the result of peasants' petitions to Moscow. When crops failed, the local administration was advised to distribute seeds for new planting; during epidemics among domestic animals, the voevodas received orders to provide horses or to loan money for their purchase. After the Kalmuck invasion of the Turinsk and Tiumen uezds in 1634, when several villages were burned down, cattle driven away, and the harvest destroyed, the government ordered the voevoda of Tobolsk to send considerable money for the relief and restoration of farms. In general, the Muscovite government on many occasions proved its interest in the welfare of agricultural colonists.[78]

The development of a prosperous farmer class, however, was hindered by the ambition of local administrators to make a reputation for efficiency. In attempting to increase the quantities of government food supplies, the voevodas imposed upon the peasants demands for grain delivery which could be met only with difficulty. In addition to that, they called upon the peasants to provide labor for different government enterprises without regard for weather, season, or detrimental effects on farm economy. The peasants of Turinsk, for instance, complained in 1632 that in the middle of the harvest, the voevodas, as soon as the government grain was delivered, made them repair the town jail, build fences, and construct the *gostinnyi dvor*. When the peasants were through with the work, they found the season was too advanced to attend to their crops. In another complaint the peasants of the same uezd told how they lost their horses, because the voevoda insisted on their bringing heavy timber to town during severe frosts for the building of a new ostrog. In most Siberian towns the peasants had to

[77] Butsinskii, *op. cit.*, pp. 35, 46, 69, 266–268.
[78] *Ibid.*, pp. 72, 265.

provide wood for the town, pick hops, prepare malt for government breweries, and catch fish for the officials, as well as perform many other odd jobs. The most burdensome of all was the *sudovoe delo*, mentioned above. In connection with it the voevodas developed quite a profitable business. For a bribe, they would allow regular carpenters to earn high wages in private employ and force inexperienced peasants to build government boats, while their farms suffered from neglect.[79]

VILLAGE ADMINISTRATION

To take charge of the administrative and judicial affairs in the village, the voevodas appointed special officials, the *prikashchiks*. These officials were usually chosen from the boiar sons or, at the end of the century, from local nobles who had become unfit to continue military service.[80] The voevodas issued instructions to them concerning the management of their respective villages. From these instructions it is possible to learn about their duties. In judicial matters a prikashchik could handle all petty cases, but he had to refer to the voevoda cases of murder, robbery, theft, claims involving more than 10 rubles, and cases dealing with the natives. He had also the police duties of keeping order, apprehending runaway peasants, and checking the documents of people passing through his village.[81] In this he was assisted by *starostas* (elders) and *desiatniks* (tithing men) elected by the peasants themselves.[82] Among the financial obligations of a prikashchik were included the collection of taxes in coöperation with the sworn men, supervision of the "sovereign's ploughing field," and the checking of the obrok delivered by the peasants. His special duty was to enlist new peasants and to provide assistance for them when they settled in his village.[83]

In their administrative methods the prikashchiks followed the

[79] *Ibid.*, pp. 271–272, 275–276. The voevoda of Tobolsk in 1640 reported that among the peasants whom he had impressed for the boat duty "some strangled themselves and some cut themselves to death." *Ibid.*, p. 276.

[80] Instructions to Tobolsk, 1697, *P.S.Z.*, III, 346; Ogloblin, III, 29. Ogloblin speaks of a pod'iachei, and Ogorodnikov of a peasant who were appointed as prikashchiks. Ogloblin, III, 29–30; Ogorodnikov, "Tuzemnoe i russkoe zemledelie na Amure," p. 73.

[81] Instructions to the prikashchik of the village of Aiat, 1685–1687, *A.I.*, V, 226–232.

[82] Instructions to Verkhoturie, 1632, *A.I.*, III, 316; Ogorodnikov, "Tuzemnoe i russkoe zemledelie na Amure," pp. 73–74.

[83] B. Chicherin, *Oblastnyia uchrezhdeniia ...*, pp. 381–383.

examples set by the voevodas. Like their superiors, they regarded their office as a financial opportunity, and sometimes became so hated for their injustices that peasants rioted and even murdered prikashchiks.[84] In the absence of complaints from the peasants, a prikashchik was granted a term of office of six or seven years, because as the government instructions explain, "when they are in office for only a short time, they try to get rich in a hurry and oppress the peasants."[85] The office of a prikashchik was regarded as a lucrative one, and in 1659 it was decided to discontinue the payment of their salaries.[86] Later, however, instructions mention a small salary "enough to keep him from starvation, but not enough to make him rich." The same instructions recommend that the voevodas show "no mercy" if they find a prikashchik guilty of extortion.[87]

Another village official was the *slobodchik,* a term used in the administration of the Russian villages in the sixteenth century. In Russia this officer was a village head, elected by the peasants. In Siberia he carried the some duties as a prikashchik, but instead of being the voevoda's appointee, he was a free man, a townsman or a peasant who had started a new village, and who, after it was organized, applied to the government for permission to take charge of it. He arranged the terms of the peasants' obligations to the government, as well as the privileges and exemptions they were to receive during the first few years.[88] The role of the slobodchiks in the history of peasant colonization can hardly be overestimated. According to Ogloblin, they founded as many villages as did the government itself.[89]

Among the Siberian population, the slobodchiks represent an interesting group of what in modern Russian terminology would be called *kulaks.* They were wealthy, enterprising peasants who usually combined the organization of agricultural settlements with moneylending, and kept the peasants of their village in a state of perpetual debt. Butsinskii mentions the history of one such slobodchik, Tsipania, who founded a village in the uezd of Mangazeia

[84] Butsinskii, *op. cit.,* p. 47; report from Tobolsk, 1626, *R.I.B.,* VIII, 388–399.

[85] Instructions to Tobolsk, 1697, *P.S.Z.,* III, 346, 371.

[86] Message from Tobolsk to Turinsk, 1659, *D.A.I.,* IV, 185.

[87] Instructions to Tobolsk, 1697, *P.S.Z.,* III, 361–362.

[88] Chicherin, pp. 383–384.

[89] Ogloblin, III, 145.

with sixteen households, and had enough money to spend 1,500 rubles for the building of a church.[90] In the territory of the river Lena there operated on a large scale a peasant Sverchkov and a merchant (formerly a peasant), the famous and versatile adventurer Erofei Khabarov, a warrior, an organizer, a speculator, and a moneylender.[91]

The Development of Agriculture in Siberia

The government used every means to make Siberia self-supporting. Until the end of the first quarter of the seventeenth century, however, there was a definite scarcity of grain in Siberia.[92] From then on there was a marked improvement. The outward sign of this change was the gradual reduction of the grain salary. For instance, in Verkhoturie in the year 1626 there were 162 men who received a grain salary. In 1633 their number decreased to 100, and in 1634 to 94.[93] Agriculture was taken up by everybody in this town, which "became depopulated in the summer time, because the serving men and townsmen attended to their ploughing fields."[94] In 1656, grain was so plentiful in Verkhoturie that the government asked for the payment of obrok in money instead of in grain.[95] The shipments of grain from European Russia gradually decreased,[96] and then, around 1683–1684, stopped altogether.[97] The data of the 1698–1699 census seem to indicate that the total amount of locally raised grain at the disposal of the voevodas was sufficient to meet the needs of the administration.[98]

However, the removal of the necessity of bringing grain from European Russia did not solve the Siberian food problem. There

[90] Butsinskii, *Mangazeia*, pp. 32–35; Ogloblin, III, 145.

[91] Petitions of Sverchkov and Khabarov, 1641, "Kolonial'naia politika," pp. 151–152; report from Iakutsk, 1641, *D.A.I.*, II, 252; Ogloblin, III, 146.

[92] Account of profitable revenues, compiled by the former voevoda Trubetskoi around 1628, quoted by Ogloblin, I, 27.

[93] Butsinskii, *Zaselenie*, p. 23; "There is enough grain in Verkhoturie to provide for its serving men," instructions to Verkhoturie, 1632, *A.I.*, III, 317.

[94] Voevoda's report, around 1654, Butsinskii, *Zaselenie*, p. 258.

[95] Instructions to Verkhoturie, 1656, *D.A.I.*, IV, 45.

[96] "In the future it will be easier for the people of Perm, since they will supply less food to Siberia with each coming year." Instructions to Cherdyn, 1622, *A.I.*, III, 159.

[97] I. V. Shcheglov, *Khronologicheskii perechen' vazhneishikh dannykh iz istorii Sibiri*, p. 132; A. A. Lappo-Danilevskii, "Organizatsiia priamogo oblozheniia," pp. 414–416; instructions to Verkhoturie, 1685, *A.I.*, V, 199.

[98] Account of revenues and expenditures ... in Siberia, 1698–1699, *R.I.B.*, VIII, 690–892.

were certain regions where agriculture was impossible, and the towns located there always depended on grain imported from other parts of Siberia. Chief among such towns were Mangazeia, Berezov, and Iakutsk.[99] The provisioning of Iakutsk was especially difficult. The grain transports from western Siberia (probably because the grain boats were large) went by a long route: Irtysh, Ob', Gulf of Ob', Gulf of Taz, Taz portage, Enisei, Upper Tunguzka and Angara, portage of Ilim, Lena. The dangerous storms in the Gulf of Ob' and the currents and rapids in the rivers Enisei and Angara continually threatened the safety of the cargoes and the lives of the crews, and the failure of the grain caravan to arrive meant starvation for eastern Siberia.[100]

In view of the hazards of transportation, the government insisted that the Iakutsk voevodas find arable lands along the river Lena and settle colonists there.[101] The voevodas followed the instructions and made the terms for the Lena settlers considerably easier than were the terms in other parts of Siberia.[102] Still, colonization in the uezd of Iakutsk progressed very slowly, partly because the available free men preferred to hunt sables. In 1679 the shortage of grain in Iakutsk was so serious that the government ordered the voevoda of Iakutsk to spend 3,000 rubles for purchasing grain, in addition to shipments he was to receive from Eniseisk.[103] In 1698 Iakutsk needed 2,590 *chets*[104] of grain, of which only 661 were raised locally. In 1699, to satisfy the demand for 2,979 chets, the officials had only 455 chets at their disposal.[105]

Because of the difficulties with food in eastern Siberia it is easy to imagine the effect produced on the administration by the first

[99] *Ibid.*, VIII, 837–838, 855–858, 799–804; instructions to Berezov, 1652, *D.A.I.*, III, 375–376.

[100] Ogorodnikov, "Tuzemnoe i russkoe zemledelie na Amure," p. 8.

[101] "The voevoda and diak must survey without delay lands along the Lena River and other rivers with the purpose of establishing farms near the ostrog ... they must put on the land peasants who will cultivate enough grain for the serving men on the Lena ... so it will not be necessary to send grain there from Tobolsk and Eniseisk. ... They must invite free peasants and guliashchie liudi and give them subsidies, exemptions, and loans, the amount of subsidy according to the former instructions or the need." Instructions to Iakutsk, 1644, 1651, 1658, *D.A.I.*, II, 269, III, 303, IV, 105.

[102] Report from Iakutsk, 1641, *D.A.I.*, II, 252–253; instructions to a serving man from Iakutsk, 1644, *D.A.I.*, II, 178–179; survey of lands in the Lena basin, 1640–1641, *D.A.I.*, II, 246–248; report from Iakutsk, 1653, *D.A.I.*, III, 402.

[103] Instructions to Iakutsk, 1679, *D.A.I.*, VIII, 157.

[104] One *chet* is equal to 5.77 bushels.

[105] Account of revenues and expenditures ... in Siberia, 1698–1699, *R.I.B.*, VIII, 799–804.

information about the existence of agriculture on the Amur River.[106] It seemed that the half-century-long struggle with food scarcity in Siberia would be settled forever, especially when the Baikal and Irkutsk regions were so conveniently connected by a number of navigable rivers. Following the report of Poiarkov about the wealth of the Amur region,[107] Frantsbekov, the voevoda of Iakutsk, was the first to suggest to the government that the Amur basin could be used as a food base for the whole of eastern Siberia.[108]

The Russian occupation of the Amur, however, ended in fiasco, and, by the treaty of Nerchinsk, in 1689 this region was lost. Further Russian expansion to Kamchatka and Alaska made the food problem even more pressing than before. In their attempt to find food, the Russians in the beginning of the nineteenth century penetrated into distant California, but the eventual solution of the problem was not reached until the middle of the nineteenth century when Murav'ev-Amurskii once more obtained the Amur Valley for Russia.[109]

---

[106] G. F. Mueller, "Istoriia o stranakh pri reke Amure lezhashchikh," *Ezh. soch.*, August, 1757, II, 102; Ogorodnikov, "Tuzemnoe i russkoe zemledelie na Amure," p. 9; survey of lands in the Lena basin, 1640–1641, *D.A.I.*, II, 246–248; reports of serving men, 1641 and 1652, *D.A.I.*, II, 251, III, 372.

[107] Documents about the journey of Poiarkov, 1646, *D.A.I.*, III, 56.

[108] Report from Iakutsk, 1651, *A.I.*, IV, 76.

[109] R. J. Kerner, "Russian Expansion to America," pp. 111–112, 114–115.

CHAPTER IX

STATE AND CHURCH

ENCOURAGEMENT OF CHURCH ACTIVITIES BY THE STATE

Subordinate position of the church.—The church began to play a prominent part in the development of the Siberian administration only after the establishment of the Siberian archbishopric in 1621. Until that time the Siberian clergy was under the ecclesiastical jurisdiction of the archbishop of Vologda and Perm Velikaia.[1] The latter was too far away from the Siberian towns to exercise any effective control, and the early activities of the church in Siberia were directed almost exclusively by the secular authorities.

The clergy appeared in Siberia from the beginning of its conquest. Even Ermak is supposed to have had priests and a portable chapel in his train.[2] Whenever a new town was established in Siberia, a church was among the first buildings to be erected, and the voevodas had instructions to build the church within the walls of the ostrog for its better protection.[3] The first two churches in Siberia were those built in Tiumen in 1586, the year of the founding of the town,[4] to which the government added a third and larger one in 1600.[5] At Tobolsk the pismennyi golova Chulkov erected a temporary church in 1587, as soon as the town had been established. This church was constructed of timber procured by dismantling the boats which transported his army of 500 men. In the following year another church was built in Tobolsk.[6] At Pelym the voevoda Gorchakov erected a church in 1595, two years after the founding of the town.[7] In Verkhoturie the church was built in 1598, at the same time as was the town.[8] By 1621 churches had been built in Turinsk (1601), Berezov (1605), Mangazeia (1603), Narym, Tara, Surgut, Ketsk, Tomsk, Kuznetsk, and Eniseisk.[9] This church-

[1] N. Abramov, "Materialy . . . ," *Zh.M.N.P.*, Vol. LXXXI (1854), Pt. 3, pp. 3, 19.
[2] *Ibid.*, p. 16.
[3] Instructions to Tobolsk, 1611, G. F. Mueller, *Opisanie*, p. 253.
[4] G. F. Mueller, "Sibirskaia istoriia," *Ezh. soch.*, January, 1764, p. 9.
[5] Instructions to Tiumen, 1600, *R.I.B.*, II, 75–76.
[6] Rukopisnaia rukopis (Chronicle in manuscript) quoted by Abramov, p. 17.
[7] Abramov, *loc. cit.*
[8] Mueller, *Opisanie*, p. 271.
[9] Abramov, p. 17; Mueller, *Opisanie*, p. 314; instructions to Tiumen, 1600, *R.I.B.*, II, 72–73; V. K. Andrievich, *Istoriia Sibiri*, 1, 188–190.

building activity of the government was the result of the genuine needs of its serving men, as is clearly evidenced by the petitions which they sent to the government from the towns where churches were as yet lacking. The government usually responded quickly to such petitions by sending instructions to the local officials with orders to build churches where they were requested.[10]

All the necessary church equipment, such as bells, icons, robes for the priests, service books, and wine for the sacraments, were also furnished by the government. This equipment usually was sent from Perm, Kazan, or Moscow.[11] The government, likewise, provided for the maintenance of the clergy. The priests and the minor unordained clerics received a *ruga* (salary) in the form of money and foodstuffs (chiefly grain). The earlier documents show the yearly salaries of priests ranging from 6 to 10 rubles and from 7 to 9 chets (from 39 to 52 bushels, a chet being equal to 5.77 bushels) of grain. The minor officials received less—the *diachek* (sexton) in Tiumen, for instance, received every year 4 rubles in money and about 39 bushels of grain.[12]

The government was interested not only in churches, but in monasteries as well, although the latter often originated as a result of private enterprise. According to Andrievich, the earliest monasteries were built in Tobolsk (1588), in Turinsk and Verkhoturie (both in 1604), and in Tiumen (1616).[13] The participation of the government in the founding of monasteries may be illustrated by the history of the monastery in Verkhoturie. From here in 1602 the monk Iona sent a petition to the Tsar Boris, stating that he had made a vow to build a monastery but the local voevodas refused him lumber. The tsar instructed the voevodas to satisfy Iona. The voevodas gave lumber, but as a loan. In 1604 the tsar canceled the debt and granted more building material in answer to Iona's second petition. The same year Iona went to Moscow and obtained a salary of 8 rubles a year for himself and 3 rubles a year for his diachek. Instead of the grain salary he received land for the monastery.[14]

---

[10] Instructions to Tiumen, 1600, *R.I.B.*, II, 72–73; instructions to Tiumen, 1601, Mueller, *Opisanie*, pp. 287–288.

[11] Instructions to Tiumen, 1600, *R.I.B.*, II, 72–75; Mueller, *Opisanie*, p. 272; instructions to Perm, 1607, *A.I.*, II, 110.

[12] Instructions to Tiumen, 1600, *R.I.B.*, II, 72–73; instructions to Verkhoturie, 1601, *A.I.*, II, 34; instructions to Tiumen, 1601, Mueller, *Opisanie*, pp. 287–288; instructions to Tara, 1627, *R.I.B.*, VIII, 461.

[13] Andrievich, *op. cit.*, I, 183–185; Abramov, p. 18.

[14] P. N. Butsinskii, *Zaselenie*, pp. 20, 21; instructions to Verkhoturie, 1604, *A.I.*, II, 59.

It is easy to see why the government was so anxious to start and to assist the development of a church organization in Siberia. The absence of the church functions would have entirely upset the life of Siberian settlers. The clergy was needed to baptize the children, to perform marriages, and to give absolution to the dying. The monasteries were looked upon as natural and desirable places for the aged. In 1612 when the monastery of Tobolsk was transferred to another place, a petition by the monks asking for a grant of land was warmly supported by the local serving men.[15]

One of the reasons for the foundation of the monastery in Eniseisk in 1639 was to provide "for the crippled and aged . . . an asylum and a place of salvation of the soul in time of death."[16] Later, in 1680, after the government ordered the confiscation of some of the monastery lands, the serving men again presented a petition: "the *igumen* (abbot) and the founders of the Spasskii monastery pledged that they would admit into the orders the aged among us, and that they would take us until death." On account of the confiscation of lands the monastery refused to accept petitioners, because it had no means of providing them with "food and drink."[17] This petition illustrates how in the absence of any state aid to the sick or the aged, the charitable work of the monasteries was of great value.

Furthermore, the church played an important part as a colonizing agency. The monasteries were more than cultural and religious centers, for, owing to special privileges which they enjoyed, they could offer security and protection to the peasants; being exempt from taxation, they could lease their lands on comparatively easy terms. In this way the monasteries stabilized private colonization and, with the increase of their land possessions, they became instrumental in bringing new settlers. These additional colonists spread further the area of agricultural activity.[18]

The church also took part in important civic functions. The

---

[15] "Ataman Durynia and his comrades . . . who have suffered all kinds of privations in the service, present to the boiars their humble petition. The serving men ask the boiars to grant to the monastery the lands [there follows enumeration of lands desired] in consideration of their service and wounds, so as to provide them with a place where they may find a refuge in old age." Petition of the monks in Tobolsk and of the serving men, 1612, Butsinskii, *op. cit.*, 118–119.

[16] N. N. Ogloblin, *Obozrenie stolbtsov* (cited hereafter as Ogloblin), III, 298.

[17] Ogloblin, III, 298.

[18] Butsinskii, *op. cit.*, pp. 118–122, 124–126, 129, 135–136.

clergy administered the oath to the serving men, given either as a pledge of loyalty when a new tsar ascended the throne, or as a guarantee upon enlisting into the service that they would faithfully discharge their duties. Through its missionary activity the church aided the state in placating the Siberian natives, performing the functions of "a school of citizenship." Baptized natives were considered by the government as being on equal terms with Russians; the men were often enrolled as "serving men" (streltsy or cossacks); the women were encouraged to marry Russians, which, as we have seen, was a method of relieving the shortage of Russian women in Siberia.[19]

These services of the church were recognized by the Muscovite government. Unfortunately during the period known as the "Time of Troubles," Moscow was too busy to pay very much attention to Siberian affairs or to look after the welfare of the Siberian church. Around 1620 life became more settled and the government began to take notice of the disquieting reports from Siberia concerning the abuses of the local administration and the demoralization of the Siberian churchmen. Apparently the Siberian clergy was not discharging its duties properly, either through its own fault or because the local officials interfered. Under the circumstances the interests of both church and state pointed toward the establishment of a special archbishopric in Siberia with its seat in Tobolsk. The church naturally preferred an active control over the Siberian clergy through its local archbishop to a merely fictitious one by the distant archbishop in Vologda. The state wished to see the Siberian church administration in better shape and to use the archbishop as the "sovereign's eye" over the secular authorities. With the interests of church and state thus concurring, the question was settled in 1620, and in 1621 the first Siberian archbishop, Kiprian, arrived in Tobolsk.[20]

The establishment of the Siberian archbishopric.—Upon his arrival Kiprian found the local churchmen insufficient in number, largely illiterate, and completely dominated by the voevodas. The latter treated the clergy with disrespect and often forced them to act as clerks or grain collectors, "while the churches were closed,

---

[19] Instructions to Verkhoturie, 1603, *A.I.*, II, 56; instructions to Verkhoturie, 1615, *A.I.*, III, 40; report of the voevoda of Kuznetsk, 1627, *R.I.B.*, VIII, 467–468; instructions to Tobolsk, 1632, *A.I.*, III, 314.

[20] Abramov, p. 20; Ogloblin, II, 18.

infants remained without baptism, and people died without absolution."[21] In the monasteries, affairs were even worse. In Turinsk,
for instance, the monks and the nuns lived together in the same
monastery.[22] A vivid picture of conditions then found in Siberia is
described in a message written by the patriarch Filaret, who contended that Kiprian was too slow in correcting the evils prevailing
in Siberia.[23]

The organization of the Siberian church and the improvement of
the low moral standards in Siberia, as described in the patriarch's
message, was not an easy task, nor could it be accomplished by
the efforts of one man. Accordingly, a number of ecclesiastics were
sent with Kiprian to assist him in his work. But, instead of co-
operating, the members of his staff were among the first to defy the
orders of the archbishop. In 1622 Kiprian reported their disobedience in his letter to the Tsar Mikhail Fedorovich and the
"holy" patriarch Filaret.[24] In another letter of the same year
Kiprian informed the authorities in Moscow that these priests, dis-

---

[21] Complaint of Kiprian (*ca.* 1621–1624), quoted by Butsinskii, *op. cit.,*
pp. 189–190, 291–292; S. Prutchenko, *Sibirskiia okrainy,* I, 31–32.

[22] Abramov, p. 22.

[23] "Many men and women become monks and nuns while sick, and upon their
recovery return home and live as before. Many nuns keep their relations with
their former husbands and lovers and beget children.... The monks and the
nuns live together with laymen in ordinary houses and do not differ from
them....

"The serving men and settlers in Siberian towns do not live in accordance
with Christian customs.... They do not wear crosses, do not observe fast days.
... They eat and drink with pagans.... They live with Tatar, Ostiak, and Vogul
women ... and have children by them.

"Some serving men ... use their own wives as security in payment of debts
... and the creditors live with these women until their husbands have paid the
debts. If the payment is not made on time, the creditors sell these women for
debauchery or work.... The unprotected widows and girls, the wives of the
poor are taken by force and tricked into serfdom.... These women as well as
such women as were taken in pledge for debt, are sold into serfdom or married
off to other men. The Siberian priests do not prohibit such doings and marry
people not in accordance with the Christian custom.... The Siberian *prikaznye
liudi* who arrive in Moscow with the sable treasury lure many women and girls
to come along ... to Siberian towns. Then they keep the women as their concubines, or turn them into serfs, or sell them to Lithuanians, foreigners, and
Tatars.

"We are informed that there is in Siberia a charter signed by the diak Ondrei
which allows the Siberian men to bring women and girls from other towns ...
and these women cannot be taken away from them.... Order this charter to be
brought to you, and have it sent to us, to Moscow." Message of Filaret, 1622,
S.G.G.D., III, 246–247.

[24] "These priests, Ivan ... and his comrades, do not participate in the archbishop's service, they defy the archbishop himself, they complain and refuse
to accept the sovereign's salary in money and grain." Report of Kiprian, 1622,
Butsinskii, *op. cit.,* p. 186.

satisfied with their life in Siberia, had attempted to run away. They had been intercepted, however, and returned to Tobolsk. In answer to his reports, Kiprian received advice from Moscow to punish the offenders severely by sending them to remote towns.[25] The instructions were not carried out. The records show that the recalcitrant priests were still in Tobolsk during the next reign. Probably it would have been impossible to replace them, and the priests, fearing punishment, became reconciled to their fate.[26]

The reluctance on the part of the members of Kiprian's staff to remain in Siberia demonstrates that the position of the clergy there was none too enviable. That the difficulty was not merely a question of remuneration is shown by the fact that the clerics who came with Kiprian had relatively good salaries.[27] On such salaries it was possible to live well in Siberia at that time. They were equal to the salaries received by the serving men of the upper rank.[28]

The successors of Kiprian continued to have the problem of finding new priests for Siberia and of overcoming their desire to escape Siberian appointments. In the correspondence between the Tsar Mikhail Fedorovich and the archbishop Varlaam of Vologda, we find that in 1635 the tsar ordered Varlaam to find one archmandrite, five monks, and from ten to twelve priests for the Siberian churches and monasteries. They were to be "good men, of sound life, not drunkards." Varlaam reported that although local priests raised from 30 to 40 rubles to cover the traveling expenses of every priest, and the monasteries raised 20 rubles for every monk, still the local priests were afraid of the long journey and, if appointed, made efforts to run away. Then the tsar ordered a grant of assistance from the state to the amount of 40 rubles for every ordinary monk or priest. In addition to that the priests were to receive free transportation and free board on the journey to Siberia for themselves, for their families, and for their servants. The total of 60 rubles received by a common priest on this occasion was a very large sum for that time. It was only after such inducements that Varlaam succeeded in finding ten churchmen for Siberia, and six additional

---

[25] "Send to the remote towns of Siberia these loafers and miscreants in punishment for their rebellion and disobendence." Message to Kiprian, 1623. *Ibid.*, p. 187.

[26] *Ibid.*, pp. 186–187.

[27] The archpriest received 25 rubles and 60 chets of grain annually; the archdeacon 15 rubles and 36 chets of grain; the priests 10 rubles and 26 chets of grain each. *Ibid.*, p. 186.

[28] *Loc cit.*

priests were sent from Moscow.[29] In spite of the fact that the government was constantly sending numbers of priests to Siberia, there always seemed to be a shortage of them, and in 1638 we find again the complaints of the archbishop Nektarii: "We greatly need ordained priests in Siberia; there is only one monk in Tobolsk who is an ordained priest . . . and in Mangazeia, Pelym, Kuznetsk, and in new monasteries there is not a single ordained monk, so that those who wish to become monks are unable to take orders." Reports like this are very numerous.[30]

The Siberian hierarchs were themselves somewhat responsible for the desire of the clergy to leave Siberia. With every new archbishop there were new clerics brought from Russia. Sometimes the archbishops were too partial to their own men at the expense of the staff of their predecessors. For instance, when the archbishop Makarii arrived at Tobolsk to replace Kiprian, the former treasurer of Kiprian as well as some of the boiar sons who served under Kiprian sent a petition to Moscow, asking permission to return to Russia. As the reason for their request they reported that Makarii molested them and refused to pay the salaries due them.[31]

The scarcity of priests made the enforcement of discipline among them much more difficult. Some of the most conspicuous evils were stopped by Kiprian when he separated monks from nuns in the monasteries of Tobolsk and Turinsk.[32] But the general moral standards of the Siberian clergy remained a matter of serious concern to the archbishops. The complaint of Simeon in 1653 that some clerics "do not observe dignity, drink, do not conduct services properly," was typical of the situation.[33]

Growth in importance of the church.—In order to meet successfully the difficult task of reforming the Siberian church, Kiprian tried from the very beginning of his activity as archbishop to raise the Siberian archbishopric to the same height of spiritual prestige as was already enjoyed by the other archbishoprics. He hoped that the establishment of local Siberian shrines of worship and the setting up of local saints and local miracles would be an effective means toward this end. Kiprian started by bringing from Russia

[29] Instructions to Varlaam . . . , 1635, *R.I.B.*, II, 582–596; Butsinskii, *op. cit.*, pp. 187–188.

[30] Butsinskii, *op. cit.*, pp. 188–189.

[31] The petition of Savatei . . . , 1626, *R.I.B.*, VIII, 344–349.

[32] Abramov, p. 23; Butsinskii, *op. cit.*, p. 121.

[33] Instructions to Verkhoturie, 1643, *A.I.*, III, 381; Butsinskii, *op. cit.*, p. 293.

the relics of sixteen different saints.[34] During his second year of office Kiprian thought of making the buccaneering cossack, Ermak, who perished in the conquest of the Siberian khanate, a martyr for the Christian faith and a special patron of Siberia. That explains his interest in collecting material about Ermak and starting the Siberian chronicles. Hestitating to canonize Ermak and his companions on his own authority, Kiprian established a special solemn service in their honor. Through the efforts of the archbishop Nektarii the "glorification" of Ermak was recognized in 1635 by the tsar, the patriarch, and the church council.[35] The same religious policy, pursued by succeeding archbishops, led to the canonization of Vasilii of Mangazeia and other Siberian saints, and influenced the appearance of the miraculous Madonna of Abalak.[36]

In the spreading and strengthening of a network of churches and monasteries over Siberia, Kiprian and his successors saw another method of building up the prestige and influence of the archbishopric. Kiprian especially must be noted for his energy in increasing the number of monasteries and reorganizing the ones already in existence. Two monasteries on the river Neiva, one on the river Tagil, the monasteries of Tara and Eniseisk owe their origin to his efforts.

As has been seen from the message of Filaret, the position of women in Siberia was not enviable. The church was the only agency championing their cause, and Kiprian was the first of the hierarchs to provide refuge and protection for women by establishing women's monasteries in Eniseisk, Tiumen, and Verkhoturie. His successors continued his efforts in this respect. Soon after the departure of Kiprian another monastery for women was founded in Turinsk, in 1629 a monastery for women was built in Tobolsk, in 1650 two more monasteries made their appearance on the Iset River, in 1653 a monastery was founded on the Konda River, and in 1660 a monastery was built in Turukhansk.[37]

It is important to remember that the establishment of a new monastery often resulted from the private initiative of individual monks and nuns supported by the local population.[38] The arch-

---

[34] "Dopolneniia k dvortsovym razriadam," *Chteniia*, Part I, 1882, p. 237.

[35] S. V. Bakhrushin, *Ocherki po istorii kolonizatsii . . .* , pp. 4–5.

[36] Abramov, p. 27; I. V. Shcheglov, *Khronologicheskii perechen . . .* , pp. 62–63.

[37] Andrievich, *op. cit.*, I, 183–185; instructions to Verkhoturie, 1621, *A.I.*, III, 140–142.

[38] Instructions to Verkhoturie, 1621, *A.I.*, III, 140–142.

bishops, however, used at the outset to assume control over the affairs of the monastery. They immediately sent ordained monks for supervision and tried to help the new monasteries in every way. The new monasteries, in order to secure a firm financial basis, appealed to the government. The latter usually required the local voevodas to gather information on the origin and resources of the newly founded monastery and then instructed the voevodas to pay the monks' salaries and to grant them land. In some monasteries, salaries were assigned only to the head of the monastery and to his assistants, while the rest of the monks were supposed to make a living by the cultivation of land. In others, salaries were granted to every monk in the monastery. The annual salaries varied and were stated in the instructions. In 1645, in Verkhoturie the nuns received 2 rubles each. In 1689, in Selenginsk the head was paid 5 rubles, the priest 3 rubles, the deacon 2 rubles, and thirty-two monks received 1 ruble each. Earlier, documents of 1621 and 1627 show somewhat higher schedules. Perhaps the government became less generous in the course of time, or it is possible that the monks of the remote monasteries as a rule received lower salaries.[39]

Besides money, the monasteries, as has been indicated, also received land. Sometimes the instructions specified the exact lands to be granted,[40] whereas in others the voevodas were instructed to use their own judgment in determining the location and amount of land, so that "the monasteries shall not suffer from need." The decision of the voevodas, of course, had to be reported to Moscow.[41] In addition to the salaries and land, the government supplied church equipment and helped the monasteries in erecting and repairing their buildings.[42]

Further assistance from the government was given in the form of important privileges. Thus, by a charter granted in 1623 the peasants of the Uspenskii monastery in Tobolsk were freed from all obligations to the state treasury.[43] In the Nikolskii monastery in Verkhoturie the peasants who rented their land from the monastery as *polovniks* (paying one-half of their crop to the monastery) had

---

[39] Instructions to Verkhoturie, 1621, *A.I.*, III, 140–142; instructions to Tiumen, 1623, *R.I.B.*, III, 481–482; instructions to Verkhoturie, 1627, *A.I.*, III, 239; instructions to Selenginsk, 1689, *A.I.*, V, 312.

[40] Butsinskii, *op. cit.*, p. 119.

[41] Instructions to Verkhoturie, 1627, *A.I.*, III, 239–240.

[42] Instructions to Verkhoturie, 1645, *A.I.*, III, 407; instructions to Verkhoturie, 1651, *A.I.*, IV, 151–152; instructions to Selenginsk, 1689, *A.I.*, V, 312.

[43] Butsinskii, *op. cit.*, p. 119.

to deliver every fifth sheaf to the treasury, but the hired peasants who cultivated land for the monastery directly and who were old servants of the monastery were declared exempt from taxation "if such was the custom in Siberia."[44] The "if" points rather significantly to a lack of uniform practice.

BUSINESS ACTIVITIES OF THE CHURCH

The efforts of the Siberian archbishops and the generous policy of the government paved the way for the prosperity of the monasteries. The monks themselves soon developed excellent business ability and in a very short time were able to accumulate a great deal of land. This was done by different methods. Sometimes pious serving men, either persuaded by their spiritual fathers or on their own iniative, would make a gift of land to the monastery. The monks made such contributions—*vklady,* a condition for the later acceptance of the donors into the monastery. Some lands were purchased. With an increase in wealth the monastery began to issue loans to private individuals with land as *zaklad* (security), and an enormous amount of land fell into the hands of the monks by this method. On several occasions the monasteries did not even stop short of outright seizure of land both from Russians and natives, provided they could manage to do so.[45]

According to the regulations of the church councils, which will be discussed later, the monasteries were forbidden to acquire lands from sources other than the sovereign himself. Being aware of this rule, the monks, after every acquisition of land, used to send tearful petitions to the tsar, asking him to confirm their new possessions "so that they would not die in poverty, and the monastery would not be deserted."[46] Such petitions were often satisfied, giving the monks valid claims to the new property. Parallel with the growth of monastery lands went an increase in the number of monastery peasants who were either in a state of bondage or rented the monastery land as polovniks. According to Andrievich the monastery of Tobolsk in 1621 had 50 peasants, in 1642 it had 260 peasants, in 1660, 402 peasants, in 1760, 2,140 peasants.[47]

While the monasteries used the means described above to estab-

[44] Instructions to Verkhoturie, 1627, *A.I.,* III, 239–240.
[45] Butsinskii, *op. cit.,* p. 119; Ogloblin, III, 298; instructions to Verkhoturie, 1621, *A.I.,* III, 140; instructions to Tara, 1678, *P.S.Z.,* II, 176.
[46] Butsinskii, *op. cit.,* p. 120.
[47] *Ibid.,* p. 121; Andrievich, *op. cit.,* I, 188.

lish and enhance their prosperity, the archbishop's see, or so-called "House of St. Sofia" went even further afield for this purpose. The archbishop Kiprian laid the foundation for land ownership and peasant colonization by the see. Upon Kiprian's appointment the voevoda of Tobolsk ordered that there be delivered to the archbishop every year 1,236 chets of grain, 60 puds of honey, 100 buckets of strong wine, and 609.65 rubles in money. In 1622 Kiprian asked for a grant of land, and in response to his two petitions he received 200 desiatinas of cultivated land as well as meadows yielding every year 800 sheaves of hay. In 1623 Kiprian asked again for two more fields of 200 desiatinas each and received them from the Tsar Mikhail Fedorovich. The businesslike archbishop further acquired by gift or through purchase 44 desiatinas of cultivated land, meadows, and other holdings from the people of Tobolsk. He also established four villages near Tobolsk, and settled some peasants there. Altogether Kiprian left to his successor a substantial land estate, 68 peasants not including those in his own household, and 133 mortgage deeds payable in "money or grain."[48]

His successor, Makarii, collected on these mortgage deeds 1,405 rubles in money[49] and 211 chets of grain. Makarii did not increase the land; instead he erected a number of storehouses, barns and other useful buildings, and received a government subsidy to cover the expense incurred. He also filled the archbishop's possessions with settlers, leaving to the next archbishop 91 *pashennye* peasants (those who cultivated the land for the see) and 33 *obrochnye* peasants (those who paid rent for use of the land). Furthermore there were 14 men who bonded themselves to the archbishop and about 70 men of his own household: boiar sons, choristers, diaks and pod'iacheis, and servants.[50]

The next archbishop, Nektarii, (1636–1640) was a very capable manager. After his arrival he returned some runaway peasants and settled new ones on the church lands. His salary, however, was reduced from 609.65 rubles to 321.65 rubles. In 1638 the voevoda of Tobolsk received instructions to substitute money for the grain salary and in 1640 to stop even that. The latter instructions stated

---

[48] Butsinskii, *op. cit.*, pp. 122–124; instructions to Tiumen, 1621, *R.I.B.*, II, 387.

[49] Soon after his death, the government was able to borrow from his successor 2,000 rubles to pay salaries of the serving men. Ogloblin, IV, 19.

[50] Butsinskii, *op. cit.*, pp. 124–125; instructions to Tobolsk, 1626, *R.I.B.*, VIII, 424–425.

that "in the future the archbishop should not count on the sovereign's grain salary but should cultivate his own fields." Nektarii, realizing that these orders came not from the tsar but from the Siberian Prikaz, sent to the tsar two plaintive petitions. In one of them he complained that "he cannot cultivate the land, because he does not have enough peasants" and in another dated 1639, that the voevodas were cheating him when they paid money instead of grain. The voevodas estimated 1 chet of grain as being worth half a ruble, while the market price was 1.25 rubles. The tsar could not resist these petitions, and an order was issued to restore the grain salary, which was paid until 1642.

To illustrate what little truth there was in Nektarii's complaints, Butsinskii quotes the inventory of 1636 which shows 39,100 puds (688.4) tons of grain in the archbishop's storehouses, besides enormous quantities of other foodstuffs. Butsinskii remarks that the archbishop who talked about starvation not only had enough provisions for his men but also could have fed Ermak's whole army for two years. As to complaints of Nektarii that he did not get any grain from his lands, the books show that he received that year 4,535 puds of grain from only a single *sloboda* (village). Nektarii left to his successor 427 adult males under the "House of St. Sofia" and 18,125 puds of grain in storehouses.[51]

The successor to Nektarii, Gerasim (1640–1650), upon his departure from Moscow, received a loan of goods to the value of 69.78 rubles and 1,000 rubles in money. As soon as he arrived in Tobolsk he immediately asked that this loan be considered paid in compensation for the grain borrowed by the treasury from the archbishop Nektarii. This request was granted. Gerasim continued the practice of lachrimose petitions. In response to one of them the tsar extended to him the grain salary for three more years after 1642. In 1641 the monks of Tiumen monastery made a donation of 150 desiatinas to the archbishop's see, and Gerasim asked the tsar's permission to accept it. In Moscow this was interpreted as an attempt of the archbishop to seize monastery land. The petition was refused, and the voevoda in Tobolsk was instructed to prevent the change of ownership of this land. The instruction of 1643 further stated that "the voevoda must watch very carefully that no one makes any donations to the archbishop's see, and that the archbishop does not seize anybody's land in the future." Gerasim mean-

---

[51] Butsinskii, *op. cit.*, pp. 126–130.

while realizing a possible refusal hurried to put his settlers on the donated land and build a church there. Thus, when the unfavorable reply was received, Gerasim sent another pitiful petition stating that the settlements were already established and the churches were built, and once more asked permission to keep this land. This time the request was granted. In 1645 the grain salary was to be stopped. This gave Gerasim an excuse to ask for more land in 1644, and in spite of the previous decision not to increase the amount of the archbishop's land under any circumstances a new grant was made.[52] At the same time (December, 1644) the voevoda of Tobolsk again received instructions that "in the future" new appropriations of land by the church should be strictly forbidden.[53] Gerasim had already learned that such decrees remained dead letters, so immediately after the accession of Aleksei Mikhailovich to the throne, he sent another petition asking for more land. This was granted again, and the voevoda of Tobolsk received another instruction that "in the future . . ."[54]

The energy of the archbishops and the generosity of the tsars account for the fact that the archbishop Gerasim controlled thousands of desiatinas and 650 adult males. At that time the whole population of the Tobolsk region was composed of 2,330 Russian families.[55] The possessions of the archbishop's see and of the monasteries created a sort of state within the state. The government was concerned over the welfare of the church, but the excessive land appropriation by the church finally called for a change of attitude. It has already been indicated that in 1643, '44, and '45 the Siberian Prikaz tried to check the archbishop and the monasteries. But so far this policy had not been brought into execution and neither the monasteries nor the archbishops were seriously hampered in their activities, largely because of the benevolence of the pious tsars.

GOVERNMENT OPPOSITION TO THE ACQUISITIVENESS OF THE CHURCH

In 1649 a significant event took place in Moscow—the *Ulozhenie,* a code of laws, was compiled by the order of the tsar. This code

---

[52] *Ibid.,* p. 130.
[53] "In the future no lands, meadows . . . should be allowed to pass to the archbishop's see or to the monasteries from either Russians, or Tatars, or Ostiaks, and if after this decree any such transfer should take place, then the transferred land should be taken over by the great sovereign irrevocably and without compensation. The voevoda of Tobolsk and other voevodas must strictly observe this order." Butsinskii, *op. cit.,* p. 135.
[54] *Loc. cit.*   [55] Butsinskii, *op. cit.,* pp. 135–136.

definitely prohibited the bishops and monasteries from acquiring land, otherwise than from the sovereign himself.[56] The regulations of the church councils of 1551, 1573, 1581, and 1584 now became laws, thus settling a long-standing problem. It is very likely that the discussions and decisions of the compilers of the Ulozhenie had an effect upon the policy of the government in Siberia. At least after the middle of the century the opposition of the government to further expansion of church lands became much more vigorous. The instructions issued in 1678[57] are especially significant. They repeated the contents of the previous instructions of 1644, 1646, and 1662, and stressed that severe punishments were to be inflicted on those who either donated or mortgaged their land to the church. Furthermore, the Siberian hierarchs and the monasteries were prohibited from engaging peasants who had fled from the state lands, towns, or from private individuals. Reference was made to reports recently received in Moscow, according to which the metropolitan,[58] Kornilii, had seized fisheries and land from the natives and from the Russian serving men and peasants. The boiar son in the service of the archbishop mistreated natives, stole their hay, and carried away a native woman. The head of the monastery in Verkhoturie drove peasants from the land which had already been planted, and settled men from the monastery there.

The instructions recommended that the voevodas make a careful census of the possessions of the "House of St. Sofia" and of monasteries, investigate their policy with regard to the Russian settlers and the natives, and confiscate all land acquired by the church since 1659. The peasants who had settled on the church lands since 1659 were to be transferred to the "sovereign's fields." In order "to save the treasury from any deficit in the collection of either grain or iasak," the voevodas were further instructed to prevent in the future any possible molestation by the church officials of either Russians or natives. The iamshchiks were relieved from transporting church officials, who henceforth were to use horses belonging to the metropolitan or the monasteries.[59]

These instructions must have been followed fairly well. The petition of the Spasskii monastery in Eniseisk and the letter of the

---

[56] Ulozhenie, Article XVII, Part 42, *P.S.Z.*, I, 97.

[57] Result of the boiars' decision, 1676, *P.S.Z.*, II, 120.

[58] In 1668 the archbishops of Siberia were raised to the rank of metropolitan.

[59] Instructions to Turinsk, 1678, *P.S.Z.*, II, 175–178; see the same instructions to Kuznetsk, 1678, *A.I.*, V, 37–38, 48–50.

metropolitan Pavel indicate that in 1679 the voevodas took over cultivated lands, meadows, saltworks, and fisheries from the Spasskii monastery. The monks also had to surrender all legal title to these possessions. The petition begins with a story of past oppression at the hands of the voevodas. In 1642 the monastery received some lands by the sovereign's orders. When the monastery cleared them and made them tillable, the voevoda took these lands away for the state peasants. In 1648, acting on the sovereign's instructions, the voevoda assigned to the monastery new "wild" lands along the river Taseeva, together with saltworks. The instructions of 1678 demanded confiscation only of lands which the monasteries possessed without the sovereign's permission. But the voevoda Bariatinskii confiscated all lands of the monastery, even though the monastery owned them on the basis of sovereign's instructions and had a title to them based on *otvodnyia, dannyia, zakladnyia,* and *kupchiia* (grants, gifts, pledges, and purchases). The petition pleaded for permission to keep the lands. It admitted also that the monastery had 159 *vkladchiks* (donors) who were either in the sovereign's service or who paid taxes as townsmen or peasants, and who made their gifts voluntarily out of their own property. But the monastery had to take care of 45 *startsy* and 29 *beltsy,* and of the crippled and blind. The support of the vkladchiks alone was insufficient; the monastery was not receiving any sovereign's salary, and the confiscation of lands would result in the starvation of the "brothers" and the abandonment of the monastery.

The verdict of the Siberian Prikaz was to return to the Spasskii monastery the lands given to it by the orders of the sovereigns and by the voevodas' grants, and to allow the monastery to hold them until the census of the monastery lands, to be made by the census taker Artem Durnovo, was completed. The saltworks were also to be returned to the monastery because it did not get any subsidy. However, the lands given to the monastery by the serving men and by settlers as a *v zaklad* (pledge) or as *vklad* (gift), without permission of the great sovereign, must be returned to the sovereign, "because these allotments were given to them [the serving men] out of vacant lands in place of grain salary, on the basis of paying the fifth sheaf" and were still considered as state property.[60]

The opposition of the government to further acquisitions by the Siberian church, already apparent in the instructions of 1678,

---

[60] Ogloblin, III, 297–298.

became even more pronounced by the end of the century.[61] In 1695 there was the merchant Tomilov who donated his town property to the metropolitan Ignatii, to be used for works of charity. A local official attached this property. The metropolitan appealed to the tsar. In answer to his petition the government explained that no one had the right to make gifts of land to the church. Such gifts must be confiscated and turned over to the treasury.[62]

In order to overcome the reluctance of the government to see any further increase of church wealth, the Siberian hierarchs tried a policy more subtle than before. In 1696 the metropolitan Ignatii asked Peter I to grant to the "House of St. Sofia" a certain "small votchina" in place of the *ruga* (salary in money and grain) which had been assigned to him from the treasury. The metropolitan gave, as the reason for his request, his poverty and the delay in the delivery of the ruga. Concerning the "House of St. Sofia," Ignatii modestly admitted that it had only a little more than 300 peasant households under its control. According to the information of the Siberian Prikaz, however, this "little more" amounted to 125 households, making a total of 425 households with 852 male peasants.

The "small votchina" about which Ignatii inquired was composed of 485 households with a population of 1,372. In 1695 this votchina yielded an income of over 528 rubles to the treasury. Ignatii was receiving from the government about 518 rubles. It looked as though he had asked for an increase of 10 rubles, but in reality the transaction was to bring the metropolitan much greater profit. Ignatii knew that under proper management the "votchina" could probably double or triple the amount it had been yielding. Peter I in somewhat caustic terms refused to make the grant.[63]

In 1697 the financial activity of the church received another blow. At that time the government issued orders to the church hierarchs and to the monasteries forbidding construction of all but the most necessary buildings. The church was asked to send to Moscow regular detailed reports of its income in money and grain.[64]

[61] Although in 1684 the metropolitan Pavel acquired the new privilege of importing every year 200 rubles worth of goods without paying taxes. P. A. Slovtsov, *Istoricheskoe obozrenie Sibiri*, I, 156; decree of 1684, *P.S.Z.*, II, 626–627.

[62] Instructions to Verkhoturie, 1695, *A.I.*, V, 458–460.

[63] Ogloblin, III, 134–135.

[64] Instructions to metropolitans, 1697, *P.S.Z.*, III, 425.

In 1698 the government prohibited the foundation of new monasteries in Siberia without permission : "there are enough monasteries in Siberia for men and for women to take care of those who would like to take the vows."[65] In the same year government subsidies to some monasteries (as in Verkhoturie) were stopped.[66]

This brief survey of the growth of the church in Siberia seems to suggest that at first, especially during the time of the patriarch Filaret (1619–1633), the government was very active in supporting the church. The same attitude prevails to a lesser degree during the reign of the pious Aleksei Mikhailovich (1645–1676). The exaggerated economic aspirations of the Siberian church did not meet with approval but there was no serious interference with the church. However, during the reign of Aleksei Mikhailovich there was prepared the *Ulozhenie* limiting the growth of the church wealth; also the meeting of the Church Council of 1667 took place. This Council deposed the patriarch Nikon and definitely established the domination of the state over the church. As a result of these events, in the beginning of the reign of the next tsar, Fedor (1676–1682), the prohibitions against land ownership by the church were strictly enforced.[67] During the reign of Peter I, when the state pursued a definite policy of subjugating the church, an antagonistic attitude was adopted against the church in Siberia.

The Siberian church itself was largely to blame for the change of policy by the central government. The Siberian hierarchs served the church first and the state afterward. They developed vigorous methods of land seizure which interfered with government colonization. To make matters worse, the church was not scrupulous, taking lands by force from Russian settlers and from natives. Thus, it interfered with the organization of the food supply for the serving men, and, in its oppression of the natives, it affected the collection of the iasak. Another cause of dissatisfaction on the part of the state was the forced Christianization of the natives carried on by the church. There are several instructions extant in which the government prohibits baptism by force.[68] The government was

[65] Instructions to Siberian voevoda Glebov, 1698, *P.S.Z.*, III, 450.
[66] Instructions to Verkhoturie, 1698, *P.S.Z.*, III, 529–530.
[67] Several instructions of 1678.
[68] "If any of the natives should desire to be baptized into the orthodox Christian faith, then you are ordered to accept and baptize them. But you are prohibited from converting any native against his wish. You are ordered to make an inquiry among the newly converted as to whether they were free men or were

naturally anxious not to antagonize the natives. Forcible baptism was prohibited "so that the Siberian territory of the Lena should not become deserted," in the words of many instructions to Iakutsk. Apparently the government weakened its watchfulness over the welfare of the natives in the late 'nineties when the amount of iasak was on a decline. Many complaints dated from 1698–1699 are preserved in which the natives protest against conversion by force.[69]

There mght have been a difference of opinion between the church and the state as to what was of greater importance, the salvation of the natives' souls or the amount of iasak they paid into the treasury; but when it came to the question of the "old-believers," the church and the state were in complete harmony. In 1684, the government issued orders to burn any old-believers who failed to see the true light after the triple torture.[70] The churchmen gladly coöperated, and one of the Siberian metropolitans, Pavel, left in Siberia a particularly gruesome memory, for during his office (1678–1691) thousands of old-believers preferred to burn themselves rather than to submit to his prosecutions.[71]

CONFLICT BETWEEN LOCAL ECCLESIASTICAL AND CIVIL AUTHORITIES

Although the tension of the relations between the central government and the Siberian church became apparent only at the end of the century, the friction between the Siberian civic and ecclesiastical officials started from the moment the archbishopric was established.[72] The appearance of the powerful church dignitary in Tobolsk constituted an immediate threat to the tyrannical tendencies of the local Siberian administration. The original instructions to the first archbishop are not preserved,[73] but the message of

---

bought by anybody, whether they want to live with the metropolitan, or in monasteries, or whether they would enter into the service of the great sovereign. . . ." Instructions to Kuznetsk, 1625, *A.I.*, III, 221; instructions to Verkhoturie, 1632, *A.I.*, III, 314; instructions to Iakutsk, 1670, *A.I.*, IV, 449; instructions to the metropolitan Pavel, 1685, *P.S.Z.*, II, 662; instructions to Nerchinsk, 1696, *P.S.Z.*, III, 245; instructions to Tobolsk, 1697, *P.S.Z.*, III, 355–356.

[69] Ogloblin, III, 51; instructions to Tobolsk, 1697, *P.S.Z.*, III, 355.

[70] "About punishment of . . . heretics and seceders," 1684, *P.S.Z.*, II, 647.

[71] Shcheglov, pp. 127–128, 133, 135; Andrievich, *op. cit.*, II, 334–335.

[72] "There is no need to attach much weight to the letter of Fedor [voevoda of Kuznetsk] because he is quarreling with these priests." Annotation on the report from Kuznetsk, 1627, *R.I.B.*, VIII, 472.

[73] N. N. Ogloblin, "Delo . . . Simeona," *Russkaia starina*, LXXX (1893), 162.

the patriarch Filaret, quoted above, already strongly indicates that the government expected the archbishops to exercise a degree of supervision over the voevodas.[74] The instructions to the second archbishop, Makarii, establish more definitely the relationship between an archbishop and the local civil officials.[75]

In the language of the instructions, the voevodas now possessed in the person of an archbishop "an eye of the sovereign"[76] in Siberia. It is evident how unwelcome to the Siberian officials was the appointment of the Siberian hierarchs. The trouble started immediately after the arrival of Kiprian, who, assured of support in Moscow, complained about the voevoda of Tobolsk, M. Godunov. The government responded with the sending of a special *syshchik* (investigator), to look into the matter.[77]

As an archbishop, Kiprian had his own staff of diaks and boiar sons; he also held his own ecclesiastical court and employed special officials called *desiatilniks*. The archbishop's court had jurisdiction over cases involving the clergy or offenses against the church and canon law. Of the composition of the court we learn from a record of the case of the boiar Suleshov *vs.* the boiar son Nizovtsev. On this occasion the court consisted of the priest and the deacon of the cathedral church, two sacristans, the archbishop's treasurer, and a monk. In addition to these ecclesiastics the voevoda second in

---

[74] "The voevodas ... pay no attention to these evils ... and themselves take part in such doings. ... They also use violence and otherwise oppress the local merchants and other people as well as the Voguls, Tatars, and Ostiaks. The unfortunate people who have suffered ... have appealed to you ... and you do nothing ... tolerating the most repulsive deeds and acts of cruelty ... you resort to no punishment, either spiritual or corporal. ... The poor people have no protection against the criminal trespassers of the law, and you do not send any reports to us. ...

"You must order the boiar and the voevodas to assemble in the cathedral church where this message shall be read." Message of the patriarch Filaret, 1622, *S.G.G.D.*, II, 245–253.

[75] "The archbishop must hold a council with the boiar [chief voevoda], with the voevodas, and with the diaks about the great affairs of the state, unless these affairs concern murders. ... If the archbishop should hear about any misconduct ... on the part of the boiar himself, or of the voevodas, or the diaks, then the archbishop must admonish them, at first mildly, and then, if they should not listen, in strong terms. If the persuasion should have no effect, then the archbishop must write about this misconduct to the sovereign tsar and to his father, the patriarch. And should the archbishop hear about neglect of duties, or violence, or oppression, he should speak to the boiar, and the voevodas, and the diaks, twice and thrice, and, in case of disobedience, the archbishop should write to the sovereign." Instructions to Makarii, Ogloblin, "Delo ... Simeona," pp. 162–163.

[76] Ogloblin, III, 18.

[77] Bakhrushin, *op. cit.*, p. 4.

command in Tobolsk, two diaks, and a pismennyi golova were present.[78] The desiatilniks, until the end of the seventeenth century, were appointed from among boiar sons attached to the archbishop. They carried out his orders and the decisions of the court. They also checked the contributions of the churches to the archbishop's see, collected fees imposed by the ecclesiastical court, issued permissions to marry, and had some other duties.[79] To aid the ecclesiastical officials, the voevodas were supposed to appoint *pristavs*.[80]

The Siberian officials refused to coöperate with members of the ecclesiastical administration. Kiprian was forced to report this fact to Moscow:

> Sovereign, thy voevodas and prikaznye liudi interfere with our church affairs and courts.... They try and punish the members of the clergy, remove them from churches, take off their vestments, put them in jail, and flog them.[81]

The government replied with the following instructions:

> It has become known to us that serving men and others in the Siberian towns do not obey, in spiritual matters, our archbishop Kiprian and his desiatilniks; they do not wish to appear in the archbishop's court and they incite the prikaznye liudi and others to defy the archbishop, and you voevodas encourage them.... In the future, you should not interfere in the ecclesiastical matters of our archbishop Kiprian; you should restrain the serving men and others from lawlessness. Should anybody disobey the archbishop or his officials, you should impose the appropriate punishment, according to the guilt and to what the archbishop and his officials may write you.[82]

These instructions, however, remained only a dead letter for the voevodas and their prikaznye liudi. In the time of Kiprian and after, the desiatilniks of the archbishop complained that the prikaznye liudi protected offenders and prevented church-trials.

In turn the voevodas reported that the desiatilniks oppressed and annoyed the people of the towns and of the uezds, and accepted large bribes. Conflicts between the archbishop's men and the voevodas were common[83] because the jurisdiction of the desiatilniks was very wide. New controversies arose daily because the population was accustomed to going to the voevodas' court, a practice

---

[78] Rasprosnyia rechi, 1625, *R.I.B.*, VIII, 330–331.

[79] Case of desiatilnik..., 1642, *R.I.B.*, II, 1014–1015; messages of the metropolitan Ignatii, 1699, *A.I.*, V, 456, 532–533.

[80] B. Chicherin, *Oblastnyia uchrezhdeniia Rossii*, p. 107.

[81] Quoted by Butsinskii, *op. cit.*, pp. 189, 291–292; Prutchenko, pp. 31–32.

[82] Instructions to Verkhoturie, 1622, *A.I.*, III, 167–168.

[83] Message from the metropolitan..., 1691, *A.I.*, V, 362–363.

which was encouraged by the voevodas, who did not want to have their authority diminished. Kiprian in his messages to the voevodas tried to establish the line between the jurisdiction of the voevodas and that of the desiatilniks. He asked the voevodas not to interfere with the affairs of the desiatilniks, not to protect offenders, and to assist the desiatilniks in apprehending culprits.[84]

In practice everybody sought justice where it was most to his advantage: the plaintiff would present his case to the desiatilnik, the defendant would go to the voevoda. As a result there was unavoidable confusion, and Kiprian was unable to fulfill the task imposed upon him by the patriarch Filaret. Neither the desiatilniks nor the archbishop himself could do much without the coöperation of the secular administration. Thus, in 1623, the nuns of the monastery of Tiumen complained of their mother superior, who "did not live according to the vows." An important witness refused to appear before the desiatilnik. The latter asked the voevoda to put the recalcitrant witness in jail, but the voevoda refused to do so, thus ending the case. On the whole, the population hated the strict desiatilniks and continued to live as it had lived before.[85]

The supervisory functions of the archbishops also provided ample opportunity for conflict because the archbishops frequently interfered in matters of civil administration or made reports upon them to Moscow. The *otpiski* (reports) and *gramoty* (writings) of the church officials were similar in form to analogous documents of the voevodas, and they touched upon many aspects of the voevodas' activities. The Siberian archbishops and metropolitans not only were quite independent of the voevodas, but often were superior to them, even in the voevodas' administrative affairs. In general, during the seventeenth century, the high dignitaries of the church, sometimes voluntarily, but more often upon the demand of Moscow acted as "eyes of the sovereign." At times they were open in their criticisms of the civil administration, but, as a rule, they limited themselves to written reports to Moscow. The church documents of 1628 include the case of the insubordination of Semen Vasiliev Chaplin, pismennyi golova of Tobolsk, who was sent on a commission to Tomsk and departed from there to Moscow, without stopping to make a report to Tobolsk; his other various misde-

---

[84] Message of Kiprian to Mangazeia, 1624, quoted by Butsinskii, *op. cit.*, p. 290.
[85] *Ibid.*, pp. 289–290.

meanors are also listed. Another document describes the misconduct of the former voevoda of Eniseisk, Andrei Oshanin, and in the same year, 1628, Archbishop Makarii reports the smuggling of tobacco into Siberia by the prikaznye liudi and also describes their matrimonial abuses (they had been marrying in Russia and selling their wives to their comrades in Siberia). In its answer the government reaffirmed the prohibition of the use of tobacco and prescribed to the archbishop *sud i sysk* (conduct of the investigation and trial) in cases of immorality. Makarii again reported the misdemeanors of the voevoda of Eniseisk, Vasilii Argamakov, his associates, and serving men. Archbishop Simeon in 1655 reported disorders and great excitement in Tiumen, where the local voevoda would not let petitioners leave for Moscow. The archbishop issued passports to them from his own office.[86] Metropolitan Ignatii, satisfying the petition of merchants, ordered the customs head to remove the seals from the shops at the Irbitskaia fair.[87]

If such activity irritated the voevodas they could always retaliate by causing the archbishops trouble in matters concerning the allotment of new lands, payment of salaries, the taking of the census of the church lands, and in other ways. The mutual interference in each other's affairs caused continual clashes of authority. One of the most serious conflicts took place in 1661, when the archbishop Simeon had to leave for Moscow because of his trouble with the local voevodas.[88] In 1682 the metropolitan Pavel excommunicated one voevoda and publicly humiliated another.[89] The climax of the discord between the church and civil authorities came toward the end of the century. In reply to the report of the voevoda regarding the metropolitan Ignatii and his subordinates, the government enumerated misdemeanors of the church officials,[90] and ended

---

[86] Ogloblin, III, 20–21.

[87] Boiars's decision, 1695, *P.S.Z.*, III, 210.

[88] Ogloblin, "Delo ... Simeona," *passim;* Shcheglov, pp. 110–111; Ogloblin, III, 50–51.

[89] Shcheglov, pp. 129–132; see also the message of the metropolitan Pavel, 1691, *A.I.*, V, 362–363.

[90] "It became known to us that the metropolitan Ignatii excommunicated ... the voevodas Andrei Naryshkin and his son Andrei Naryshkin, together with their whole household. ... He closed the church which was attended by the voevodas and prikaznye liudi. ... He did not admit the voevodas to the cathedral church and had it closed. ... When the diak Aleksei Protopopov came to his *krestovaia palata* (chamber of the Holy Cross) to get a benediction, Ignatii ordered him locked up and wanted to disrobe and flog him. He cursed and denied admittance to the church to the diak Afonasii Gerasimov. ... He imposed a

with a demand for a vigorous investigation and a report. Meanwhile the metropolitan Ignatii was ordered not to employ boiar sons as desiatilniks, but to replace them with members of the clergy.

The church rendered very valuable service to the government in the occupation of Siberia and in organizing the administration. It satisfied the spiritual needs of the serving men and of the colonists; it helped to pacify natives by converting them to Christianity; it stabilized colonization through the establishment of monasteries and the building of churches; it played an important part in colonization by clearing and cultivating new lands and settling them; it restrained the abuses of the local administration by disciplining local officials and protesting against their actions as well as by reporting them to Moscow; it improved the social life by raising moral standards; it carried on the work of charity by taking care of the aged and crippled.

The government recognized the service of the church by lending financial aid in building churches and monasteries, by paying salaries to the clergy, by liberal grants of land, and by granting various privileges, such as exemption from taxes. It demanded from the local officials respect for the clergy and coöperation when force was needed to carry out the policies of the church. It took an active part in settling disorders within the church organization and especially in suppressing heretical old-believers who were the common foes of state and church. Nevertheless, the government did not give a free hand to the church, but kept it under supervision and control.

This was because certain activities of the church interfered with the plans of the government. The church developed an insatiable craving for land, which impeded government colonization, and owing to its privileged position it was able to offer to peasant

---

penalty of 100 rubles upon the boiar son of Tobolsk, Leontii Redrikov, and he took others to punish in his yard. All this was done without the permission or knowledge of the voevoda Andrei Naryshkin.

"In Tiumen the desiatilnik of the House of St. Sofia, the boiar son, Ivan Zakharov, is ruining, taxing, and greatly persecuting the people. He takes daughters and sisters from the men of all ranks and flogs and tortures them ... whether guilty or innocent, without anybody accusing them. He orders girls and widows to accuse some good and prosperous men of immorality and makes them accuse five men or more. Then he seizes these men and extorts from them 10 rubles and more, and after receiving the bribe, lets them free ... and he marries these girls to men, that nobody would let his daughter marry ... and some of the girls he sells in serfdom." Instructions to Tiumen, 1697, *D.A.I.*, XII, 391; instructions to Verkhoturie, 1698, *A.I.*, V, 495–496.

colonists more advantages than were offered on state-owned lands. The missionary zeal of the church obstructed the collection of the iasak, although the government looked favorably on voluntary conversion of the natives. The representatives of the church administration were often no better than the other officials when it came to corruption, bribery, extortion, and general misconduct.

In accordance with the Muscovite administrative practice, the church and the secular administration in Siberia were placed on a basis of mutual control and supervision. This peculiar situation, together with the reluctance to define clearly the sphere of action of each (another typical feature of the Muscovite administration) led to administrative confusion and to several conflicts between the churchmen and the local civil authorities.

CHAPTER X

GENERAL SURVEY OF THE SIBERIAN COLONIAL ADMINISTRATION

THE SIBERIAN colony represented a huge business enterprise on the part of the Muscovite government. The management of this enterprise was in the hands of the Siberian Prikaz, an institution headed by some exalted noble, but controlled by the Muscovite bureaucracy. Acting as business directors, the officials of this "Colonial Office" for the most part adopted deliberate and farsighted policies with respect to the colony, with the purpose of putting business on a solid basis. In order to insure the regular delivery of the iasak, they tried by various methods to win the goodwill of the natives and to protect them from oppression. Conversion to Christianity by force, and enslavement of the natives were forbidden, because such practices would affect the economic interests of the state. Likewise, in order to supply the colony with grain, the Siberian Prikaz recommended extensive peasant colonization and advanced liberal aid to the government colonists. This paternalistic attitude of the government, for obvious reasons, was not extended to its business rivals, the merchants and promyshlenniks.

As its local agents, the Siberian Prikaz used the voevodas and their associates. It must be remembered that in European Russia at the end of the sixteenth and the beginning of the seventeenth centuries a struggle took place between two privileged groups, the old feudal nobility and the new nobility which arose as a result of its service to the Muscovite tsar. This struggle manifested itself in the inauguration by Ivan IV of the system of political terror which exterminated many distinguished members of the old nobility, and in the events of the civil wars which raged all over Russia during the "Time of Troubles." When, finally, political equilibrium was more or less restored, Mikhail Fedorovich Romanov, the choice of the serving nobility, ascended the throne. Thereupon, this lesser nobility filled the principal positions both in the provincial and the colonial administrations, especially the offices of the voevodas.

Many representatives of this class may have been good warriors, but most of them were amateurs in administrative matters. Taking advantage of the inability of the voevodas to attend the technical details of their office, the Siberian Prikaz succeeded in introducing bureaucratic officials, the diaks and pod'iacheis s pripis'iu, as the voevodas' associates. Although these officials remained in the background, they exercised considerable influence and represented a step toward the bureaucratic administration of more modern times. Likewise, the most important financial functions were transferred to the customs heads and their sworn men, who were chosen from among middle class businessmen. The political significance of the introduction of these two elements will be explained later. Below the voevodas and their staff were numerous lesser officials, who have been described in previous chapters. It is significant, however, that within the Siberian administrative hierarchy the right to hold a post was determined by the affiliation of a candidate with a definite social order. This can be illustrated by the following table:

RELATION BETWEEN ADMINISTRATIVE RANK AND SOCIAL STATUS IN THE SIBERIAN ADMINISTRATIVE PERSONNEL

Administrative Rank	*Social Status*
Voevodas	Muscovite nobles
Diaks Pod'iacheis s pripis'iu	Bureaucratic officials of Muscovite prikazes
Pismennye golovas	Muscovite and provincial nobles
Commissioned officers Commandants of ostrogs	Boiar sons, later also Siberian nobles
Customs heads	Prominent businessmen
Noncommissioned officers	Serving men of higher type
Sworn men	Small businessmen
Ordinary pod'iacheis Serving men Iamshchiks	Various free men of lower class

In European Russia the government was liquidating political feudalism, but it left intact its social and economic features, which even became intensified. The landed estates of the pomeshchiks were increasing in size and becoming hereditary votchinas, while free peasants rapidly disappeared, becoming serfs. These particular features did not develop in Siberia, because the government needed peasants for its own grain fields and because frontier conditions made escape from serfdom easy. In the absence of serf labor, the noblemen were not anxious to acquire estates in Siberia, and preferred to return to Russia when their term of office had expired. Only the church possessed extensive tracts of land in Siberia, but, as has previously been shown, its appetite was checked.

With the exception of serfdom, the feudal class differentiation was preserved in Siberia, partly because a wholesome respect for one's social superiors was regarded as a check upon anarchical elements, especially the cossacks, but mostly because the government found it convenient to distribute different duties and services among definite social groups. An attempt to shift from one social group to another was usually looked upon as an attempt to escape one's responsibilities and obligations to the state. It has been shown above that the government demoted cossacks who were made boiar sons, or returned to their fields peasants who enlisted as serving men. In order to keep men within their own station, the government insisted on a mutual pledge and mutual responsibility whenever serving men were enlisted, iamshchiks engaged, or peasants settled in their villages.

Nevertheless, the Siberian class structure was not nearly so rigid as it was in European Russia. At the top there was still a large gap between the Muscovite noble, the voevoda, and the petty nobles, the boiar sons,[1] but at the bottom the distinctions were less sharp and a shifting from one social group to another was made possible whenever such a change was in the interest of the government. Streltsy were merged with cossacks; serving men, townsmen, and peasants were allowed to become iamshchiks, and any of the lower offices were open to the guliashchie liudi, who themselves were a rather ill-assorted group. Sometimes there was even a transfer from the nonprivileged to the privileged group, and some of the serving men who were raised to the rank of boiar sons remained in this station.

Although the social position of the serving nobility was well established at the top of the administrative ladder in Siberia, its political aspirations there were effectively checked. After all, the new aristocracy, which now also included many absorbed members of the old nobility, was not different in its general tendencies from

---

[1] For an illustration, see the case of the boiar Suleshov *vs.* the boiar son Nizovtsev, 1625, *R.I.B.*, VIII, 327–331, also the petitions about "blemished honor," N. N. Ogloblin, *Obozrenie stolbtsov* (cited hereafter as Ogloblin), III, 89–90.

the class it displaced. As likely as not it was ready to revive the old political feudalism. The Siberian Prikaz, however, took steps to prevent any such possibility in Siberia, even if this meant inefficiency and administrative confusion. In Siberia as a whole, the establishment of strong local administrative centers was avoided. In the organization of a single town, the concentration of authority in the hands of a single voevoda was prevented by a diak, whose consent was necessary in administrative decisions, and by customs officials, who kept the voevoda from sharing in the state revenues. Incidentally, this policy of the Siberian Prikaz discouraged administrative initiative among the Siberian voevodas.

With the outlet for their political ambitions thus closed, the Siberian voevodas sought compensation in the revival of the time-honored practice of kormlenie. In 1652, for instance, the investigation of the activities of the former voevoda of Iakutsk, Frantsbekov, disclosed that he had accumulated an enormous fortune while in office. The investigator attached the voevoda's furs, which were worth 2,123 rubles, and his cash to the amount of 3,855.84 rubles. In addition to this, the local people owed the voevoda 6,763 rubles (including 1,363.76 rubles which Frantsbekov had loaned to Erofei Khabarov). The Prikaz ordered the confiscation of most of Frantsbekov's possessions, with the exception of 2,000 rubles' worth of furs and 300 rubles in cash, which represented a rather generous "feeding" at that.[2] Although, as in this case, the Prikaz tried to keep the "feeding" within certain limits and issued general instructions prohibiting the export of cash from Siberia beyond a certain sum, the practice of "feeding" flourished. In 1699 an investigation in Iakutsk led to the discovery of the practice by voevodas of charging from 50 to 400 rubles for appointments as prikashchiks of ostrogs. It was estimated that the voevodas in Iakutsk during the years 1695–1698 collected 16,975 rubles in this fashion.[3]

Since the office of the voevodas was regarded as inseparable from "feeding," it is not surprising to find that some appointments were made with the purpose of giving the appointee a chance to repair his fortune. Sometimes father and son were appointed together as voevodas[4] and it appeared that the office was granted to a family rather than to an individual. One appointment particularly at-

---

[2] Ogloblin, III, 181–182.   [4] *D.R.V.*, III, 131–132, 151, 236, 275, 288.
[3] *Ibid.*, III, 332.

tracts attention. In 1698 the voevoda of Nerchinsk died, and the local people presented a petition asking that his son be appointed to the office. The fact that the boy was very young did not deter the assent of the Muscovite government, which stipulated, however, that his uncle, the voevoda of Irkutsk, should look after the new voevoda.[5] The voevodas themselves held an even more liberal view of their office as being a family affair. Like the old kormlenshchiks, not content with being appointed themselves, they used to bring to Siberia with them a number of relatives and friends, with the intention of distributing profitable jobs among them. This practice finally drove the government to the necessity of issuing special instructions limiting the importation of the relatives of voevodas.[6]

The thriving of kormlenie was responsible for certain distinct features of the Siberian administration. It made Siberia a land famous for administrative abuses, because under its system it was impossible to distinguish "voluntary gifts" from bribes and extortions, or to draw a line between "feeding" and outright graft. Several times in the pages of this study reference has been made to the discrepancies of the policies of the central and of the local governments. The existence of the deeply rooted conception of "feeding" furnishes an explanation of these discrepancies. The Siberian Prikaz wanted to reap all the possible profits from the colony for the tsar's treasury, while the voevodas were intent on the collection of their own "feeding."

In their attempts to amass a fortune in Siberia, the voevodas, however, were handicapped by the fact that the government claimed all possible sources of profit for itself. It collected furs from the natives, taxes from visiting merchants and from the colonists, and even set up its own business enterprises. With other opportunities for profit closed, the voevodas, who felt themselves entitled to "feeding," could enrich themselves only by selling offices,

---

[5] Instructions to Irkutsk, 1698, *A.I.*, V, 516.

[6] "The voevodas appointed last year to Siberian towns were advised not to take along any friends to Siberia ..., not to give those friends any employment in the service of the tsar. These friends of the voevodas caused great harm on previous occasions ... they insulted and oppressed the people. Now we are informed that by your connivance your friends are in service in the uezd of Verkhoturie ... and the peasants are being ruined [by them].

"The Siberian Prikaz did not appoint any of your friends. And in your instruction you have been advised to choose the prikashchiks over peasants from the best local men, who are fit [for this service] and are familiar with the cultivation of land." Instructions to Verkhoturie, 1696, *A.I.*, V, 466–467.

by accepting bribes in court, by extortions from the population, and, at best, by moneylending or by manufacturing and selling wine; in other words, by disregarding and violating the orders from the Siberian Prikaz.

As a result of this, although the Siberian Prikaz was unable to suppress the practice of "feeding," it had grounds for the prosecution of the voevodas as administrative offenders whenever they tried to make a personal profit on a large scale. The supervision and control of the local officials, however, was one of the weakest details in the Siberian administration. It has been shown in this study that in order to achieve some control the government ordered the voevodas to check upon their predecessors, enlisted the aid of the Siberian archbishop as the "sovereign's eye," sent numerous investigators, and listened to the petitions from the oppressed Russian population and from the natives. Occasionally some of the voevodas were removed from office and even imprisoned,[7] but, on the whole, any approach toward efficient and honest administration could not be made so long as the feudal elements of the administrative system were allowed to exist.

A general view of the Siberian colonial administration presents a picture in which the elements of feudal society are blended with the new ideas of the bureaucratic centralized monarchy. The whole system lacked orderliness and cohesion and was marred by corrupt practices and oppression. It seemed, however, to satisfy the needs of the Muscovite state at its particular stage of development at that time.

---

[7] *D.R.V.*, III, 146, 151, 160–161; Ogloblin, III, 12–13.

BIBLIOGRAPHICAL ESSAY

THE FIELD OF Siberian historiography was opened by A. N. Pypin, who in his history of Russian ethnography discussed the sources and literature of Siberian history. Recent contributions to Siberian historiography have been made by V. I. Ogorodnikov and S. V. Bakhrushin. Ogorodnikov, in his yet unfinished history of Siberia, has presented a critical survey of Siberian historical literature, and Bakhrushin in addition to an historiographical essay in his book on the history of Siberian colonization, has written an excellent article on Gerhard Mueller, which appeared in a new edition of Mueller's Siberian history. Bakhrushin has also written notes on the historiography of Siberia in the second volume of the *Sibirskaia sovetskaia entsiklopediia*. In speaking of the historiographers of Siberia, perhaps one should also mention Professor V. S. Ikonnikov, who prepared a monumental work on Russian historiography in which some pages are devoted to the Siberian chronicles.

Among contributors to the study of Siberian historical bibliography V. I. Mezhov and Robert J. Kerner, the latter of the University of California, should be especially noted. Mezhov's fundamental Russian and Siberian bibliographies are still considered classics in spite of serious defects in organization. His bibliographies, however, should be consulted only for works published before the close of the nineteenth century. A selected list of works published during the first four decades of the twentieth century is to be found in *Northeastern Asia: a Selected Bibliography*, prepared by Professor Kerner, which contains about 3500 titles of books and articles written on Asiatic Russia in Russian, Chinese, Japanese, and other languages. It must also be noted that prior to the preparation of *Northeastern Asia*, Professor Kerner had already made contributions to Russian historical bibliography with his *Slavic Europe* and a short bibliographical essay on Russian expansion in America. In addition to these bibliographies, a very good bibliography for the Amur and Okhotsk-Kamchatka region, prepared by V. A. Grachev, should also be mentioned.

The primary sources of Siberian history consist of chronicles and official documents found in the government archives. The Siberian chronicles fall into two groups. The larger group was written by pious churchmen to whom the predatory raid of Ermak was a holy crusade against the pagans. These chroniclers saw the guiding hand of Providence in the cossack exploits and embellished their narrative with fantastic stories of the miracles which enabled the Russians to conquer Siberia. In spite of the presence of supernatural elements, these chronicles are very valuable to a historian, because, however unreliable, they form the main source for the study of the early conquest of Siberia. Another and a considerably smaller group of chronicles was prepared by government officials. Written in a dry, matter-of-fact style, the chronicles of this group contain information about the founding of different towns, the names of officials, some comment about the activities of the local voevodas and members of their staff, and brief accounts of such events as fires or epidemics. This last group of chronicles has a special significance for the history of the Siberian administration. The most important Siberian chronicles were published by the Archeographic Commission at the Russian Academy of Sciences. One of the best administrative chronicles appeared in the third volume of Novikov's *Drevniaia rossiiskaia vivliofika.*

The chief sources, largely unexplored, of Siberian history, are the administrative documents stored in the government archives in Russia and in the town archives in Siberia. They are exceedingly numerous—according to Ogorodnikov there are "hundreds of thousands" of them.[1] Most of them were kept in the archives of the former Siberian Prikaz until recently, and became accessible for research only in the last quarter of the nineteenth century. Only a comparatively small part of them is yet published. But this is to a large extent compensated by the labors of N. N. Ogloblin, who prepared a rather remarkable survey of all the material found in the archives of the Prikaz. Under four main headings he described in detail the documents dealing with the different phases of administration, and added to this description not only scholarly comment but numerous significant quotations as well, which make his work a mine of information for those who, for one reason or another, cannot use the archives.

The documents of town archives in Siberia became available to historians much earlier than did those of the Siberian Prikaz. In 1733 the Russian Senate and Academy of Sciences sent an expedition to Siberia, which included among its members "the father of

[1] V. I. Ogorodnikov, *Ocherki istorii Sibiri*, I, 41.

Russian historical science," G. F. Mueller. For ten years Mueller investigated the local archives and supervised the copying of various documents. As the result of extensive, patient, and careful research, he returned with a wealth of historical material, which has acquired special value because many of the original documents which he copied are now lost, having been destroyed by fire or in other ways. Many of the documents brought from his travels Mueller incorporated in his history of Siberia, which for that reason is listed in this study among the primary sources, and a great number of his documents are included in various collections of published sources.

The source collections which are essential for a study of Siberian administration first of all include two large official publications, *Polnoe sobranie gosudarstvennykh gramot i dogovorov* and *Polnoe sobranie zakonov*. The first contains many communications of the central government to Siberian officials during the early time of the conquest, and the second embraces the government decrees and regulations issued after 1648.

The most important and extensive collections of Siberian documents were published by the Archeographic Commission founded in 1834 at the Academy of Sciences. Among its publications the most valuable for this study were *Akty istoricheskie, Dopolneniia k aktam istoricheskim*, and *Russkaia istoricheskaia biblioteka*, although other publications of the Archeographic Commission, which are listed in the Bibliography, were also used.

Most of the documents published by the Archeographic Commission are orders sent from Moscow to voevodas in Siberia, reports of these voevodas to the central government, orders from voevodas to their subordinates, reports of various petty officials to the voevodas and to Moscow, petitions and complaints of serving men, Russian colonists and natives, the government replies to these petitions, and other similar official papers.

With the exception of the *Pamiatniki sibirskoi istorii*, the publications of the Archeographic Commission, as well as the official publications already mentioned, have Siberian documents scattered among other Russian documents, apparently without any definite system or plan except chronological order. Not all regions of Siberia are equally represented. *Akty* includes mostly documents of Verkhoturie, Tobolsk, and Iakutsk, *Dopolneniia* has a preponderance of Iakutsk documents, and *Russkaia istoricheskaia biblio-teka* covers the towns of the Tobolsk razriad during the first half of the seventeenth century. There is a marked shortage of documents from Tomsk and Eniseisk, both of which were important administrative centers. The compilers of these documents also failed to present sufficient statistical data.

After the Revolution, the Archeological Commission no longer existed, but the Academy of Sciences continued publication of Siberian sources through the newly organized Historico-Archeographic Institute and the Institute of the Northern Peoples. Under their auspices there recently appeared collections of documents dealing with Kamchatka, Chukotka, and Iakutsk. A set of over 200 Iakutsk documents published under the title *Kolonial'naia politika Moskovskogo gosudarstva v Iakutii,* accompanied by the introductory article of I. M. Trotskii, *Nekotorye problemy istorii Iakutii,* proved very helpful for this study.

To the wealth of sources published by the government and by the organizations attached to the Academy of Sciences must be added numerous documents published by the Russian historical societies. Although provincial societies have been interested chiefly in local material, the historical society at the Moscow University has shown a great deal of interest in Siberian history. Several important documents dealing with the history of Siberian administration have appeared in the pages of the society's journals, *Chteniia* and *Vremennik,* and in addition, the society sponsored the publication of Ogloblin's survey of archival material discussed above, and of Gnevushev's collection of documents covering the short reign of Vasilii Shuiskii.

Private initiative has also contributed its share in the gathering and publishing of Siberian sources. The private efforts are best represented in the collections of documents dealing with the history of towns such as Tomsk, Iakutsk, Nerchinsk, and Selenginsk. A noteworthy private collection of Siberian documents edited by I. P. Kuznetsov-Krasnoiarskii was published in two volumes covering the period from 1633 to 1699.

Finally, a great many documents have appeared in historical periodicals, such as *Russkaia starina, Russkii arkhiv,* and, after the Revolution, in the *Krasnyi arkhiv,* in which recently the sources of the history of Buriatia were published.

Among the published sources the most numerous and most valuable for the present study are the instructions of the Siberian Prikaz to the voevodas in Siberia. The government aims, the government requisites from the local officials, the extent of governmental control over the local administration, the attitude of the government toward different groups of the Siberian population, and the government concern in the interests of these groups are all outlined in these documents, which thus represent an excellent and unique source of material for the reconstruction of the government policies in Siberia.

At first glance, an investigator is somewhat puzzled by the apparent resemblance to each other of the instructions issued under different circumstances, at different times, and sent to different regions. The resemblance is due to the methods of the Muscovite clerks, who, rather than compose an entirely new document, sought inspiration in the previous instructions, and, having substituted new names, reproduced in a sort of official formula a considerable part of the former documents. After that had been done, the clerks used to append a summary of recent reports sent in by the local officials and lay down recommendations concerning these reports. This last part of the instructions is the one which has historical importance, although it might disagree with the directions given in the first, obsolete part of the document. The Muscovite clerks evidently realized the possible confusion to a reader which might be caused by these contradictions as well as by obscurities in the quaint official language of the seventeenth century. Therefore they proceeded to repeat significant passages several times, in the course of the document to be sure that the government orders would be understood and be duly impressed upon the obtuse minds of their recipients.

Turning now to a consideration of secondary writings, it is worth while to note that in spite of the considerable interest in Siberian administration, no one has attempted so far to write about its origin and development. More than eighty years ago Chicherin wrote a monograph on the provincial administrative institutions of Russia in the seventeenth century, and in this book he described the administration by the voevodas but without special reference to Siberia. Prutchenko, in his *Sibirskiia okrainy*, devoted largely to the reforms of Speranskii, has an introductory sketch of the

earlier administration. The American historian Golder in his work
on the Russian expansion on the Pacific has a short chapter on the
administration in eastern Siberia. None of these accounts is sufficiently complete. All of them suffer from the tendency to look for
dramatic dark colors and to neglect the somewhat drab details
of administration. Some are marred by comments of doubtful
historical value.[2]

There exists, however, a large body of secondary literature from
which important information may de drawn. In the preparation of
this study a great deal of material was obtained from the writings
of Kotoshikhin, a government official of the seventeenth century,
who left a detailed and accurate description of the Muscovite
prikazes. Many recent secondary works have been written on the
basis of archival research and provide useful and reliable material,
even if administrative matters are mentioned there only incidentally. Among these works are Bakhrushin's *Ocherki po istorii kolonizatsii Sibiri* and Ogorodnikov's *Ocherk istorii Sibiri*, which deal
mainly with Russian expansion and conquest in Siberia. Likewise,
Zaselenie Sibiri, Mangazeia, and *K istorii Sibiri*, prepared by
Butsinskii, throw light on many problems concerning both private
and government colonization in western Siberia during the first
half of the seventeenth century. One of the chief merits of Butsinskii's writings is the abundance of quotations from the documents
of the Siberian Prikaz, which he uses to illustrate his statements.
Fisher's monograph, *The Russian Fur Trade*, written in English,
contains a great deal of material about the financial administration
of Siberia.

Some of the best secondary material based on published and
unpublished sources is found in both scholarly and general periodicals. Within this group fall articles written by Ogloblin,
Ogorodnikov, Bakhrushin, Vernadskii, and a few others. From the
standpoint of administrative history, special consideration should
be given to Ogorodnikov's "Russkaia gosudarstvennaia vlast'..."
and "Tuzemnoe i russkoe zemledelie na Amure" and to Bakhrushin's "Iasak v Sibiri." The first of these articles discusses the
relations between the Russian administration and the natives, the

---

[2] "One can hardly believe that these [Siberian officers—voevodas] were so
low and ... depraved. ... They were without fear of God and without feelings
of shame." F. A. Golder, *Russian Expansion on the Pacific*, p. 19.

second, the development of agriculture on the Amur River, and the third, the origin, meaning, and methods of collection of iasak.

In this short bibliographical essay no attempt has been made to comment upon material which, although pertinent to the topic of the present investigation, is of a general nature. The study of such material, however, is necessary for a better understanding of the origin and the function of Siberian administration. Only the most important primary and secondary sources have been discussed here. The following bibliography has been prepared to aid the reader in securing additional information on the subject. The titles which make up the bibliography have been classified according to (1) bibliographical and historiographical literature, (2) sources, (3) contemporary accounts, (4) secondary works, and (5) articles and essays. The periodicals cited most frequently have been shortened according to the list of abbreviations found opposite page 1. When there is more than one edition of a work only the edition used in this study is listed.

BIBLIOGRAPHY

Bibliographical and Historiographical Literature

Andreev, A. I. "Trudy G. F. Millera o Sibiri" (Works of G. F. Mueller on Siberia). See no. 45, G. F. Mueller, *Istoriia Sibiri*, pp. 57–144.

Aziatskaia Rossiia. See no. 17, Pereselencheskoe upravlenie...

1. Bakai, N. N. *K voprosu ob izuchenii istorii Sibiri* (The problem of the study of Siberia). Krasnoiarsk, 1890.

2. ———. *Pamiati P. A. Slovtsova kak istorika Sibiri* (In memoriam. P. A. Slovtsov, historian of Siberia). Krasnoiarsk, 1890.

Bakhrushin, S. V. "Glavnye techeniia v sibirskoi istoriografii s XVIII veka" (Main currents in Siberian historiography since the eighteenth century). See no. 75, S. V. Bakhrushin, *Ocherki po istorii kolonizatsii Sibiri...*, pp. 36–58.

———. "Miller kak istorik Sibiri" (Mueller as a historian of Siberia). See no. 45, G. F. Mueller, *Istoriia Sibiri*, pp. 3–55.

Baklanova, N. A., and Andreev, A. I. "Obzor rukopisei G. F. Millera po istorii, geografii, etnografii i iazykam norodov Sibiri, khraniashchikhsia v moskovskikh i leningradskikh arkhivakh i bibliotekakh" (Survey of the manuscripts, preserved in the archives and libraries of Leningrad and Moscow, of G. F. Mueller, concerning the history, geography, ethnography, and languages of the peoples of Siberia). See no. 45, G. F. Mueller, *Istoriia Sibiri*, pp. 541–569.

Bazilevich, K. V. "Tamozhennyia knigi kak istochnik ekonomicheskoi istorii Rossii" (The customs books as a source of the economic history of Russia). See no. 162, *ibid.*

3. Belov, A. M. *Materialy k ukazateliu literatury o Sibiri na evropeiskikh iazykakh s 1917 po 1930 g.* (Material for a guide to the literature on Siberia in European languages from 1917 to 1930). Leningrad, 1931.

4. Chernevskii, P. O. *Ukazatel' materialov dlia istorii torgovli, promyshlennosti i finansov v predelakh rossiiskoi imperii. Ot drevneishikh vremen do kontsa XVIII stoletiia* (Guide to the material for the history of trade, industry, and finance, within the limits of the Russian Empire, from earliest times to the end of the eighteenth century). St. Petersburg, 1883.

5. Golitsyn, N. N. *Portfeli G. F. Millera* (G. F. Mueller's portfolios). Moscow, 1899.

6. Grachev, V. A. "Obzor istochnikov po istorii Priamur'ia i Okhotsko-Kamchatskogo kraia" (Survey of sources pertaining to the history of the Amur and Okhotsk-Kamchatka regions), *Trudy gosudarstvennogo dal'nevostochogo universiteta*, Series III, No. 5. Vladivostok, 1927.

7. Ikonnikov, V. S. *Opyt russkoi istoriografii* (An attempt at Russian historiography). 2 vols. in 4. Kiev, 1891–1908.

8. Kaidanov, N. *Sistematicheskii katalog delam sibirskago prikaza* (Systematic catalogue of the transactions of the Siberian Prikaz). St. Petersburg, 1888.

9. KERNER, ROBERT J. *Northeastern Asia: A Selected Bibliography. Contributions to the Bibliography of the Relations of China, Russia, and Japan, with Special Reference to Korea, Manchuria, Mongolia, and Eastern Siberia, in Oriental and European Languages,* Publication of the Northeastern Asia Seminar of the University of California. 2 vols. Berkeley, Calif., 1939.

10. ———. "Russian Expansion to America: Its Bibliographical Foundations," The Papers of the Bibliographical Society of America, XXV (1931), 111–129.

11. ———. *Slavic Europe: A Selected Bibliography in the Western European Languages, Comprising History, Languages, and Literatures.* Harvard Bibliographies, Library Series, Vol. I. Cambridge, Mass., 1918.

12. *Krizhnaia letopis'* (Book Chronicle). Vols. I– . Rossiiskaia tsentral'naia palata pri gosudarstvennom izdatel'stve. Moscow, 1907– .

13. LAMBIN, P. P. *Russkaia istoricheskaia bibliografiia* (Russian historical bibliography). 10 vols. in 5. St. Petersburg, 1861–1884.

14. MEZHOV, V. I. *Russkaia istoricheskaia bibliografiia za 1865–1876 g.g.* (Russian historical bibliography for 1865–1876). 8 vols. in 4. St. Petersburg, 1882–1890.

15. ———. *Sibirskaia bibliografiia. Ukazatel' knig i statei o Sibiri na russkom iazyke i odnekh tol'ko knig na inostrannykh iazykakh za ves' period knigopechataniia* (Siberian bibliography. Guide to the books and articles about Siberia in Russian, and to books in foreign languages for the whole period of book printing). 3 vols. in 2. St. Petersburg, 1903.

16. ———. *Supplément: Bibliographie des livres et articles russes d'histoire et sciences auxiliaires de 1800–1854.* 3 vols. St. Petersburg, 1892–1893.

OGLOBLIN, N. N. *Obozrenie stolbtsov i knig sibirskago prikaza, 1592–1768 g.g.* (Survey of the rolls and books of the Siberian Prikaz, 1592–1768). See no. 52, *idem.*

OGORODNIKOV, V. I. *"Vvedenie"* (Introduction [an essay on the historiography of Siberia]). See no. 121, V. I. Ogorodnikov, *Ocherki istorii Sibiri,* Vol. I, pp. 1–90.

17. Pereselencheskoe upravlenie glavnago upravleniia zemleustroistva i zemledeliia (Chief Bureau of Colonization and Agriculture). *Aziatskaia Rossiia* (Asiatic Russia). 3 vols. St. Petersburg, 1914. Volume III contains bibliography of Asiatic Russia.

PLATONOV, S. F. *"Vvedenie"* (Introduction). See no. 128, S. F. Platonov, *Lektsii . . . ,* pp. 1–48.

18. PUTSILLO, M. N. *Ukazatel' delam i rukopisian otnosiashchimsia do Sibiri* (Guide to files and manuscripts concerning Siberia). Moscow, 1879.

19. PYPIN, A. N. *Istoriia russkoi etnografii* (History of Russian ethnography). 4 vols. St. Petersburg, 1890–1892. Volume IV contains historiography of Siberia.

20. Tikhomirov, M. N., and Nikitin, S. A., *Istochnikovedenie istorii SSSR* (Sources for the history of the U.S.S.R.). 2 vols. (Vol. I by M. N. Tikhomirov; Vol. II by S. A. Nikitin). Moscow, 1940.

21. TYZHNOV, I. *Zametki o gorodskikh letopisiakh Sibiri. Chast' 1. Letopis' goroda Tobolska* (Notes on the town chronicles of Siberia. Part 1. Chronicle of the town of Tobolsk). St. Petersburg, 1898.

22. UL'IANOV, N. A., AND UL'IANOV, V. N. *Ukazatel' zhurnal'noi literatury, alfavitnyi, predmetnyi, sistematicheskii, 1896–1905 g.g.* (Guide to periodical literature, alphabetic, topical, systematic, 1896–1905). 2d ed. Moscow, 1913.

23. VIKTOROV, A. G. *Opisanie zapisnykh knig i bumag starinnykh dvortsovykh prikazov, 1584–1725 g.g.* (Description of the record books and papers of the old court prikazes, 1584–1725). 2 vols. Moscow, 1877–1883.

24. *Zhurnal'naia letopis'* (Periodical chronicle), since 1938 the title has been changed to *Letopis' zhurnal'nykh statei* (Chronicle of periodical articles), *Sistematicheskii ukazatel' statei iz zhurnalov i sbornikov SSSR* (Systematic guide to magazine and other articles published in the U.S.S.R.). Vols. I– . Tsentral'naia knizhnaia palata. Moscow, 1926– .

SOURCES

25. Akademiia nauk (Academy of Sciences). *Akty arkheograficheskoi ekspeditsii,* cited as *A.A.E.* (Acts of the archeographic expedition)—a generally accepted abbreviation of *Akty sobrannye v bibliotekakh i arkhivakh rossiiskoi imperii arkheograficheskoi ekspeditsiei imperatorskoi akademii nauk* (Acts collected in the libraries and archives of the Russian Empire by the archeographic expedition of the Imperial Academy of Sciences). 4 vols. St. Petersburg, 1836; Index, 1838.

26. ———. *Akty moskovskago gosudarstva* (Acts of the Muscovite state). 3 vols. St. Petersburg, 1890–1901.

27. ALKOR, IA. P., AND DREZEN, L. K., comps. *Kolonial'naia politika tsarizma na Kamchatke i Chukotke v XVIII veke. Sbornik arkhivnykh materialov* (Colonial policy of tsarism in Kamchatka and Chukotka in the eighteenth century. Collection of the archival material). Leningrad, 1935.

28. Arkheograficheskaia kommissiia (Archeographic commission). *Akty istoricheskie,* cited as *A.I.* (Historical acts). 5 vols. St. Petersburg, 1841–1842; Index, 1843.

29. ———. *Akty iuridicheskie* (Legal acts). St. Petersburg, 1838.

30. ———. *Dopolneniia k aktam istoricheskim,* cited as *D.A.I.* (Supplements to the historical acts). 12 vols. St. Petersburg, 1846–1872; Index, 1875.

31. ———. *Pamiatniki sibirskoi istorii XVIII v.* (Records of Siberian history of the eighteenth century). 2 vols. St. Petersburg, 1882–1885.

32. ———. *Polnoe sobranie russikikh letopisei,* cited as *P.S.R.L.* (Complete collection of Russian chronicles). 24 vols. St. Petersburg, 1841–1914.

33. ———. *Russkaia istoricheskaia biblioteka,* cited as *R.I.B.* (Russian historical library). 39 vols. St. Petersburg, 1875–1927.

34. ———. *Sibirskiia letopisi* (Siberian chronicles). St. Petersburg, 1907.

35. BANTYSH-KAMENSKII, N. N., MALINOVSKII, A. F., and others, eds. *Sobranie gosudarstvennykh gramot i dogovorov, khraniashchikhsia v gosudarstvennoi kollegii instrannykh del*, cited as *S.G.G.D.* (Collection of state charters and treaties preserved in the state college of foreign affairs). 5 vols. Moscow, 1813–1894.

36. BOGOIAVLENSKII, S. K., AND RIABININ, I. S., comps. *Akty vremeni mezhdutsarstviia* (Acts of the time of interregnum). Moscow, 1915.

37. "Drevniia gramoty XVI i XVII v.v. otnosiashchiiasia k osnovaniiu i pervonachal'nomu ustroistvu g. Verkhoturiia" (Old official documents of the sixteenth and seventeenth centuries dealing with the foundation and original organization of the town of Verkhoturie), *Vremennik imperatorskago moskovskago obshchestva istorii i drevnostei rossiiskikh* (cited as *Vremennik*). XXV (1856), 4–12.

38. GNEVUSHEV, A. M., comp. *Akty vremeni pravleniia tsaria Vasiliia Shuiskago, 1606 g. 19 maia–17 iiulia 1610* (Acts of the time of the rule of tsar Vasilii Shuiskii, May 19, 1606–July 17, 1610). Moscow, 1914.

Also in *Chteniia v imperatorskom obshchestve istorii i drevnostei rossiiskikh pri moskovskom universitete* (cited as *Chteniia*), Vol. CCLIII (1915), Bk. II, sec. 1, pp. i–xix, 1–422. Moscow.

39. GOLOVACHEV, P. M., ed. *Tomsk v XVII veke* (Tomsk in the seventeenth century). St. Petersburg, 1907.

40. GOLOVIN, P. P. "Instruktsiia pismianomu golove Poiarkovu" (Instructions to the *pismennyi golova* Poiarkov), *Chteniia* (January–March, 1861), Bk. I, pt. 5, pp. 1–14, Moscow.

41. GREKOV, B. D., ed. *Pravda russkaia* (Russian law). Izdatel'stvo akademii nauk SSSR. Leningrad, 1940.

42. "Istoricheskie akty o podvigakh Erofeia Khabarova na Amure v 1649–1651 g.g." (Historical acts concerning the exploits of Erofei Khabarov on the Amur in 1649–1651), *Zhurnal dlia chteniia vospitannikam voenno-uchebynykh zavedenii*, 1840, No. 105, St. Petersburg.

43. KUZNETSOV-KRASNOIARSKII, I. P., comp. *Istoricheskie akty XVII stoletiia, 1633–1699. Materialy dlia istorii Sibiri* (Historical acts of the seventeenth century, 1633–1699. Sources for the history of Siberia). Vol. I, 1890; Vol. II, 1897, Tomsk.

44. MAKSIMOVICH, L., comp. *Ukazatel' rossiiskikh zakonov* (Guide to the Russian laws [containing a collection of Russian laws for the period 996–1649]). St. Petersburg, 18—[?].

45. MUELLER, G. F. *Istoriia Sibiri* (History of Siberia). 3 vols. projected; Vol. I was published Moscow–Leningrad, 1937 and is the revised edition of:

46. ———. *Opisanie sibirskago tsarstva i vsekh proisshedshikh v nem del ot nachala a osoblivo ot pokoreniia ego rossiiskoi derzhave po sii vremena* (Description of the Siberian kingdom and all events occurring there from the beginning, but especially from its subjugation to the Russian power, up to the present time). 2d ed. St. Petersburg, 1787.

47. N., A. N., comp. *Irkutsk. Materialy dlia istorii goroda* (Irkutsk. Sources for the history of the town). Moscow, 1883.

48. ———. *Sibirskie goroda. Materialy dlia ikh istorii. Nerchinsk, Selenginsk, Iakutsk* (Siberian towns. Sources for their history. Nerchinsk, Selenginsk, Iakutsk). Moscow, 1886.

49. ———. *Tobolsk. Materialy dlia istorii goroda v XVII i XVIII st.* (Tobolsk. Sources for the history of the town in the seventeenth and eighteenth centuries). Moscow, 1885.

50. "Nakaz narymskago ostroga voevode Vasil'iu Ivanovu 1662 goda, o iasachnom i denezhnom sbore i kazennom khlebopashestve" (Instruction to the voevoda of the ostrog of Narym, Vasilii Ivanov, regarding iasak and money collection and state agriculture), *Vremennik*, Vol. XVII (1853), Pt. 3, pp. 4–8, Moscow.

51. NOVIKOV, N., comp. *Drevniaia rossiiskaia vivliofika, soderzhashchaia v sebe: sobranie drevnostei rossiiskikh, do istorii, geografii i geneologii rossiiskiia kasaiushchikhsia*, cited as *D.R.V.* (Ancient Russian library, which contains a collection of Russian antiquities concerning history, geography, and genealogy). 20 vols. 2d ed. Moscow, 1788–1791.

52. OGLOBLIN, N. N. *Obozrenie stolbtsov i knig sibirskago prikaza, 1592–1768 g.g.* (Survey of the rolls and books of the Siberian Prikaz, 1592–1768). 4 vols. Moscow, 1895–1900.

53. OKUN', S. "K istorii Buriatii v XVII v" (Concerning the history of the Buriats in the seventeenth century), *Krasnyi Arkhiv*, Vol. LXXVI (1936), No. 3, pp. 156–191. Moscow.

54. "Otnosheniia voevod i diakov v sibirskikh gorodakh Mangazee i Iakutske" (Relations between the voevodas and diaks in the Siberian towns, Mangazeia and Iakutsk), *Chteniia*, Vol. CCXXXIII (1910), Bk. 11, pt. 5, pp. 1–16. Moscow.

Polnoe sobranie zakonov . . . (Complete collection of laws . . .). See no. 58.

55. "Smetnyi spisok 139 godu" (Active list of 1631), *Vremennik*, Vol. IV 1849), Pt. 3, pp. 18–51. Moscow.

Sobranie gosudarstvennykh gramot i dogovorov . . . (Collection of state charters and treaties . . .). See no. 35.

56. Sobstvennaia ego imperatorskago velichestva kantseliariia (His majesty's own office). *Dvortsovye razriady* (Court registers). 4 vols. St. Petersburg, 1850–1855.

57. ———. *Knigi razriadnyia* (Register books). 4 vols. St. Petersburg, 1853–1855.

58. ———. *Polnoe sobranie zakonov rossiiskoi imperii s 1649 goda*, cited as *P.S.Z.* (Complete collection of laws of the Russian empire since 1649). Series I, 44 vols. St. Petersburg, 1830.

59. STRELOV, E. D., ed. *Akty arkhivov iakutskoi oblasti* (Acts of the archives of the region of Iakutsk). Iakutsk, 1916.

60. TROTSKII, I. M., comp. "Kolonial'naia politika moskovskogo gosudarstva v Iakutii XVII v." (Colonial policy of the Muscovite state in Iakutiia in the seventeenth century). *Trudy istoriko-arkheograficheskogo instituta akademii nauk S.S.S.R.*, Vol. XIV, No. 5 (1936), Leningrad.

61. VVEDENSKII, A. A. *Torgovyi dom XVI–XVII vekov* (A commercial firm of the sixteenth and seventeenth centuries). Leningrad, 1924.

Contemporary Accounts

62. Kotoshikhin, G. *O Rossii v tsarstvovanie Aleksiia Mikhailovicha* (Russia in the reign of Aleksei Mikhailovich). 3d ed. St. Petersburg, 1884.

63. Križanić, Iu. *Russkoe gosudarstvo v polovine XVII veka. Rukopis' vremen tsaria Alekseia Mikhailovicha* (The Russian state in the middle of the seventeenth century. A manuscript of the time of tsar Aleksei Mikhailovich). 1 vol. in 6 pts. Moscow, 1859–1860.

64. "Puteshestvie chrez Sibir' ot Tobol'ska do Nerchinska i granits Kitaia russkago poslannika Nikolaia Spafariia v 1675 godu" (Journey across Siberia from Tobolsk to Nerchinsk and the borders of China of the Russian ambassador Nikolai Spafarii in 1675), *Zapiski imperatorskago russkago geograficheskago obshchestva po otdeleniiu etnografii*, Vol. X (1882), No. 1, pp. 1–214, St. Petersburg.

65. Spafarii, N. G. "Pis'mo Nikolaia Spafariia k boiarinu Artemonu Sergeevichu Matveevu" (Letter of Nikolai Spafarii to the boiar Artemon Sergeevich Matveev), *Russkii arkhiv*, 1881, No. 1, pp. 52–57, St. Petersburg.

66. "Stateinyi spisok posol'stva N. Spafariia v Kitai" (Detailed account of the embassy of N. Spafarii to China), *Vestnik arkheologii i istorii*, Vol. XVII (1906), Pt. 2, pp. 162–339, St. Petersburg.

67. Titov, A. A., ed. *Sibir' v XVII veke. Sbornik starinnykh russkikh statei o Sibiri i prilezhashchikh k nei zemliakh* (Siberia in the seventeenth century. A collection of old Russian accounts of Siberia and the lands bordering it). Moscow, 1890.

68. *Zhitie protopopa Avvakuma im samim napisannoe i drugie ego sochineniia* (Autobiography of the priest Avvakum, and his other works). Moscow, n.d.

Secondary Works

69. Akulinin, I. G. *Ermak i Stroganovy* (Ermak and the Stroganovs). Paris, 1933.

70. Andreevskii, I. E. *O namestnikakh, voevodakh i gubernatorakh* (Namestniks, voevodas, and gubernators). St. Petersburg, 1887.

71. Andrievich, V. K. *Istoriia Sibiri* (History of Siberia). 5 vols. St. Petersburg, Irkutsk, Tomsk, St. Petersburg, Odessa, 1887–1889.

72. ———. *Kratkii ocherk istorii Zabaikal'ia ot drevneishikh vremen do 1762* (Short outline of the history of the Trans-Baikal region from ancient times to 1762). St. Petersburg, 1887.

73. Baddeley, John F. *Russia, Mongolia, China* ... 2 vols. London and New York, 1919.

74. Bakhrushin, S. V. *Kazaki na Amure* (Cossacks on the Amur). London, 1925.

75. ———. *Ocherki po istorii kolonizatsii Sibiri v XVI i XVII v.v.* (Essays on the history of colonization of Siberia in the sixteenth and seventeenth centuries). Moscow, 1927–1928.

76. BALKASHIN, N. *Khronologicheskii ukazatel' vazhneishikh sobytii iz istorii Zapadnoi Sibiri s 1465 po 1881 g.* (Chronological guide to the most important events in the history of western Siberia from 1465 to 1881). N.p., n.d.

77. BELIKOV, D. N. *Pervye russkie krest'iane nasel'niki tomskago kraia* (First Russian peasant colonists of the Tomsk district). Tomsk, 1898.

78. BRIX, H. O. R. *Geschichte der alten russischen Heeres-Einrichtungen von den fruehesten Zeiten bis zu den von Peter dem Grossen gemachten Veraenderungen.* Berlin, 1867.

79. BUTSINSKII, P. N. *K istorii Sibiri: Surgut, Narym i Ketsk do 1645 g.* (Concerning the history of Siberia: Surgut, Narym, and Ketsk to 1645). Kharkov, 1893.

80. ———. *Mangazeia i mangazeiskii uezd, 1601–1645 g.g.* (Mangazeia and the uezd of Mangazeia, 1601–1645). Kharkov, 1893.

81. ———. *Zaselenie Sibiri i byt eia pervykh nasel'nikov* (The settlement of Siberia and the life of its first settlers). Kharkov, 1889.

82. CAHEN, GASTON. *Histoire des relations de la Russie avec la Chine sous Pierre le Grand (1689–1730).* Paris, 1912.

83. CHICHERIN, B. *Oblastnyia uchrezhdeniia Rossii v XVII veke* (Provincial institutions in Russia in the seventeenth century). Moscow, 1856.

84. COXE, WILLIAM. *Account of the Russian Discoveries between Asia and America; to Which Are Added, the Conquest of Siberia, and the History of the Transactions and Commerce between Russia and China.* 2d ed., rev. London, 1780.

85. DIAKONOV, M.A. *Ocherki obshchestvennago i gosudarstvennago stroia drevnei Rusi* (Essays on the social and political structure of old Russia). 4th ed., rev. St. Petersburg, 1912.

86. DUROV, A. *Kratkii istoricheskii ocherk kolonizatsii Sibiri* (Brief historical essay on Siberian colonization). Tomsk, 1891.

87. FIRSOV, N. A.
——. *Polozhenie inorodtsev severo-vostochnoi Rossii v Moskovskom gosudarstve* (Position of the non-Russian natives of northeastern Russia in the Muscovite state). Kazan, 1866.

88. FIRSOV, N. N. *Chteniia po istorii Sibiri* (Readings on the history of Siberia). 2 vols. in 1. Moscow, 1920–1921.

89. FISCHER, J. E. *Sibirskaia istoriia s samago otkrytiia Sibiri do zavoevaniia sei zemli rossiiskim oruzhiem . . .* (Siberian history from the first discovery of Siberia to the complete conquest of this land by Russian arms . . .). St. Petersburg, 1774.

90. FISHER, RAYMOND H. "The Russian Fur Trade 1550–1700" University of California Publications in History Vol. 31. Berkeley, Calif., 1943.

91. GAZENVINKEL, K. B. *Gosudarevo zhalovan'e posluzhnikam sibirskim* (Sovereign's salaries to the Siberian state servants). Tobolsk, 1892.

92. ———. *Knigi razriadnyia v offitsial'nykh ikh spiskakh, kak material dlia istorii Sibiri v XVII v.* (Official copies of the register books as material for the study of Siberia in the seventeenth century). Kazan, 1892.

93. ———. *Sistematicheskii perechen' voevod, diakov, pismennykh golov i pod'iachikh s pripis'iu v sibirskikh gorodakh i glavneishikh ostrogakh s ikh osnovaniia do nachala XVIII v.* (Systematic list of voevodas, diaks, pismennye golovas, and pod'iacheis s pripis'iu in Siberian towns and most important ostrogs from their foundation to the beginning of the eighteenth century). Tobolsk, 1892.

94. GOLDER, FRANK A. *Russian Expansion on the Pacific, 1641–1850: An Account of the Earliest and Later Expeditions Made by the Russians along the Pacific Coast of Asia and North America, including Some Related Expeditions to the Arctic Regions.* Cleveland, 1914.

95. GOLUBINSKII, E. *Istoriia russkoi tserkvi* (History of the Russian Church). Moscow, 1881.

96. GRADOVSKII, A. D. *Istoriia mestnago upravleniia v Rossii* (History of local government in Russia). St. Petersburg, 1868.

97. IADRINTSEV, N. M. *Sibir' kak koloniia* (Siberia as a colony). St. Petersburg, 1882.

98. IONIN, A. A. *Novyia dannyia k istorii Vostochnoi Sibiri XVII v.* (New data concerning the history of eastern Siberia of the seventeenth century). Irkutsk, 1895.

99. *Istoriia reki Amura, sostavlennaia iz obnarodovannykh istochnikov s planami reki Amura* (History of the Amur River based on published sources and accompanied by maps of the Amur River). St. Petersburg, 1859.

100. *Kak zaselialas' Sibir'* (How Siberia was colonized). Tomsk, 1885.

101. KARAMZIN, N. M. *Istoriia gosudarstva rossiiskago* (History of the Russian state). 12 vols. 2d ed. St. Petersburg, 1818–1829.

102. KATANAEV, G. E. *Kratkii istoricheskii obzor sluzhby sibirskago kazach'ego voiska s 1582 po 1908* (Brief historical survey of the service of the Siberian cossack army, 1582–1908). St. Petersburg, 1908.

103. ———. *Zapadno-sibirskoe sluzhiloe kazachestvo i ego rol' v obsledovanii i zaniatii russkimi Sibiri i Srednei Azii. Vypusk I. Konets shestnadtsatago i nachalo os'mnadtsatago stoletii* (West-Siberian serving cossacks and their role in the Russian exploration and occupation of Siberia and Central Asia. Part I. From the end of the sixteenth to the beginning of the eighteenth centuries). St. Petersburg, 1908.

104. KERNER, ROBERT J. *The Urge to the Sea: The Course of Russian History—the Role of Rivers, Portages, Ostrogs, Monasteries, and Furs.* Berkeley, Calif., 1942.

105. KLIUCHEVSKII, V. O. *Kurs russkoi istorii* (The course of Russian history). 5 vols. Moscow, 1908.

106. ———. *Russkii rubl' XVI–XVIII v. v ego otnoshenii k nyneshnemu. Opyt opredeleniia menovoi stoimosti starinnago rublia po khlebnym tsenam* (The Russian ruble of the sixteenth to eighteenth centuries and its relation to the present day ruble. An attempt to evaluate the purchasing value of the old ruble by the prices of grain). Moscow, 1884.

107. KORF, S. A. *Administrativnaia iustitsiia v Rossii* (Administrative justice in Russia). St. Petersburg, 1910.

108. KOSTOMAROV, I. N. *Iz nashego proshlago. Sibirskie zemleiskateli* (From our past. Siberian land prospectors). Berlin, 1922.
109. KOSTOMAROV, N. I. *Ocherki torgovli moskovskago gosudarstva v XVI i XVII stoletiiakh* (Essays on the trade of the Muscovite state in the sixteenth and seventeenth centuries). St. Petersburg, 1905. (Book VIII, Vol. XX of the complete works of N. I. Kostomarov, *Istoricheskiia monografii i issledovaniia.*)
110. ―――. *Russkaia istoriia v zhizneopisaniiakh eia glavneishikh deiatelei* (Russian history portrayed in biographies of its principal actors). 3 vols. St. Petersburg, 1880–1888.
111. KOZMIN, N. N. *Ocherki proshlago i nastoiashchego Sibiri* (Essays on the past and present of Siberia). St. Petersburg, 1910.
112. KULESHOV, V. *Nakazy sibirskim voevodam v XVII v.* (Instructions to Siberian voevodas in the seventeenth century). Tashkent, 1888.
113. KULISHER, I. M. *Istoriia russkago narodnago khoziastva* (History of Russian national economy). 2 vols. Moscow, 1925.
114. LIKHACHEV, N. P. *Razriadnye diaki XVI veka* (Ranking diaks of the sixteenth century). St. Petersburg, 1888.
115. LODYZHENSKII, K. *Istoriia russkago tamozhennago tarifa* (History of the Russian customs tariff). St. Petersburg, 1886.
116. MAKSIMOV, S. V. *Sibir i katorga* (Siberia and penal servitude). 3 vols. St. Petersburg, 1871.
117. MANYKIN-NEVSTRUEV, A. I. *Zavoevateli vostochnoi Sibiri iakutskie kazaki* (Conquerors of the eastern Siberia—the Cossacks of Iakutsk). Moscow, 1883; also in *Russkii vestnik*, 1883, No. 4, pp. 469–522.
118. MEL'GUNOV, P. P. *Ocherki po istorii russkoi torgovli IX–XVIII v.v.* (Essays on the history of Russian trade from the ninth to the eighteenth centuries). Moscow, 1905.
    MUELLER, G. F. *Istoriia Sibiri.* See no. 45.
    ―――. *Opisanie sibirskago tsarstva* . . . See no. 46.
119. NEBOL'SIN, P. *Pokorenie Sibiri* (Conquest of Siberia). St. Petersburg, 1849.
120. OGORODNIKOV, V. I. *Iz istorii pokoreniia Sibiri. Pokorenie iukagirskoi zemli* (From the history of the Siberian conquest. The conquest of the land of the Iukagirs). Chita, 1922.
121. ―――. *Ocherki istorii Sibiri do nachala XIX veka* (Essays on the history of Siberia to the beginning of the nineteenth century). Vol. I, *Istoriia do-russkoi Sibiri* (History of pre-Russian Siberia). Irkutsk, 1920. Vol. II, Part 1, *Zavoevanie russkimi Sibiri* (The conquest of Siberia by the Russians). Vladivostok, 1924.
122. OKLADNIKOV, A. P. *Ocherki iz istorii zapadnykh buriat-mongolov XVII–XVIII v.v.* (Essays on the history of the western Buriats-Mongols). Leningrad, 1937.
123. OKUN', S. V. *Ocherki po istorii kolonial'noi politiki tsarizma v Kamchatskom krae* (Essays on the history of the colonial policy of tsarism in the region of Kamchatka). Leningrad, 1935.

124. Osokin, E. *O poniatii promyslovago naloga i ob istoricheskom ego razvitii v Rossii* (Taxation of business, and its historical development in Russia). Kazan, 1856.

125. ———. *Vnutrennıa tamozhennyıa poshlıny v Rossıı* (Internal customs taxes in Russia). Kazan, 1850.

126. Pavlov-Silvanskii, N. *Feodalism v drevnei Rusi* (Feudalism in early Russia). Petrograd, 1924.

127. ———. *Gosudarevy sluzhilye liudi, proiskhozhdenie russkago dvorianstva* (Sovereign's serving men, the origin of the Russian nobility). St. Petersburg, 1898.

128. Platonov, S. F. *Lektsii po russkoi istorii* (Lectures on Russian history). 8th ed. St. Petersburg, 1913.

129. ———. *Proshloe russkago severa; ocherki po kolonzatsii Pomor'ia* (The past of the Russian north; essays on colonization of the north-European maritime country). Petrograd, 1923.

130. Pokrovskii, M. N. *Russkaia istoriia s drevneishikh vremen* (History of Russia from the earliest times). 5 vols. 2d ed. Moscow, 1913–1914.

131. Popov, G. A. *Ocherki po istorii Iakutii* (Essays on the history of Iakutia). Iakutsk, 1924.

132. Potapov, L. P. *Ocherk istorii Oirotii. Altaitsy v period russkoi kolonizatsii* (Essay on the history of Oirotia. The Altai natives during the period of Russian colonization). Novosibirsk, 1933.

133. Prutchenko, S. *Sibirskiia okrainy* (Siberian borderlands). 2 vols. St. Petersburg, 1899.

134. Rozhkov, N. A. *Russkaia istoriia* (Russian history). 12 vols. in 10. Petrograd-Moscow, 1919–1926.

135. Semevskii, V. I. *Krest'ianskii vopros v Rossii* (The peasant problem in Russia). 2 vols. St. Petersburg, 1888.

136. Serebrennikov, I. N. *Pokorenie i pervonachal'noe zaselenie Irkutskoi gubernii* (Conquest and first settlement of the Irkutsk gubernia). Irkutsk, 1915.

137. Sergeevich, V. I. *Russkiia iuridicheskiia drevnosti* (Russian legal antiquities). Vol. I, 1890; Vol. II, 1893. St. Petersburg.

138. Sgibnev, A. *Istoricheskii ocherk glavneishikh sobytii v Kamchatke s 1650 po 1856 g.* (Historical outline of the most important events in Kamchatka from 1650 to 1856). St. Petersburg, 1869.

139. Shcheglov, I. V. *Khronologicheskii perechen' vazhneishikh dannykh iz istorii Sibiri, 1032–1882* (Chronological summary of the most important data from the history of Siberia, 1032–1882). Irkutsk, 1883.

140. Slovtsov, P. A. *Istoricheskoe obozrenie Sibiri* (Historical survey of Siberia). 2 vols. in 1. 2d ed. St. Petersburg, 1886.

141. Solov'ev, S. M. *Istoriia Rossii s drevneishikh vremen* (History of Russia from earliest times). 29 vols. in 7. St. Petersburg, 1894–1895.

142. Sukachev, V. P. *Irkutsk. Ego mesto i znachenie v istorii i kul'turnom razvitii Vostochnoi Sibiri* (Irkutsk. Its place and significance in the history and cultural development of eastern Siberia). Moscow, 1891.

143. SVATIKOV, S. G. *Rossiia i Sibir* (Russia and Siberia). Prague, 1929.
144. TOKAREV, S. A. *Dokapitalisticheskie perezhitki v Oirotii* (Precapitalist survivals in Oirotia). Leningrad, 1936.
145. USTRIALOV, N. *Istoriia tsarstvovaniia Petra Velikago* (History of the reign of Peter the Great). 6 vols. (Vol. 5 not published). St. Petersburg, 1853–1863.
146. VERNADSKII, G. V. *Nachertanie russkoi istorii* (Sketch of Russian history). Pt. I. Prague, 1927.
147. VORONETS, E. N. *Pravoslavnaia missiia v Sibiri i otnosheniia k nei gosudarstvennago pravitel'stva* (Greek Orthodox mission in Siberia and its treatment by the state government). Moscow, 1887.
148. *Zamechatel'nye russkie liudi. Erofei Khabarov i Semen Dezhnev* (Outstanding Russians, Erofei Khabarov and Semen Dezhnev). St. Petersburg, 1897.
149. ZOLOTOV, [?] *Materialy dlia istorii sibirskago voiska* (Material for the history of the Siberian armed forces). Omsk, 1878.

ARTICLES AND ESSAYS

150. ABRAMOV, N. "Materialy dlia istorii khristianskago prosveshcheniia v Sibiri so vremeni pokoreniia eia v 1581 godu do nachala XIX st." (Material for the history of the propagation of Christianity in Siberia from the time of its conquest in 1581 to the beginning of the nineteenth century), *Zhurnal ministerstva narodnago prosveshcheniia* (cited as *Zh.M.N.P.*), Vol. LXXXI (1854), Pt. 1, pp. 15–56. St. Petersburg.
151. ———. "O sibirskikh dvorianakh i detiakh boiarskikh" (Concerning Siberian nobles and boiar sons), *Etnograficheskii sbornik imperatorskago russkago geograficheskago obshchestva*, V (1862), 10–18. St. Petersburg.
152. BAKHRUSHIN, S. V. "Agenty russkikh torgovykh liudei XVII veka" (The agents of the Russian merchants of the seventeenth century), *Uchenye zapiski instituta istorii rossiiskoi assosiatsii nauchno-issledovatel'skikh institutov obshchestvennykh nauk*, IV (1929), 71–88. Moscow.
153. ———. "Iasak v Sibiri v XVII veke" (Iasak in Sibera in the seventeenth century), *Sibirskie ogni*, No. 3, May–June, 1927, pp. 95–129.
154. ———. "Istoricheskie sud'by Iakutii" (Historical destinies of Iakutia), *Iakutiia. Sbornik statei*, 1927, pp. 275–322. (1–48). Leningrad.
155. ———. "Mangazeiskaia mirskaia obshchina v XVII s." (The Mangazeia community in the seventeenth century), *Severnaia Azia*, 1929.
156. ———. "Moskovskoe gosudarstvo" (Muscovite state), *Bol'shaia sovetskaia entsiklopediia*, XL, 451–474.
157. ———. "Ostiatskie i vogul'skie kniazhestva v XVI i XVII vekakh" (Principalities of the Ostiaks and Voguls in the sixteenth and seventeenth centuries), *Institut narodov severa. TsIK SSSR imeni Smidovicha,* 1935. Leningrad.
158. ———. "Sibirskie slobodchiki v XVII veke" (Siberian slobodchiks in the seventeenth century), *Trudy gosudarstvennogo kolonizatsionnogo instituta,* II (1926). Moscow.

159. ———. "Sibirskie sluzhilye tatary v XVII veke" (Siberian serving Tatars in the seventeenth century), *Istoricheskie zapiski,* I (1937), 55–80. Moscow.

160. ———. "Torgi gostia Nikitina v Sibiri i Kitae" (The trade of the merchant Nikitin in Siberia and China), *Institut istorii. Trudy pamiati Aleksandra Nikolaevicha Savina. Sbornik statei,* 1926, pp. 357–390. Moscow.

161. BAZILEVICH, K. V. "K voprosu ob izuchenii tamozhennykh knig XVII v." (Concerning the problem of the study of the customs books of the seventeenth century), *Problemy istochnikovedeniia,* II (1936), 71–90. Moscow and Leningrad.

162. ———. "Tamozhennye knigi kak istochnik ekonomicheskoi istorii Rossii" (The customs books as a source of the economic history of Russia), *Problemy istochnikovedeniia,* I (1933), 110–129. Moscow and Leningrad.

163. BELIAEV, I. D. "Sluzhilye liudi v moskovskom gosudarstve" (The serving men in the Muscovite state), *Moskovskii sbornik,* I (1852), 357–382. Moscow.

164. ———. "Zhiteli moskovskago gosudarstva" (Inhabitants of the Muscovite state), *Vremennik,* III (1849), 1–88. Moscow.

165. BOGOIAVLENSKII, S. K. "Materialy po istorii kalmykov v pervoi polovine XVII veka" (Material for the history of the Kalmucks in the first half of the seventeenth century), *Istoricheskie zapiski,* V (1939), 48–101. Leningrad.

166. BUTSINSKII, P. N. "Sibirskie arkhiepiskopy. Makarii, Nektarii i Gerasim, 1625–1650" (Siberian archbishops. Makarii, Nektarii, and Gerasim, 1625–1650), *Vera i razum,* 1891, No. 10, pp. 577–616.

167. CHULKOV, N. P. "Erofei Pavlov Khabarov: dobytchik i pribyl'nik XVII veka" (Erofei Pavlov Khabarov: freebooter and profiteer of the seventeenth century), *Russkii arkhiv,* 1898, No. 2, pp. 177–190. Moscow.

168. FRIEDE, M. A. "Russkie dereviannye ukrepleniia po drevnim literaturnym istochnikam" (Russian wooden fortifications according to early literary sources), *Izvestiia rossiiskoi akademii istorii material'noi kul'tury,* III (1924), 113–143. Leningrad.

169. GOLOVACHEV, D. M. "Chastnoe zemlevladenie v Sibiri" (Private landownership in Siberia), *Sibirskie voprosy,* 1905, No. 1, pp. 122–170. St. Petersburg.

170. GOLOVACHEV, P. M. "Blizhaishiia zadachi istoricheskago izucheniia Sibiri" (Immediate problems of historical research on Siberia), *Zh.M.N.P.,* Vol. CCCXLIII (1902), No. 9, pp. 49–68. St. Petersburg.

171. GRADOVSKII, A. D. "Obshchestvennye klassy i administrativnoe delenie Rossii do Petra I" (Classes of society and administrative divisions of Russia to Peter I), *Zh.M.N.P.,* Vol. CXXXVIII (1868), April, pt. 2, pp. 1–91, May, pt. 2, pp. 405–436, June, pt. 2, pp. 631–698; CXXXIX (1868), July, pt. 2, pp. 72–241. St. Petersburg.

172. IADRINTSEV, N. M. "Trekhsotletie Sibiri 26 okt. 1881" (Tercentenary of Siberia, October 26, 1881), *Vestnik evropy,* 1881, December, pp. 834–850. St. Petersburg.

173. IONOVA, O. "Iakuty v XVII veke" (Iakuts in the seventeenth century), *Istorik-marksist*, 1939, V–VI, 175–191. Moscow.

174. IURTSOVSKII, N. "Administrativnoe delenie" (Administrative division), *Sibirskaia sovetskaia entsiklopediia*, I (1929), 20–27. Novosibirsk.

175. KISELEV, S. V. "Razlozhenie roda i feodalism na Enisee" (Feudalism and the decline of the clan system in the Enisei region), *Izvestiia gosudarstvennoi akademii istorii material'noi kul'tury*, No. 65, 1933. Leningrad.

176. KLIUCHEVSKII, V. O. "Boiarskaia duma drevnei Rusi" (Council of boiars in early Russia), *Russkaia mysl'*, 1880, January, pp. 40–76; March, pp. 45–74; April, pp. 1–37; October, pp. 64–95. Moscow.

177. ———. "Po povodu zametki Golovacheva" (Concerning the article by Golovachev), *Russkii arkhiv*, 1889, No. 2, pp. 138–145. Moscow.

178. KOZMIN, N. N. "Istoriia Sibiri" (History of Siberia), *Sibirskaia sovetskaia entsiklopediia*, II (1929), 380–399. Novosibirsk.

179. KRASSOVSKII, M. A. "Russkie v iakutskoi oblasti v XVII v." (Russians in the region of Iakutsk in the seventeenth century), *Izvestiia obshchestva istorii, arkheologii i etnografii pri kazanskom universitete*, Vol. XII (1894), No. 2. Kazan.

180. KURTS, B. G. "Kolonial'naia politika Rossii i Kitaia v XVII–XVIII vv." (Colonial policies of Russia and China in the seventeenth and eighteenth centuries), *Novyi vostok*, XIX (1927), 194–206. Moscow.

181. LAPPO-DANILEVSKII, A. A. "Organizatsiia priamogo oblozheniia v moskovskom gosudarstve so vremen smuty do epokhi preobrazovanii" (Organization of direct taxation in the Muscovite state from the Time of Troubles to the era of reform), *Zapiski istoriko-filologicheskago fakul'teta S.-Peterburgskago universiteta*, XXIII (1890), 1–557. St. Petersburg.

182. LIKHOVITSKII, A. "Prosveshchenie v Sibiri v pervoi polovine XVIII stoletiia" (Education in Siberia during the first half of the eighteenth century), *Zh.M.N.P.*, CCCLX (1905), July, 1–29. St. Petersburg.

183. MAMET, L. "Kolonial'naia politika tsarizma v Iakutii" (Colonial policy of tsarism in Iakutia), *Sbornik. 100 let iakutskoi ssylki*, 1934. Moscow.

184. MIKHAILOV, K. P. "Krepostnichestvo v Sibiri" (Serfdom in Siberia), *Sibirskii sbornik*, 1886, Bk. I, pp. 93–137. St. Petersburg.

185. MILIUKOV, P. N. "Feodalism v Rossii" (Feudalism in Russia), Brockhaus and Efron, eds., *Entsiklopedicheskii slovar'*, LXX (1902), 548–550. St. Petersburg.

186. ———. "Gosudarstvennoe khoziaistvo Rossii v sviazi s reformoi Petra Velikago" (State economy of Russia in relation to the reform of Peter the Great), *Zh.M.N.P.*, CCLXXI (1890), September, 1–107, October, 301–357; CCLXXII (1890), November–December, 1–79; CCLXXIII (1891), January–February, 1–47; CCLXXIV (1891), March–April, 30–146; CCLXXVI (1891), July–August, 289–393; CCLXXVII (1891), October, 408–482; CCLXXIX (1892), January, 65–124, February, 261–347. St. Petersburg.

187. Moskvin, I. S. "Voevody i nachalniki g. Iakutska i ikh deistviia" (Voevodas and superior officials of the town of Iakutsk and their activities), *Pamiatnaia knizhka iakutskoi oblasti*, 1863. Iakutsk (?).

188. Mueller, G. F. "Istoriia o stranakh pri reke Amure lezhashchikh" (History of countries situated on the Amur River), *Ezhemesiachnyia sochineniia akademii nauk* (cited as *Ezh. soch.*), 1757, July, pp. 1–39; August, pp. 99–130; September, pp. 195–227; October, pp. 291–328. St. Petersburg.

189. ———. "Sibirskaia istoriia" (Siberian history), *Ezh. soch.*, 1763, October, pp. 354–368; 1764, January, pp. 3–43, February, pp. 99–135, March, pp. 195–237, April, pp. 291–324, May, pp. 387–418, June, pp. 483–528. St. Petersburg.

190. Nevolin, K. A. "Obrazovanie upravleniia v Rossii ot Ioanna III do Petra Velikago" (Russian government from Ioann III to Peter the Great), *Zh.M.N.P.*, Vol. XLI (1844), No. 1, pt. 5, pp. 1–32; No. 2, pt. 5, pp. 33–86; No. 3, pt. 5, pp. 87–149. St. Petersburg.

191. Ogloblin, N. N. "Bunt i pobeg na Amur vorovskogo polka M. Sorokina" (The rebellion and flight to the Amur of the traitorous detachment of M. Sorokin), *Russkaia starina*, LXXXV (1896), 205–224. St. Petersburg.

192. ———. "Bytovyia cherty XVII veka" (Sketches of lfe in the seventeenth century), *Russkaia starina*, LXXIII (1892), 449–458, 675–682; LXXIV (1892), 681–694; LXXVI (1892), 165–182; LXXXI (1894), 223–236. St. Petersburg.

193. ———. "Delo o samovol'nom priezde v Moskvu arkhiepiskopa Simeona" (The case concerning the unwarranted arrival of the archbishop Simeon to Moscow), *Russkaia starina*, LXXX (1893), 162–184.

194. ———. "Iakutskii rozysk o rozni boiarskikh detei i kazakov" (Investigation in Iakutsk concerning the conflict between the boiar sons and cossacks), *Russkaia starina*, XCI (1897), 375–392. St. Petersburg.

195. ———. "Nerchinskii zagovor o pobege na Amur, na ostrova Vostochnago okeana" (The Nerchinsk conspiracy concerning the flight to the Amur and islands of the Pacific Ocean), *Russkaia starina*, LXXXVIII (1896), 121–129. St. Petersburg.

196. ———. "Ostiatskie kniaz'ia v XVII veke" (Ostiak chiefs in the seventeenth century), *Russkaia starina*, LXXI (1891), 395–401. St. Petersburg.

197. ———. "Proiskhozhdenie provintsial'nykh pod'iachikh" (Origin of the provincial pod'iacheis), *Zh.M.N.P.*, Vol. CCXCV (1894), September, no. 9, pp. 118–150, October, no. 10, pp. 222–241. St. Petersburg.

198. ———. "Sibirskie diplomaty XVII veka" (Siberian diplomats of the seventeenth century), *Istoricheskii vestnik*, Vol. XLVI (1891), No. 10, pp. 158–171. St. Petersburg.

199. ———. "Tomskii bunt 1637–1638," *Istoricheskii vestnik*, LXXXV (1901), 229–250. St. Petersburg.

200. OGORODNIKOV, V. I. "Russkaia gosudarstvennaia vlast' i sibirskie inorodtsy v XVI–XVIII v.v." (The Russian administration and the Siberian natives in the sixteenth to eighteenth centuries), *Sbornik professorov i prepodavatelei gosudarstvennogo irkutskogo universiteta*, Section I, Nauki gumanitarnye, I (1921), 69–113. Irkutsk.

201. ———. "Tuzemnoe i russkoe zemledelie na Amure v XVII v." (Native and Russian agriculture on the Amur in the seventeenth century), *Trudy gosudarstvennogo dal'ne-vostochnogo universiteta*, 1927, Series III, No. 4. Vladivostok.

202. OZEROV, I. "Obshchaia kartina oblozheniia v Rossii v XVII v." (General view of taxation in Russia in the seventeenth century), *Russkaia mysl'*, 1899, No. 6, pp. 42–66. Moscow and St. Petersburg.

203. PEIZEN, [?] "Istoricheskii ocherk kolonizatsii Sibiri" (Historical essay on the colonization of Siberia), *Sovremennik*, Vol. LXXVII (1859), Bk. IX. St. Petersburg.

204. PLATONOV, S. F. "Ocherk nizovskoi kolonizatsii severa" (Essay on the colonization of the north), Russkoe geograficheskoe obshchestvo, komitet severa. *Ocherki po istorii kolonizatsii severa*, 1922, pp. 47–69. St. Petersburg.

205. "Po povodu sibirskago iubileia" (Concerning the anniversary of the acquisition of Siberia), *Zh.M.N.P.*, CCXXV (1883), 1–23. St. Petersburg.

206. POLIAKOV, V. P. "Proshloe i nastoiashchee goroda Verkhotur'ia" (The past and present of the town of Verkhoturie), *Istoricheskii vestnik*, LXIV (1896), 587–604. St. Petersburg.

207. POLNER, T. "*Kolonizatsiia kraia v proshlom*" (Colonization of the region [of the Amur] in the past), *Priamur'e. Fakty, tsifry, nabliudeniia. Prilozhenie k otchetu obshchezemskoi organizatsii za 1908 god*, 1909, pp. 1–70. Moscow.

208. POPOV, G. A. "Rasselenie iakutov v XVII i XVIII st." (Distribution of the Iakuts in the seventeenth and eighteenth centuries), *Izvestiia iakutskogo otdela gosudarstvennogo russkogo geograficheskogo obshchestva*, III (1928). Iakutsk.

209. POTANIN, G. N. "Privoz i vyvoz tovarov goroda Tomska v polovine XVII stoletiia" (The import and export of goods at Tomsk in the middle of the seventeenth century), *Vestnik imperatorskago russkago geograficheskago obshchestva*, Vol. XXVII (1859), Pt. 2, pp. 125–144. St. Petersburg.

210. PRUSSAK, A. V. "Krest'iane Vostochnoi Sibiri vo vtoruiu polovinu 17-go veka" (Peasants of eastern Siberia during the second half of the seventeenth century), *Arkhiv istorii truda v Rossii*, VI–VII (1923), 75–89.

211. ———. "Zametka o nesvobodnom naselenii Vostochnoi Sibiri vo vtoroi polovine XVII v." (Notes on the non-free population of eastern Siberia during the second half of the seventeenth century), *Izvestiia vostochnosibirskago otdela russkago geograficheskago obshchestva*, XIV (1916).

212. PYPIN, A. "Pervyia izvestiia o Sibiri i russkoe eia zaselenie" (First information about Siberia, and its settlement by Russians), *Vestnik Evropy*, XXVI (1891), July, 764–765; August, 742–789. St. Petersburg.

213. RAISKII, V. "Zametki iz del iakutskago arkhiva" (Notes from the files of the archives of Iakutsk), *Zapiski sibirskago otdeleniia imperatorskago russkago geograficheskago obshchestva*, VI (1898), 38–39. Irkutsk.

214. SEREDONIN, S. M. "Istoricheskii ocherk zavoevaniia aziatskoi Rossii" (Historical essay on the conquest of Asiatic Russia), *Aziatskaia Rossiia*, I (1914), 1–38. St. Petersburg.

215. SHCHAPOV, A. P. "Istoriko-geograficheskoe raspredelenie russkago narodo-naseleniia" (Historico-geographical distribution of the Russian population), *Sochineniia* (3 vols., St. Petersburg, 1906–1908), II (1906), 182–364. St. Petersburg.

216. SHPAKOVSKII, N. I. "Strel'tsy" (Shooters), *Zh.M.N.P.*, CCCXIX (1898), September–October, 135–151. St. Petersburg.

217. SHUMAKHER, P. V. "Pervyia russkiia poseleniia na sibirskom vostoke" (First Russian settlements in eastern Siberia), *Russkii arkhiv*, 1879, No. 5, pp. 5–36. Moscow.

218. SPASSKII, G. I. "Svedeniia russkikh o reke Amure v XVII stoletii" (Information of the Russians in the seventeenth century concerning the river Amur), *Vestnik imperatorskago russkago geograficheskago obshchestva*, Vol. VII (1853), Pt. 2, pp. 15–42. St. Petersburg.

219. STEPANOV, N. N. "Mezhplemennyi obmen v vostochnoi Sibiri, na Amure, na Okhotskom poberezh'e v XVII veke" (Barter among the natives in eastern Siberia, on the Amur, on the coast of the Sea of Okhotsk in the seventeenth century), *Leningradskii gosudarstvennyi universitet. Uchenye zapiski. Seriia istoricheskikh nauk*, 1939, No. 5, pp. 53–79. Leningrad.

220. STROEV, S. "Statistiko-finansovaia kartina v Sibiri v 1698–1700" (A view of statistics and finances in Siberia in 1698–1700), *Moskovskii telegraf*, 1825, No. 21, pp. 45–57; No. 22, pp. 139–150. Moscow.

221. TOKAREV, S. A. "Iz istorii iakutskogo naroda" (Notes on the history of the Iakut people), *Vestnik drevnei istorii*, I (2), 1938, 216–227. Moscow.

222. ———. "Kolonial'naia politika moskovskogo gosudarstva v Sibiri v XVII veke" (Colonial policy of the Muscovite state in Siberia in the seventeenth century), *Istoriia v shkole*, IV (1936), July–August, 73–99. Moscow.

TROTSKII, I. M. "Nekotorye problemy istorii Iakutii XVII veka" (Some problems on the history of Iakutia in the seventeenth century). An introductory chapter to his compiled sources, "Kolonial'naia politika . . . ," pp. iii–xxx. See no. 60.

223. VERNADSKII, G. V. "The Expansion of Russia," *Transactions of the Connecticut Academy of Sciences*, XXXI (1933), July, 393–425.

224. ———. "Gosudarevy sluzhilye i promyshlennye liudi v vostochnoi Sibiri XVII veka" (The sovereign's serving men and the enterprisers in eastern Siberia during the seventeenth century), *Zh.M.N.P.*, New Series, LVI (1915), March–April, 332–354. St. Petersburg.

225. ———. "Protiv solntsa" (Against the sun), *Russkaia mysl'*. XXXV (1914), January, 56–79. Moscow and St. Petersburg.

226. VOLENS, N. V. "Ocherk khoziaistvennago stroia Iakutii" (Essay on the economic organization of Iakutia), *Iakutiia. Sbornik statei*, 1927, pp. 675–702. Leningrad.

227. ZAMYSLOVSKII, E. E. "Zaniatie russkimi Sibiri" (Russian occupation of Siberia), *Zh.M.N.P.*, Vol. CCXXIII (1882), No. 10, pp. 223–250. St. Petersburg.

INDEX OF TERMS, WITH PAGE REFERENCES

(An accented vowel indicates that, in pronunciation, the stress is to fall
on that syllable in which the accented vowel occurs.)

[233]